HARVARD STUDIES IN URBAN HISTORY

Series Editors
Stephan Thernstrom
Charles Tilly

Clyde and Sally Griffen

Natives and Newcomers

The Ordering of Opportunity
in Mid-Nineteenth-Century
Poughkeepsie

Harvard University Press
Cambridge, Massachusetts, and London, England 1978

Library of Congress Cataloging in Publication Data

Griffen, Clyde, 1929-
  Natives and newcomers.

  (Harvard studies in urban history)
  Bibliography: p.
  Includes index.
    1. Occupational mobility — New York (State) — Pough-
keepsie — History.   2. Labor and laboring classes —
New York (State) — Poughkeepsie — History — Social
conditions.   3. Poughkeepsie, N.Y.   I. Griffen,
Sally, 1936-   joint author.   II. Title.
III. Series.
HD8085.P713G74   331.1'27'0974733   77-3553
ISBN 0-674-60325-7

For John, Sarah, and Robert
who grew up with it and were clerks, too

Preface

THIS INVESTIGATION BEGAN, as have most historical mobility studies, with the aim of assessing conventional ideas about opportunity in America through a case study of occupational mobility in one community. Our early grapplings with problems of occupational classification soon persuaded us that clarifying the meaning of mobility frequencies by microscopic examination of occupations should become a primary purpose. We also found that this refinement in mobility analysis had a valuable by-product, a variety of clues to the processes by which industrialization and immigration transformed the structure of opportunity in nineteenth-century America.

We are aware of the limitations of occupational mobility as a surrogate for social mobility; it does not comprehend all those changes in residence, voluntary association, education, and way of life that in cumulative interaction result in a change in social class. But we are not persuaded that mobility studies for the United States should focus solely upon changes in social class. In a society where class boundaries have been so indistinct, most people accordingly have tended to think of improvement in their situation in more immediate and less inclusive forms.

Unless historians are to disregard entirely how individuals usually defined opportunity to rise they must not underestimate the importance of specific improvements, most notably in occupation, income, property, or residence, which did not eventuate in changes in social class. While we sympathize with recently expressed desires to see mobility studies relate a wider range of variables, we also believe — and hope our study demonstrates — that much more remains to be learned about changes in the nature of opportunity over time through more refined examinations of occupational mobility.

A brief account of how our purposes developed may suggest the usefulness we hope our book will have for social history. Our immediate inspiration was local. Long before the pioneering mobility studies by Merle Curti and his associates and by Stephan Thernstrom, Edna C. Macmahon, Professor of Economics at Vassar College, had encouraged students to trace the careers of workers, especially craftsmen, through annual city directories. The suggestiveness of these tracings not only for evaluating general impressions of social fluidity but also for understanding changes in the situation of workers in various occupations as skill dilution progressed made us want to investigate the entire labor force of Poughkeepsie over time. Describing these changes became one of our major aims.

As soon as we began the project, we confronted a major problem of historical mobility studies: whether to forgo the more precise and refined description which some but not all of the evidence permits in favor of comparability and systematic analysis. We deliberately favored comparability in our general methodology—specifically by proceeding as much as possible on the same lines as Thernstrom's model study of Boston—rather than create idiosyncratic classifications and measurements that might not relate easily to those of other studies. Any inclination we had to elaborate Thernstrom's five strata vertical ranking in order to recognize finer gradations in the skill, status, and reward of occupations was quickly removed by limitations in the evidence available for nineteenth-century studies, especially the failure of occupational designations in censuses and directories to reflect with any consistency progress in the division of labor.

Yet the more we learned about variation within the unskilled, semiskilled, and skilled manual and low and high nonmanual ranks, the more important refinement in analysis of the resulting frequencies of movement between these ranks seemed. Otherwise, readers might assume a distinctness and comparable social distance between these categories that the historical evidence does not justify. To specify as much as possible the limitations of these twentieth-century categories when applied to mobility analysis for an earlier era seemed to us an important contribution to future comparisons of opportunity across time.

The constraints imposed by the claims of comparability and systematic analysis did not pose so severe a limitation as we first imagined for our investigation of the impact of industrialization upon the opportunities of workers in various occupations. As it turns out, the behavior of workers that can be described by a tracing study, such as

persistence in the community, stability in occupation, and ownership of property, proves to be a sensitive indicator of the changing
circumstances of individual occupations or occupational groups
even when the occupational designations do not reveal the progress
of division of labor and mechanization. We believe that the resulting insights about the processes of change within the occupational
universe of the mid-nineteenth century as well as the concreteness in
describing that universe should be especially useful to historians of
labor, business, and immigration.

Computation of frequencies of mobility between broad functional
occupational groups within our five vertical ranks impressed upon
us the importance of identifying changes in the paths of mobility for
particular groups of workers. That computation revealed, for example, that clerical and sales positions became more important and
skilled trades less important as stepping stones to business proprietorships in the city and that immigrants overwhelmingly pursued
the latter path to self-employment in the city whereas natives predominated in the former. Once again, refinement through disag-
gregation seemed urgent because general analysis of vertical mobility would not reveal this shift. Specifying the changing importance
of particular paths will add a needed dimension to the impressive
similarity in frequencies in movement between broad strata in different communities over a span of more than a century, a period in
which the economic organization of the nation was transformed.

We hope our attempt at specification of paths for three decades
in a small city will encourage similar efforts for cities of different
sizes and types; only when we have a variety of case studies for different periods during the past two centuries will we be able to determine how typical the process of change in particular localities was.
Until recently social history has taken its picture of the transformation of opportunity during industrialization largely from studies of
the nation's largest cities and from mill towns, and even these studies
have paid little attention to the relative importance of different
avenues of mobility.

One important group of workers, women, has been ignored so far
by mobility studies because during the nineteenth century women
rarely persisted in the labor force long enough for career analysis.
Yet their employment influenced the opportunities for men; in
turn, major changes in the supply and attitudes of male workers in
certain industries and callings had a profound impact on the em-

ployments available to women. Analysis of changes in the importance of particular avenues of mobility for particular groups of men
without the perspective of the related changes in employment of
women gives a distorted picture of the occupational universe and
how much opportunity for advancement it provided. We hope our
chapter on women will show the importance of including this perspective in future mobility studies.

We considered Poughkeepsie for a case study initially because we
lived there and had had some preview of its nineteenth-century
occupational structure through the work of Professor Macmahon
and her students and through the classic study of mortality in its
business firms by Mabel Newcomer and the Hutchinsons. The economic diversification apparent in that preview seemed to us essential
for a localized measurement of how much opportunity changed during a period of industrialization, especially for evaluating the frequent suggestion by earlier historians of abrupt displacement of
artisans or their degradation to machine tenders. Precisely because
Poughkeepsie had a long history of manufacture of varied type and
scale and a continuing commercial vitality it afforded a much
needed comparison with mill towns like Lawrence, Lowell, Chico-
pee, and Holyoke, so long regarded as exemplifying the industrial
transformation.

The size of Poughkeepsie served our purposes. Our desire to compare the careers of all workers in each occupation precluded use of
samples, yet tracing the entire labor force of a city much in excess of
20,000 — the total population of this Hudson River town by 1870 —
seemed unmanageable. Our sense of the appropriateness of Poughkeepsie for a case study of mobility was strengthened by several
other considerations. The city lay near the geographical center of
the northeastern states, the most rapidly urbanizing and industrializing region in the United States at mid-century; its crude ratio of
manufacturing workers to total male labor force was almost the
median among the fifty largest cities in that region in 1860 as was its
population growth rate for the decade after 1860. In the following
decades the population increased very slowly; within the class of
small cities with diversified economies it belongs with those that
enjoyed periods of relatively rapid growth but failed to generate sufficient momentum to maintain their relative importance within
their region over the longer run. The net stagnation in Poughkeepsie's population during the seventies, our concluding decade, does

have the usefulness for our study of permitting comparison of variation in mobility patterns between decades of substantial and of no
growth.

Like other mobility studies, this book uses a particular city as the
locus for investigating a larger social process. It is not a form of
urban biography and focuses upon the evolution of the city only
where that evolution illuminates the process. But our emphasis
upon microscopic analysis does entail a fuller description of changes
in the city's economy than has seemed necessary so far for mobility
studies.

The richness of information in the federal census beginning with
1850 and the unavailability of the census after 1880 determined our
choice of this thirty year period as it did the span of several other
mobility studies completed before the recent, limited opening to
scholars of the 1900 census. We have done cross-sectional and tracing analyses which involve years before 1850 and after 1880, but
these analyses use sources which comprehend less of the labor force
than the census does. They have permitted us to identify some
longer-range trends for particular groups of workers, such as the
rich and members of selected trades and professions.

"Natives" in our title and text refers to white men of native parentage; the city's blacks — all native-born and mostly New Yorkers —
made up a very small proportion of the population, as in most
northeastern cities during these years. "Newcomers" refers to foreign immigrants and their children, almost entirely accounted for in
this period by the Irish, Germans, and British. We have not applied
the label newcomer to native immigrants. We cannot identify them
systematically and so generalize their traits precisely. Unless they
arrived in Poughkeepsie after 1850, we cannot tell whether natives
born in New York State had emigrated from another locality.

Our occupational classification like that of other historical mobility studies uses categories devised by investigators rather than by the
actors. The perspective of hindsight is essential in making distinctions for comparisons across time although the distinctions may not
coincide with those made by people in the period being studied.
Even the most past-minded historians do not and cannot reconstruct
the past entirely from the actors' points of view. The issue is the adequacy of the categories chosen for the purpose at hand. If that purpose is re-creation of contemporary perception, then the historian
will wish to make his own vocabulary as close as possible in meaning

and perhaps even in diction to that of the actors. If his purpose is identifying changing patterns of behavior over time, as ours is, then different considerations govern the choice of categories. We ask the reader to remember that when we speak of occupational strata and of the sharpening or blurring of the boundaries between them, we are describing change as it appears through the lens of a classification scheme.

We do not presume that the study of occupational mobility— even when it includes movements judged horizontal as well as those judged vertical—reveals the only important dimension of men's working lives, much less the cultures that defined the meaning of those lives for them. We do recognize that the very focus upon this one "objective" dimension of their experience tends to imply its supreme importance for contemporaries. We have tried throughout the book to emphasize alternative viewpoints wherever our evidence suggests their presence.

It bears mentioning here that one of our most useful sources for fleshing out the careers of men in the middling range of occupational status, primarily self-employed artisans and owners of small retail and service shops, adds to the bias. The local correspondents of R. G. Dun & Company, predecessor to Dun & Bradstreet in rating the worthiness of businesses for credit, were preoccupied with improvement or decline in the economic condition of the owners. In the assessments correspondents sent to the company at least once a year, and more often if the subject was in financial trouble, they sometimes reported behavior that suggests the owner was motivated by values other than economic success. But the suggestion usually depends upon our inference rather than upon direct statement by the correspondent.

The proper antidote to this bias in mobility studies is not to swing to the opposite extreme and to infer from evidence of the strong ties of work place or of ethnic neighborhood a full identification of workers with the dominant values of either. In a mobile society there is a constant tension for members of many groups between the group's emphasis on loyalty to a shared way of life and their own desires to improve their personal position. Our evidence for Poughkeepsie's immigrants suggests that they came with an ethos of opportunity of their own which reduced the tension. If there is an inherent danger that mobility studies will overemphasize the individual drive for success, there also is a corresponding danger that the interest of historians of labor or immigration in the occasions when their subjects express solidarity will lead these historians to overlook the simultaneous presence of individual aspirations with a different tendency.

No issue raised by mobility studies has been more acute for us than the paradox that they have been motivated largely by a desire to reconstruct the experience of the historically inarticulate and yet have so often seemed to reduce them to abstractions in the process and rather specialized abstractions at that. We hope that in describing one important dimension of the lives of workers in Poughkeepsie we have not created a portrait they would not recognize, however alien the language of mobility analysis to the way they talked about their occupational careers. We have tried to vivify our generalizations through the particular individuals who compose them. We have been haunted throughout this study by G. K. Chesterton's moral, "There is one sin: to call a green leaf grey."

While this book has been a joint effort from the beginning, we divided some responsibilities. Clyde wrote the original drafts of Chapters 1, 3, and 7 through 10 and Sally of Chapters 4 through 6 and Chapter 11. We shared equally in the writing of Chapter 2.

Acknowledgments

THE INTEREST OF Edna Cers Macmahon in the fate of crafts-men in the nineteenth century helped inspire our project. Her guid-ance in its initial stages was invaluable. The example of *Poverty and Progress* encouraged us soon after the project's inception; since then we have benefited from Stephan Thernstrom's generosity and good sense as colleague, editor, and friend.

The data gathering and analysis entailed in a full population study requires more assistance from more people and institutions than we can acknowledge here.

A Ford Foundation grant to Vassar College for student participa-tion in research made possible our initial compilation of individual records from the manuscript census schedules. A grant-in-aid from the American Council of Learned Societies for computer-oriented research in the humanities underwrote the preparation of those records for computer analysis. We are indebted to the University of California at Los Angeles for use of its computer during Clyde's year there in 1970-71 as a visiting teacher. A National Science Founda-tion Grant (GS-39632) helped provide time for the writing of the manuscript. Vassar College provided time and financial assistance at crucial points, and the staff of its library invariably proved help-ful.

Many students contributed to the gathering and preliminary analysis of data; we are grateful for their enthusiasm, industry, and carefulness. We owe special thanks to Judith Allen, Mark Barr, John Carroll, David Gazek, Mary Ruth Gross, Virginia Kozack, Lynn Larsen, Lois Marcus, Joan Moskowitz, Nancy Sahli, and Johnna Torsone, all of whom gave much more than was required.

Agnes Langdon kindly translated the Jubilee Year Book of Na-tivity parish for us. We are indebted to Valeria Herles, Thomas McCormick, the Reverend Hugh Miller, the Most Reverend Joseph Pernicone, and Mr. and Mrs. Edmund G. Rawson, Jr., for making materials available to us. Special thanks are owed to Dun & Bradstreet, Inc., for providing a rich source for scholars in the credit reports of the R. G. Dun & Company, to Robert Lovett of the Baker Library at Harvard University, who facilitated our use of the reports, and to our friend Peter Decker, who first made them known to us and has helped in other ways. Scattered material in Chapters 1, 5, and 8-9 appeared previously in essays published in Tamara K. Hareven, ed., *Family and Kin in Urban Communities, 1700-1930* (New York: Franklin Watts, 1977), and in Richard L. Ehrlich, ed., *Immigrants in Industrial America, 1850-1920* (Charlottesville, Va.: The University Press of Virginia, 1977); we are grateful for their permission to use this material in the present book.

One of the pleasures of working in a new field, especially when it has as democratic a temper as the newer social history, is the ease of collaboration. Theodore Hershberg's inspired initiative led not only to a rewarding venture in comparative analysis but also to a fraternity with him, Stuart Blumin, Laurence Glasco, and Michael Katz, which we continue to enjoy. Margo Conk enhanced our comparative perspective by sharing, in the same spirit, her analyses of the labor forces of cities in and adjacent to New Jersey. Finally, we are indebted to Tamara Hareven, John Modell, and Sam Bass Warner, Jr., for their comments on essays already published from this investigation.

The richness of evidence available to any community study depends upon those who have saved its records. Poughkeepsie has been fortunate in the zeal and intelligence of those responsible for the remarkably comprehensive local history collection at Adriance Memorial Library. We have been blessed again and again by the helpfulness of its curator, Wilhelmina Powers.

Contents

Natives
and
Newcomers

1

From Village to Small City

"I AM ABOUT to write up (in pamphlet form) a brief Puff for Poughkeepsie. This I have been requested to do by a party of gentlemen associated for the purpose of adding to the character and population of our idol city."[1] So wrote S. L. Walker, the city's first daguerreotype artist, to Benson Lossing, the historian, with a request for assistance in gathering the necessary facts. Walker's puffing belongs to the booterish years preceding the depression of 1873, one of two boom times in nineteenth-century Poughkeepsie which sparked high ambitions for the city's future importance.

By 1906, when editor Edmund Platt published his history, the failure of both booms to produce sustained rapid growth favored a soberer view. Chronicling in detail the innovations and casualties of a century among the city's industries, Platt generalized that "Poughkeepsie is not so very different from many other Eastern cities, but nevertheless has its characteristics. It has been a town of slow growth . . . Its people in the past have been by turns over-conservative and then over-enterprising, but the periods of conservatism and of enterprise have coincided with National conditions. As a result of the forces of the past Poughkeepsie is partly a manufacturing town, partly a trading town drawing upon a productive territory, partly a

1

college town, partly a residence town — the home of many persons in comfortable retirement from the cares of business — partly a railroad town, and partly a river town. Within easy reach of the metropolis, it stands apart with an independence of its own. Its loyal citizens think it the best place in the United States to live."[2] The pride remained, but with a touch of defensiveness prompted perhaps by knowledge that Poughkeepsie had declined in relative importance among Eastern cities.

Platt's overview of a small, slow-growing city with a diversified economy describes generally the context for occupational mobility. But like most local chroniclers, he made no attempt to show how the evolution of his city's industries was reflected in its labor force. To provide a more refined description than Platt's of characteristics which seem important for interpretation of occupational mobility during the thirty years after 1850, this chapter will describe population growth, labor force composition, the extent of diversification and specialization in both commerce and manufacturing, change in the occupational structure and in the scale of enterprise, the frequency, direction and apparent meanings of geographical mobility, and native actions encouraging the assimilation of immigrants.

Continuities loom largest in so short a period as three decades, but this chapter will identify short-term changes which had immediate consequences for opportunity and some consistent trends which point the direction of major changes over a longer span of time. Defining typicality is more difficult and uncertain. We will suggest what kinds of urban settings this case study may be most representative of by showing how Poughkeepsie compares with other cities, primarily in the mid-Atlantic region, in traits which can be described systematically.

The village of fewer than 8,000 inhabitants in 1840 numbered 12,763 in 1855, the year after its incorporation as a municipality. This gain of more than half was repeated in the next fifteen years, producing a population of 20,080 in 1870. In 1850 Poughkeepsie had ranked among the 60 largest urban places in the nation; in 1870 it could still claim to be America's sixty-fifth largest city. Its growth rate for the sixties alone made it almost the median case among rates for the 48 northeastern cities with more than 10,000 inhabitants at the start of that decade.[3] In a mood of high optimism about its future importance, the city sharply increased government services and expenditures.

The heady visions encouraged by the growth rate of the sixties collapsed during the next decade. Economic depression brought retrenchment in government and stagnation in population, the net gain of 127 people bringing the total to only 20,207 in 1880. Cities in the vicinity of New York, by contrast, grew rapidly. The seventies made it clear that Poughkeepsie belonged to a regional group of small cities in the Hudson valley which were declining in relative size and economic importance along with the decline of river transportation compared to railroads. The neighboring river towns of Newburgh and Kingston, both with fewer than 20,000 souls in 1880, registered only slight increases in population during the decade.

A comparison of growth for the period from 1860 to 1880 for the 22 cities in New York, New Jersey, and Connecticut which had populations of 20,000 or more by 1880 puts Poughkeepsie's slower growth in sharper perspective.[4] Between 1860 and 1870 the city had been eleventh in percentage of increase among these 22 cities, but for the twenty-year period it fell to twenty-first. It was one of five, four of them in upstate New York, which had increases of between 26 and 46 percent: Oswego, Poughkeepsie, Albany, Troy, and Hartford, Connecticut. The increases for Syracuse, Rochester, Buffalo, and Newark fell between 84 and 91 percent and at the other extreme, five Jersey cities near New York City or Philadelphia — Elizabeth, Paterson, Hoboken, Jersey City, and Camden — grew between 144 and 313 percent. In the next twenty-year period from 1880 to 1900 the growth of all these Jersey cities in metropolitan regions slowed, but except for Hoboken, none increased less than 68 percent. None of the cities in the Hudson valley above Yonkers increased as much as 40 percent. Within New York State as a whole, the cities along the western end of the Erie Canal continued to increase in relative importance. Younger manufacturing cities in the south central area bordering Pennsylvania like Elmira and Binghamton surpassed the old river towns in population.

Poughkeepsie did not provide a rapidly expanding market for labor in the last half of the nineteenth century. Despite its proximity to a major port of entry, New York City, it did not attract foreign immigrants as readily as more dynamic inland cities like Rochester and Buffalo. In 1850 Irish, German, and British immigrants comprised 21, 7, and 8 percent respectively of the city's male labor force; thereafter, with the brief exception of the Germans who increased to 12 percent in 1860, the proportion of the foreign-born of

these nationalities declined and the native-born of foreign parentage increased. Newcomers of other nationalities in both first and
second generations never comprised as much as 2 percent of the
male labor force and blacks, all native-born, remained about 3
percent at each census.

Although Poughkeepsie's labor force had been profoundly altered
by immigration by 1880, with 27 percent of all male workers
foreign-born and another 21 percent native-born of foreign parentage, the degree of transformation was less than in most cities in its
tri-state region. Using the proportion foreign-born in the total
population as crude proxy for their proportion in the labor force,
Poughkeepsie appears in 1880 as one of the four cities with less than
20 percent foreign-born compared to 17 cities with 25 percent or
more, including Newark, Rochester, and Troy with 30 percent,
Buffalo and Jersey City with 33 percent, and Paterson and Hoboken
with 37 and 42 percent respectively. As the case of slow-growing
Troy indicates, however, no invariable correlation can be presumed
between growth rate and proportion of immigrants.

Because Poughkeepsie attracted fewer foreign immigrants, white
workers of native parentage continued to form a large proportion of
manual workers at all levels of skill. As late as 1880, these native
whites comprised 47 percent of the skilled and 37 percent of the unskilled and semiskilled male wage earners. Less drastic change in
the ethnic composition of the city's labor force made it atypical for
the region. By contrast, lack of major change in the structure of its
labor force—the distribution of workers by both skill and industry—seems typical of diversified urban economies. Two previous
studies of mobility in urban America have classifications of occupations by level of skill which can be compared readily, and both
studies investigated cities with diversified economies. As the
percentages for Atlanta in 1870 and for Boston in 1880 in Table 1.1
indicate, the skill distribution of male workers did not differ much
from that of Poughkeepsie despite the wide variation in the size
and ethnic composition of the three cities.

Similarity in structure is even more pronounced in the one comparison of male labor forces at the same census which employed
identical classification of occupational titles from the manuscript
population schedules. The comparison of Buffalo, Kingston, Poughkeepsie, Philadelphia, and Hamilton in 1860 was reported in detail in the *Historical Methods Newsletter*. All of the five cities were

TABLE 1.1. Structure of the labor force at four censuses[a]

Occupation	Poughkeepsie				Atlanta	Boston
	1850	1860	1870	1880	1870	1880
Number						
Male	3,837	3,942	5,593	5,926	–	–
Female	–	1,345	1,436	1,907	–	–
Total	–	5,287	7,029	7,833	–	–
Percent						
Professional						
Male	4	5	5	5	3	3
Female	–	6	7	6	–	–
Total	–	5	5	5	–	–
Proprietorial						
Male	17	17	20	17	19	–
Female	–	3	3	3	–	–
Total	–	14	17	15	–	
						29[b]
Clerical						
Male	4	7	9	11	12	–
Female	–	1	2	2	–	–
Total	–	5	7	9	–	–
Skilled						
Male	30	36	33	29	24	36
Female	–	40	26	21	–	–
Total	–	37	31	27	–	–
Semiskilled						
Male	9	10	10	16	7	17
Female	–	4	3	13	–	–
Total	–	8	8	15	–	–
Unskilled						
Male	36	24	24	23	34	15
Female	–	.47	60	54	–	–
Total	–	30	31	31	–	–

[a]The census did not report female employment in 1850. Only women reporting occupations, regardless of age, comprise the female labor force. The male labor force was defined as men of 16 years or older, except students, and men under 16 if employed. The census in this period rarely indicated retirement; most workers reported an occupation at the last census in which they appeared in the city; additional evidence exists that too many workers continued to be employed late in life to use age as proxy for retirement; and the census did not specify retirement often enough to exclude on that basis. Men who reported no occupation, who appeared

commercial centers; none had an extreme concentration in manufacturing. Extractive industry did have special importance in Kingston's economy producing the most important exception to the general similarity, a larger proportion of unskilled workers.

Ranking occupations vertically into four strata — high and low white collar and skilled and unskilled blue collar — the proportion in the top stratum in Buffalo, Hamilton, Poughkeepsie, and Philadelphia ranged between 5 and 10 percent, in the second highest stratum, between 11 and 18 percent, in the next, between 42 and 50 percent, and in the lowest, between 30 and 32 percent. A functional grouping of occupations showed comparable similarity with between 2 and 6 percent in agriculture and extraction, between 46 and 49 percent in manufacturing and at ordinary labor, between 2 and 8 percent in transportation, between 18 and 23 percent in commerce and the professions, between 3 and 8 percent in other occupations, and between 11 and 22 percent in construction.[5]

Comparison of Poughkeepsie's entire labor force, male and female, with those of New York City, Brooklyn, Philadelphia, Camden, Jersey City, Paterson, and Newark in 1880 as classified by Margo Conk also shows broad similarity with two exceptions.[6] Manufacturing and construction accounted for 71 percent of Paterson's and 61 percent of Newark's workers compared to between 41 and 49 percent for the other cities. Trade and the professions, by contrast, accounted for between 18 and 23 percent with the single exception of Paterson which had only 10 percent so employed. Newark already was moving toward becoming a center of commerce and finance as well as manufacturing.

---

at the poorhouse or who described themselves as gentlemen composed no more than 7 percent of the total male labor force at any of our four censuses.

There is only one difference in skill classification between men and women: the semiskilled category for men includes more responsible service occupations as well as factory operatives; for women it comprises only operatives. Female service workers, almost entirely domestics, appear as unskilled; for our rationale see Chapter 11.

The recomputation for Atlanta combines the data for white, black, and immigrant males in Tables 1, 2, and 3 of Richard J. Hopkins, "Occupational and Geographical Mobility in Atlanta, 1870-1896," *Journal of Southern History,* 34 (May 1968), pp. 202-204; the percentages for Boston are from Table 4.1 of Stephan Thernstrom, *The Other Bostonians: Poverty and Progress in the American Metropolis, 1880-1970* (Cambridge, Mass., 1973), p. 50.

[b]The percentage is for proprietorial and clerical combined.

All of the cities but two reported between 4 and 7 percent of their workers in transportation, the exceptions being Paterson with 2 percent and Jersey City, a major transshipment center, with 9 percent. Data for 1870 for all but Camden and Paterson indicate little change over the decade although all the cities show some decline in the proportion of ordinary laborers, Jersey City increased its commitment to manufacturing, and the proportion of trade, professional, and transportation workers increased in Newark. The proportion of the total population in gainful occupations of any kind in tri-state region cities varied between a high of 44 percent for Paterson and a low of 35 percent for Jersey City in 1880 with Poughkeepsie at 37 percent having a slightly higher proportion than Brooklyn, Camden, Newark, Albany, and Buffalo as well as Jersey City.

Although no major change in the character of Poughkeepsie's economy occurred during our period, the direction of change was toward a greater dependence upon commerce and a lesser importance for manufacturing. Between 1860 and 1880 the proportion of the entire labor force, male and female, in trade increased from 11 to 15 percent and the proportion in manufacturing and construction decreased from 47 percent to 42 percent.

The direction of change in the distribution of skills within the labor force conformed to the general tendencies within the national economy. The seventies saw an increase in the proportion of both male and female factory operatives (distinguished from craftsmen and laborers who worked in factories) and a continuing decline in journeymen in the trades. Poughkeepsie probably had a larger remnant of the older craft manufacture than many cities in its region, but the broad tendencies in the skill composition of its labor force conformed to a national pattern, regardless of industry.

The sharp decline between 1850 and 1860 in the proportion of male unskilled workers reflected a local loss in demand for laborers with the end of construction on the Hudson River Railroad; thereafter the proportion remained similar. Workers classified as semi-skilled comprised a very similar proportion from 1850 to 1870 with service workers rather than factory operatives comprising the large majority of the men. By the end of the next decade, however, factory operatives comprised 9 percent of the male labor force as a whole and service workers, 7 percent; in the female labor force, 13 percent reported factory employment. The opening of new and more

mechanized factories explains the change; this indication of change
in the skill composition of the labor force should not be confused,
however, with estimates of the proportion of workers employed by
large manufacturing establishments. For example, specification of
place of employment in a few city directories suggests that at least
one fourth of the unspecified "laborers" in Poughkeepsie at each
census worked for factories and furnaces, but we have no evidence
to suggest that their tasks required even the limited training which
justifies the classification semiskilled for operatives.[7]

The most revealing sign of specialization appears outside manual
work in the increase of clerical and sales workers from 4 to 11 percent of the male total and in the greater specificity in their designations. By 1880 the undifferentiated title of "clerk" no longer predominated as enumerators increasingly specified type of business
and even type of work, such as accountant, salesman, store clerk, or
shipping clerk.

As late as 1880 in Poughkeepsie expansion of the proportion of
workers in clerical jobs occurred in the male labor force rather than
the female. With one other important exception, the general
patterns of stability and change in distribution among skill categories was similar for the two sexes. The decline of skilled workers
was earlier and more decisive among women and resulted in a sharp
increase in 1870 in the proportion of unskilled workers in the female
labor force. The dramatic increase in proportion of semiskilled
workers for both sexes due to new factory employment in 1880 was
accompanied by reduction in the percentage unskilled for women
and also reduction in the percentage of skilled for both sexes.

Generally, a much higher proportion of women than of male
workers throughout the period had unskilled jobs and a much lower
proportion appear as clerks and proprietors. The higher proportion
of women in professional work reflects their predominance in
teaching. Judged by rate of growth in the male and the female labor
forces, increase in job opportunities was more rapid for women
during the economic stagnation of the seventies than in the more
prosperous sixties when the male labor force grew most rapidly.

In both 1865 and 1880 Poughkeepsie had the highest ratio of fe-
males to males among inhabitants of working age of any city in New
York State. Because the river town had no leading industry which
depended heavily upon female workers, we infer that the ratio reflects the lesser attractiveness of Poughkeepsie's labor market to

male workers. Other evidence seems to support this inference. Besides having a slow growth rate, the city also had more older male workers. The differences among cities in New York State in 1865 were small, but Poughkeepsie had the highest percentage of men more than 50 years old. In the five city comparison of male labor forces, Poughkeepsie had a slightly higher proportion in the oldest age group than Philadelphia, Buffalo, or Kingston.

We did not find any consistent correlation between age distribution, sex ratio, and other urban traits in our comparisons, but we are impressed by the fact that the cities in New York State with the highest proportions of both old workers and women experienced slow growth in these years. We are further impressed by the fact that the two cities in which these traits do not relate readily to the character of local industries — Poughkeepsie and nearby Newburgh — belonged to a region declining in relative economic importance.

Commerce based upon a productive hinterland and access by water to a regional market extending from Albany to Long Island by 1800 had been the impetus to the early growth of the village. Retailing and service for a more restricted mid-Hudson valley market would be the backbone of its economy in the slowed growth after 1870. Even at moments like the eve of civil war when Poughkeepsie's manufactures seemed most prosperous, the city stood at the opposite pole from the extremes of specialization in manufacturing which Troy at that date and Paterson later represented, both of them atypical of the region's cities.

Until the opening of the Erie Canal, Dutchess County remained a major grain-growing region and the village its major point for transshipment. By 1813 eight sloops sailed weekly from Poughkeepsie's river landings for New York City and in 1814 the village became a steamboat terminal. Subsequent shift from grain to wool in the thirties did not diminish the importance of the village as a center for traffic for the county. Newspaper reports frequently mentioned the lines of farmers and teamsters waiting their turns along the roads to the landings.

With the coming of the Harlem Railroad to the eastern part of the county in 1847 and of the Hudson River Railroad to the western edge not long after, the river landings had been reduced by 1873 to a single terminal at the foot of Main Street. But the change in the dominant form of transportation did not end the importance of Poughkeepsie as a transshipment center for farmers in the central and western parts of the county, nor did it reduce its role as the major shopping center for a wider region in the mid-Hudson valley.

Local newspapers throughout the nineteenth century reminded readers that when the sun shone steadily, "there is a rush of our country friends to town daily." The importance of the farm trade for the city's prosperity brought swings between rejoicing and worry. In late 1861, after a year in which "many began to despond and to say we had got where there must be a stop and no further progress made . . . our business is more booming than usual, with rich farmers thronging in the streets and stores of Poughkeepsie." In 1865 the *Eagle* exulted that trade with some towns in the eastern part of the county had increased so much—despite their readier access to the Harlem Railroad running south to New York—as to require not only three stages a week but also regular runs of a large market wagon.[8]

As some of the city's oldest, largest, and most prosperous manufacturing enterprises closed during the nineties, most often through obsolescence, boosters emphasized regional preeminence in retailing as the abiding foundation of Poughkeepsie's prosperity. Concluding a rather sad account of the abandonment of older factories in the eighties and nineties, especially those along the river front, Edmund Platt, the historian, remarked that "much of the best enterprise of Poughkeepsie has always been devoted to retail trade, which has attained a development greater than in many cities of even larger size, in spite of the competition of the metropolis."[9]

That retail development probably benefited some from the presence of a student population drawn from other localities to the city's well-reputed private academies, seminaries, and colleges. At the height of its prosperity the Eastman Business College, opened in 1859, enrolled more than a thousand young men who lived in private homes and boarding houses throughout the city. Vassar College opened in 1865 with 353 students who resided at the college beyond the city limits. More certain as a stimulus to retailing of high quality merchandise were the gentlemen of means who found the hilltops overlooking the Hudson River both south and north of the city so attractive for estates.

Among the more modest types of retailing, the number of groceries and saloons increased with the population, providing more opportunities for manual workers especially. Neither type of business grew as fast in proportion to population as it did in Paterson during these years.[10] This difference suggests that in the smaller city with fewer immigrants established firms in older business locations did not decline as much in relative importance compared to the newer, usually smaller ventures dispersed in working-class residential areas and catering to their immediate neighborhoods.

Even before 1880 local retailing had begun to show an increase in scale and complexity of organization, notably in the evolution of its two largest dry goods firms toward the variety of the modern department store. At the same time local firms in some lines began to face competition from local branches of national chains like the Atlantic and Pacific Tea Company or, as with the Boston Clothing Store, of firms in other cities in the region. Agencies of national manufacturers — at first primarily of agricultural implements and sewing machines — became more common by 1880.

Poughkeepsie long had had substantial commission businesses specializing in flour, feed, and produce. It never became much of a regional wholesaling center except in smaller items sold to petty retailers in the city and countryside, primarily groceries and provisions, liquor, tobacco, and drugs. Annual directories show 21 wholesale firms as compared to 1,502 retail firms between 1844 and 1873; between 1874 and 1903 the ratio more than doubled but the number remained small — 48 wholesalers compared to 1,234 retailers.[11]

Although Poughkeepsie's importance as a trading center for its hinterland remained the foundation of its economy, its highly varied career in manufacturing provided the highest hopes for its future and its sharpest fluctuations in employment. Textile factories exploiting the water power of local streams had been manufacturing in the city since the first decade of the century, but the progress of manufacturing in Poughkeepsie was far from smooth.[12] Gone before 1850 were a variety of enterprises including wood screw and paperhanging factories. Some of the most ambitious and short-lived were born during the boom of the thirties. Local entrepreneurs launched a whaling industry to compete for whales in foreign waters with established centers like New Bedford and Nantucket; in 1840 they employed 180 men locally. More than 200 machinists found employment in a new locomotive engine company which preceded by a decade the actual building of a railroad to the village.

The city never developed a successful specialization such as upstate Troy did in stove manufacture, with numerous firms and auxiliary enterprises providing external economies. The largest employers by 1850 did not cluster in one or a few industries. A blast furnace and a chair factory founded in the forties joined a soon-to-be-defunct cotton factory, one carpet factory, and the much older dye wood mill and Matthew Vassar's brewery as the village's largest manufacturers in 1850.

The precariousness of Poughkeepsie's manufacturing from the beginning reflected its dependence on extralocal markets made possible by the location on the Hudson River. By the fifties a number of the city's cooperages, carriage shops, and foundries depended heavily upon the soon-to-be-ruined Southern trade. Orders for large castings were filled by local foundries for places as distant as Cincinnati and the Crystal Palace in England. Latin American markets consumed most of the production of a chair factory which employed 75 men and 99 women in 1850 but failed in 1858. Contractors organized local tailors and tailoresses to make ready-made garments for New York City and Philadelphia houses.[13] The years of Civil War and Reconstruction saw expansion of some old industries like the furnaces, a temporary decline in garment making followed by a depression-born revival in factories, decline in the relative importance of cooperage, carriage making, and foundry, and the emergence of large factories in new lines, notably agricultural implements, shoes, and in 1880, glassware.

Throughout these shifts in the fortunes of particular industries, Poughkeepsie's manufacturing remained highly varied. No one or two industries or even a group of closely related industries ever became dominant. The two largest employers in 1880, shoes and iron, accounted for less than one fifth of the labor force, placing it with other cities with diversified manufacturing like Newark, Hartford, and Bridgeport. At the other extreme, nearly half of the labor force of Trenton worked — to use manufacturing census categories — in pottery and iron and steel, of Utica, in men's clothing and shoes, and of Troy, in two garment industries — shirts and men's furnishing goods. Another pair of related industries, iron and steel and foundry and machine products, accounted for another third of that city's labor force. The greatest specialization in any of the 22 tri-state cities with more than 20,000 persons appeared in Paterson where one industry, silk, accounted for half of the workers. Troy and Paterson also had the highest proportions of workers in large factories. This combination suggests that in these two cities similar employment for a majority of the labor force would be peculiarly conducive to the development of the working-class subculture described by Herbert Gutman for Paterson.[14]

Judged by average number of workers per firm, Poughkeepsie's enterprise remained smaller in scale. In contrast to averages of 57 for Paterson and 44 for Troy, most cities in the tri-state region show averages of between 15 and 26 with Poughkeepsie at 18. Cities within this range resemble Philadelphia for which we have the fullest analysis of scale of enterprise in 1880 so far. Although three fifths of the workers in the 14 industries described by Theodore Hershberg and his associates labored in firms employing more than 50 hands, the median work force was less than 8 workers in all but one industry, iron and steel. Small (1 to 5 hands) and medium-sized (6 to 50 hands) firms continued to account for a large minority of workers in most industries and for a majority in 6 of the 14 industries.[15] In Poughkeepsie about two fifths of the workers reported in the manufacturing census labored for firms employing more than 50 hands and correspondingly employment in small and medium-sized firms accounted for a majority of hands in most industries.

The river town already lagged behind upstate manufacturing centers like Troy and Albany in scale of enterprise by 1860. It had no factories with more than 100 workers on the eve of Civil War; it counted six with more than 50 employees and 24 with 20. In 1880 the new shoe factory did have nearly 300 hands and six firms reported 100 or more, but the proportion of all manufacturing workers in firms of 20 to 49 and of 50 or more hands had not changed much between 1860 and 1880. This continued predominance of small and medium-sized shops and diversified manufacturing emphasizes the lack of abrupt change affecting large numbers of workers such as occurred in a city like Paterson when the silk industry developed so rapidly in the seventies. Nor did any entrepreneurial group with such distinct interests as the Paterson silk manufacturers emerge in Poughkeepsie. Absentee owners were the exception; new entrepreneurs came to Poughkeepsie but usually moved quickly into the city's business and professional circles. Correspondingly, while individual factory owners sometimes faced strikes or public criticism for particular actions, this city of diversified manufacturing never experienced the sense of one group of manufacturers as alien to the community or their business policies as injurious to it.

In some lines of manufacturing, especially where custom work and hand methods continued to prevail, the median size of firms decreased during the middle decades. One or two man shops were frequent among immigrants, but, regardless of nativity, large tailoring, shoe, cabinet, carriage, and harness making shops became less common in Poughkeepsie as national and regional competition increased. The invasion of goods manufactured elsewhere limited many firms to local customers and increasingly in some lines to a repairing business. Whereas 2 shoe merchants employed 14 workers each and another 2 employed 12 each to make shoes in 1850, only one firm in 1860 reported as many as 11 workers and the rest had six or fewer. An increase in the proportion of shops with 1 to 5 hands at the expense of shops with 6 to 50 hands in men's clothing and in boots and shoes in Philadelphia between 1850 and 1880 suggests that the Poughkeepsie pattern may have been common in crafts which attracted large numbers of immigrants or which were shifting toward a more localized custom and repair business as they became less competitive in wider markets.

The small scale of much of Poughkeepsie's manufacturing did not mean that native artisans avoided the subdivision of work spreading throughout the northeast in the antebellum decades. Specialization was common well before the immigrant influx. As early as the forties local shops sometimes hired boys to perform the simpler operations in some crafts and industries. The son of one Poughkeepsie shoemaker recalled that whenever he was not in school during the forties he worked at anything he could find to do; among other jobs, he stripped tobacco for a local cigar manufacturer, worked in the wallpaper factory, "pricked tile" in the Vassar brewery, primed signs for a boss painter, and "closed uppers and fitted boots on the shoe bench with my father."[16]

The change in workers' situations wrought by the uneven progress of division of labor during these years and even by the adoption of machinery can easily be exaggerated, however. In Poughkeepsie, as in Philadelphia, the majority of firms, mostly small, reported no use of water or steam power as late as 1880. And even in many large establishments with powered machinery like Poughkeepsie's mower and reaper works, furnaces, and chair and glass factories, the rhythms and control of work were much closer to earlier artisan production than to twentieth-century mass production. That situation prevailed in American manufacturing generally before the 1890s as did the great predominance of workers in consumer goods rather than in producer goods manufacturing. The frequency of small shop manufacture in Poughkeepsie does suggest that more of its work force than of the forces of most cities in the tri-state region remained close to earlier handicraft manufacture, making it a particularly useful location in which to study the lingering of that manufacture as it dwindled in the nation and the consequences for opportunities for artisans.

We presume that the less dynamic character of Poughkeepsie's manufacturing made the city less of a magnet for workers searching for employment. It is presumption only because we do not yet have the systematic studies of movement into as well as out of cities within a region which would demonstrate the relationship between the character of their economies and their relative attractiveness to immigrants, native and foreign. It does seem a reasonable presumption, however, given the low ratios of male to female adults and also of immigrants to natives in Poughkeepsie, especially when those ratios are coupled with the relatively high level of persistence of workers in the city during the sixties and seventies. As the ensuing discussion of geographical mobility will suggest, those foreign newcomers who did find a niche in the city's economy settled down. What did not happen in Poughkeepsie was that massive continuing in-migration of outsiders which transformed the labor forces of cities sustaining rapid growth between 1850 and 1880.

The slower expansion of Poughkeepsie's economy and its lesser dependence on workers born elsewhere did not necessarily mean less opportunity for occupational mobility for workers remaining in the city, however. Stephan Thernstrom's comparison of mobility rates by decade has already suggested that there is no consistent relation between rapid growth and occupational mobility. The extraordinarily high rates which Thomas Kessner has found for New York City suggest the importance of the scale of enterprise and, correspondingly, of relative opportunities for self-employment, a further reminder of how far we have yet to go in discovering the relationships between rates of growth in labor force, immigration and emigration, and occupational mobility.[17] What the following discussion of geographic mobility in Poughkeepsie will attempt to show are the implications of frequencies of movement out of the city for the opportunities of particular groups of workers.

By the most common measure, persistence in a city for a decade, Poughkeepsie's male workers share in the description of nineteenth-century Americans as "men in motion." Tracing from one federal census to the next reveals that half or more disappeared from the city through emigration or death within that ten-year interval (Table 1.2). Following workers through annual city directories reveals a much greater volatility in the labor force than determining whether they persist in the city from one census to the next.[18]

A skilled trade which looks comparatively stable in work force judged by a decadal rate of persistence — the proportion still present ten years later — looks quite different in the light of tracing from year to year. Thus, the census of 1870 showed 45 moulders; 25 of these remained in the 1880 census and were augmented by 16 recent immigrants and local boys starting in the trade. However, an additional 36 moulders had appeared and disappeared from the city directories in the intervening years, 1871 through 1879. Half of them were listed for one year only and all but seven for less than four years. Some years brought unusually large numbers of transients in

TABLE 1.2. Persistence of male workers in Poughkeepsie by occupation in three decades

Occupation	Percent 1850-60[a]	Number 1850	Percent 1860-70	Number 1860	Percent 1870-80	Number 1870
All	32	3,837	49	3,942	50	5,593
Professional	40	135	49	182	48	231
Large proprietor	41	197	63	280	54	554
Semi-professional	29	21	52	25	45	51
Clerical	33	164	45	277	45	495
Small proprietor	50	460	61	399	52	574
Skilled	35	1,149	48	1,424	52	1,824
Semiskilled	34	326	48	396	49	540
Unskilled	20	1,385	42	959	46	1,324

[a]The very low rate of persistence between 1850 and 1860 is influenced by our inability to distinguish systematically residents of the then village from those of the town of Poughkeepsie. Could we do so the total rate of persistence for that decade might rise as high as 40 percent but would still be substantially lower than the rates for the next two decades.

this and other trades. Eight moulders appeared only in the 1873-74 directory. Of a total of 38 plumbers and gasfitters listed in the same directory, 15 showed up in that year only.

Decadal measures alone prove to be particularly misleading for businessmen if their high rates of persistence are generalized into any overall impression of stability as an occupational group. Turnover in businesses, especially small ones, has been notorious in the American past as well as present. In a classic essay on the life of business firms in Poughkeepsie, Mabel Newcomer and the Hutchinsons documented that turnover from 1843 to 1936 showing that a majority of firms in different periods within that span lasted less than four years.[19] Many of the proprietors of these short-lived firms never appeared in any census as businessmen and an important minority did not even appear in Poughkeepsie censuses at other occupations. While most shopkeepers and manufacturers worked in the city before opening their businesses and remained there if they sold out or went bankrupt, credit reports show many firms started by strangers which had very short lives. In the more extreme case, a local correspondent said of one man just starting a small grocery, "Dangerous, failed in New York, in Newburgh, in Hudson, and will do same here if you give him the chance." Failure did not follow, but within a year this man had closed up his store and left Poughkeepsie to start yet another grocery in Troy, 80 miles north.[20]

Decadal measures of persistence do show one dimension of stability in a labor force which analysis of annual turnover ignores. They isolate the most settled element in the population, those workers who have remained long enough to become identified with the community. Men who appear employed in Poughkeepsie at two censuses more often than not spent much or all of their working careers there. Of all men employed at more than one census, two thirds appear in three or more censuses and so worked in the city for a span of at least twenty years. Among all workers first listed in 1850, the only group we can trace over a 30 year span in the census, two fifths of those who survived a decade still remained in Poughkeepsie in 1880.

In general, as migration theory would lead us to expect, the highest rates of persistence are found among middle-aged, married heads of household with property, and of these traits property ownership is the most useful in predicting persistence. At the other extreme, young, single boarders moved on most frequently, regard-

less of nationality. The high rate of persistence among proprietors
partly reflects the older age distribution of this occupational group,
but it does support the expectation that men who sustained their
own businesses for more than a few years tended to continue in the
same community more often than workers without this stake.[21]

Differences in the proportion of the more mobile young in the
various occupational groups does help blunt any sharp differences
between white- and blue-collar workers in frequency of emigration
from Poughkeepsie. While the generally older proprietors show
more stability than manual workers, clerical and sales workers —
disproportionately composed of young men just beginning their
careers who, therefore, should be compared with apprentices in the
crafts — left town much more often than manual workers. The census did not distinguish apprentices at skilled work with any consistency, but a rough approximation can be achieved by analyzing
workers listed at crafts during their teens. Their rates of persistence
resemble those for young white-collar workers.

Apart from the influence of age, marked differences in stability
between particular occupations at every level of skill and responsibility blur the effect of the more obvious examples of stability at the
top and transiency at the bottom of the hierarchy. By their thirties,
most bankers, lawyers, and doctors had indeed settled down for life;
at the same age, day laborers and especially farm laborers disappeared from the city much more often. But other laborers who
can be identified as employed regularly, whether in the gas house,
water works, cemeteries, or factories, prove more stable, as do gardeners and teamsters who tend to be middle-aged or older men.
Among professionals, clergymen and teachers, including proprietors
of academies, leave the city more frequently than workers in all but
a few occupations at any level.

Toward the middle and numerically the largest level of the occupational hierarchy, that of skilled artisans, rates of migration vary
greatly between trades and within particular trades at different
times. Itinerancy was usual among Poughkeepsie's stonecutters; by
contrast, the city's coopers emphasized their local roots, apparently
identifying themselves with a particular cooperage even when unemployed. English and Scottish carpet weavers, progressively displaced by the power loom, seemed to form a largely separate,
diminishing, and unstable enclave.

But other declining trades, such as cabinetmaking and shoe-making, followed a different and more common pattern, which at first glance seems contrary to common sense. Rather than increase, their rate of out-migration decreased as their work force contracted. Sharp decline in the number of new workers entering the trade explains the contraction. The old lingered on in their craft; the young rarely chose it. Since older workers tended more often to have some property, the ironic result was that crafts suffering from competition elsewhere or from the progress of mechanization tended to show a higher proportion of workers owning property than expanding trades that attracted younger workers.

This gradual attrition of the work force in response to lessening local demand for particular skills conformed nicely to the prevailing atomistic theory and condition of the labor market. As local opportunities dried up in an occupation, individuals shifted to other occupations in the same community or emigrated to another community where opportunities still existed in their occupation. The personal costs might be painful—especially in the early stages of declining demand when journeymen found themselves unexpectedly out of jobs with no other local opportunities in their craft—but for the community this individualized process of adjustment avoided any sense of communal responsibility.

The atomistic character of attrition in the crafts encourages a view of large, impersonal forces propelling individuals to move from place to place. The very magnitude of total volatility in population tends to reinforce that view and suggest a churning mass of virtual strangers, even in a small city like Poughkeepsie. At this level of analysis, our evidence offers no exception. After a decade of rapid growth, little more than a third of the city's male labor force of 1870 had been part of it in 1860. Adding to these survivors boys present in the city in 1860 who entered the local labor market thereafter, we still find that more than two fifths of the male workers of 1870 had moved into Poughkeepsie during the preceding decade, a rather awesome proportion.

The problem with such raw counting is not the accuracy of the magnitudes of emigration and immigration presented but rather the misleading impression of strangeness and even chaos created by lack of attention to the patterns of movement. To take the most elementary example, the frequency with which men repeatedly move in and out of the same community raises questions about the meaning of computations of in-migration and out-migration that do not or cannot specify the amount of repetition.

The problem becomes acute, however, in interpreting analyses of annual turnover that depend simply upon total number of listings dropped from and added to a city directory annually. People temporarily absent from a community for a year or two, perhaps sporadically absent, and people returning to live among family and friends after more extended sojourns count the same as strangers who may be in the city only a few months before moving on again. A Connecticut-born hackman first appeared in the Poughkeepsie directory in 1859, left the city by 1862, returned by 1864, left again by 1868, not to return this time until 1878. Within a twenty year period, he would have been counted three times as a newcomer and twice as an emigrant.[22]

Return to the familiar appears again and again, especially among well-established families for whom the evidence is fullest. Sometimes the return has the semblance of a thoroughly rational decision to launch a business or professional career in a known environment where personal acquaintance provides the foundation for a clientele. One boy clerked in a local drug store for four years before accepting clerkship 20 miles up the river. After five years in Kingston, he started his own drug business in Providence, Rhode Island, but after a year started up again in Poughkeepsie.[23]

Some decisions to return undoubtedly reflect an inseparable mixture of nostalgia and failure to do well enough elsewhere. The son of a builder probably would never have left home in the first place had not the outbreak of civil war brought hard times to his own line of business, sash and blind manufacture. He gave up his own shop, moving to Providence as foreman over 40 men in a large carpentry shop there. He spent three years in that city and five in Detroit before coming back to Poughkeepsie to start another unsuccessful venture, this time a saloon. When it failed, he resumed carpentry as a journeyman.[24]

But the most striking illustrations of the appeal of the familiar come in the frequent retirements in Poughkeepsie of native sons who had spent most of their adult lives elsewhere. A father and son came home to live as gentlemen, the father after a career as jeweller in Richmond, Virginia, and the son after 30 years in jewelry in Natchez, Mississippi, and in dry goods at St. Louis. To be sure, not all who returned in later life could afford to retire. A shoemaker left the city in his late twenties, coming back not long after his fiftieth birthday to practice his trade, at first in a short-lived shop with a son who had returned to the city five years earlier.[25]

The return of previous residents meant less strangeness in the tide of newcomers than analysis of turnover suggests. More important in creating a sense of orderliness and security in so geographically mobile a society was a rough sense of predictability as to who moved, when, and why. Familiarity in the patterns of migration if not in the migrants themselves made the frequency of strangers less unsettling. You expected certain kinds of strangers under certain kinds of circumstances. Americans at mid-century expected that many young men would try a number of occupations and pursue them in a number of localities before settling down. Young Poughkeepsians knew that many of the well-established businessmen of their city had been born or worked elsewhere, that migration had been no hindrance to success. They knew that opportunity could be found not only in cities but also in the smaller towns in the surrounding countryside; they knew that if they went to New York City they would find a home-town colony, some permanently settled but others expecting to return upstate.

At mid-century a young man often left home to pursue some form of apprenticeship in business or in a craft, then journeyed in search of opportunities before settling down. One native of nearby Pleasant Valley moved to Fishkill, 15 miles southward, to learn the marble cutter's trade, to Glens Falls in the northern part of the state to perfect the trade, westward to Oswego on Lake Ontario to finish his schooling, then back to Pleasant Valley in business for himself before volunteering for the Union. By age 30 he had returned to employment in Poughkeepsie, where he spent the rest of his life in business.[26]

Many young men spent several years in New York City clerking for commercial houses and sometimes engaging in business themselves for a time before returning to Poughkeepsie or other smaller cities and towns in the Hudson valley. In 1879 the *Eagle* estimated that at least 150 young Poughkeepsians were then in business in New York City. This movement toward the nation's largest city did not go entirely unreciprocated. Two men, born as well as apprenticed to their trades in New York City, left their birthplace to set up a meat market and a bookbindery respectively in Poughkeepsie, where they spent the remainder of their careers. The predominant movement from smaller to bigger cities had its opposing current.[27]

Moreover, reversing the more usual movement from country to city, some Poughkeepsians continued to leave the city to settle in surrounding rural areas. The migration from city to country did become more restricted in character as Poughkeepsie and other river towns grew in importance as retail and wholesale centers. Men planning to engage in farming, storekeeping, and trades whose services could best be rendered locally predominated in this migration. In the country blacksmiths, masons, and carpenters continued at their customary work, little affected by the increasing division of labor in urban centers. Born and apprenticed in the mason's trade in Poughkeepsie, one native went into business for himself in the nearby hamlet of Verbank in the late sixties, moving later to the larger town of Red Hook in the northern part of the county. Another, whose father ran a grocery and later followed shoemaking in Poughkeepsie, left the city as a young man to work on a farm and subsequently became a farm owner himself.[28]

Although all sources confirm the more frequent mobility of the young, they also point up the danger of overemphasizing it. The difference in rates of out-migration between age groups is clear and consistent, but not extreme. About 44 percent of both the younger and older workers of 1860 remained in the city by 1870, compared to about 55 percent of the middle-aged. Similar proportions appear for other decades. Nor does the available evidence suggest any marked difference in the age distribution of native-born immigrants to Poughkeepsie.

Rich men often moved late in life, especially large farmers coming into the city to reside. One prosperous local grocer left in 1865 at age 50 to enter business in New York City. He subsequently opened stores in Minneapolis and in San Francisco before returning to Poughkeepsie to resume business at age 62.[29]

Poor men also moved late in life, but the frequency of movements in and out of the city and of changes in occupations reported suggests necessity more than choice. Elias York reported no occupation at age 42 and employment as a carman at age 48, but he then left Poughkeepsie for several years. York reappeared working at one of the city's furnaces at age 54, disappeared once more for a few years only to crop up at age 58 listing himself as a farmer, presumably a farm worker. Gone again for more than a decade he returned to Poughkeepsie at age 71, reporting himself first with no occupation and then as an ordinary laborer. Such men drifted from place to place and job to job, usually within a limited region. Whether or not they moved as often as York, unskilled workers made up more than one fifth of all men who first reported employment in Pough-keepsie at age 50 or over and remained in the city at least a decade thereafter.

The continuing movement in search of jobs among the unskilled who had achieved no security for their old age was yet another of the familiar patterns citizens recognized in the volatility of people in their community. But this particular pattern reminds us that what might seem familiar, natural, and therefore not frightening to the community does not tell us how the individual migrants composing the pattern viewed it. Still less does it tell us anything about the out-come of emigration, whether it resulted in any improvement in occupation. Because our study captures systematically only those portions of careers spent in Poughkeepsie, it cannot adequately assess the relationship between geographical mobility and occupa-tional mobility.

We do, though, have in our evidence two hints about that rela-tionship which deserve mention. The first hint might more properly be called a caution. Most young men who left Poughkeepsie to try their fortunes elsewhere had done so by age 25 and did not appear employed in the city at more than one census. A small minority, however, emigrated before they reached age 30 but after two census enumerations. Of these emigrants who had begun at white-collar work, one third had reported manual jobs shortly before leaving Poughkeepsie — a rate of downward mobility thrice that for men re-maining in the city.

We suspect that young men who remained in their home towns until their late twenties hoped to make good there and, correspond-ingly, that disappointment with their success so far may have been the motive for departure for a substantial minority, emphasizing the fact that not all young men left their homes with high spirits or even high expectations. The son of a pillar of the German Catholic con-gregation provides an extreme example. This son reported himself as a clerk in his father's hardware store in 1870 at age 19; his father failed in business in 1875 and in 1877 the son, after an uneven rec-ord of employment, which included labor at the iron works, moved to New York City. Two years later, now employed as a private watch-man, he committed suicide in the metropolis.[30]

Those who did not leave their birthplace until their late twenties or early thirties are atypical among youthful emigrants. Moreover, we do not know their destinations or subsequent employment in most cases. Fortunately, we can examine the careers of one other group of migrants without the handicap of foreign birth, men of native parentage born in other states who came to Poughkeepsie before age 30. The occupational mobility of these immigrants during their careers in the city can be compared with the careers of men born in New York State. The result does suggest that men who moved some distance more often improved their occupational status than those who stayed closer to home but not enough to support any image of the movers as invariably more ambitious and able.

Men born in the six New England states show higher upward and lower downward mobility than the New York-born and this picture does not change if we also compare men who first appear in Poughkeepsie at more than 30 years of age. Men born in states outside New England also show mobility superior to the New York-born but the cases are fewer. The better showing of men who moved some distance undoubtedly reflects in part the fact that unskilled workers appear much less frequently in interstate migration than they do in intrastate migration. At the other extreme, highly skilled workers appear more frequently; at the 1860 census 34 percent of all workers in Poughkeepsie who had been born in New England show up as professionals or as large proprietors, managers, and officials compared to 15 percent of those born in New York State.

The largest and most visible streams of immigration at mid-century came from Europe and they consistently reported occupations with lower status more often than native-born whites from any state or region. In the 1830s the need for ordinary labor in a variety of new public and private enterprises brought enough Irish Catholics to the city to form a parish, St. Peter's. But as in most eastern towns, the ebbs and flows of earlier migration never approximated the force of the influx from Ireland and Germany in the late forties and fifties, a wave of refugees from famine, oppression, and civil war. Until 1848 no more than 26 weddings had been celebrated at St. Peter's in any year, but between 1849 and 1855, the numbers range between 73 and 87 annually, subsiding in the next three years to between 52 and 58.[31]

The completion of the railroad to Albany in 1851 left a surplus of unskilled workers from the famine immigration. Continuing arrival of newcomers during the fifties (Table 1.3) meant that many im-

TABLE 1.3. Persistence of male workers in Poughkeepsie by nativity in three decades

Nativity	1850-60		1860-70		1870-80		1870-80 20-29 years old
	Percent	Number	Percent	Number	Percent	Number	
Native-born white	35	2,263	50	2,140	48	2,874	45
Native-born black	37	104	39	105	38	178	34
Irish	25	823	50	772	53	973	43
Native-born of Irish parentage	9[a]	11	49	51	56	305	65
German	32	254	50	468	54	611	47
Native-born of German parentage	0[a]	5	53	32	65	175	70
British	28	304	45	245	45	248	42
Native-born of British parentage	35	26	66	59	60	141	55

[a]The percentage is based on fewer than 25 cases. The age distribution of immigrants and of the native-born of foreign parentage, many of them children of the immigrants, varies, especially in 1870, the first census in which the children of the late forties and fifties influx of Irish and Germans became numerous in the labor force. To eliminate the bias of age distribution, the last column in the table gives the percentages of persistence for all workers aged 20 to 29 years in each nativity group.

migrants did not find opportunities to settle in Poughkeepsie during that decade. Less than one third of the foreign born present in 1850 remained by 1860. After that first terrible decade, the Irish and Germans showed increasing stability in the city. Their rates of persistence converged with that for the native-born of native parentage in the decade after 1860. During the following decade of depression, the first and second generation of both groups remained in the city more frequently than third or more generation Americans. This tendency did not depend upon improving occupational status. Among day laborers, 55 percent of both the Irish and the Germans persisted in Poughkeepsie between 1870 and 1880 compared to 44 percent of the native-born of native parentage and 33 percent of the English and Scottish.

Judged by rates of persistence in three decades, the British as a group showed less tendency to become more settled with the passage of time. The high proportion of skilled workers, especially in textiles, among them undoubtedly made continuing movement within the United States easier, but throughout this period they remained even more migratory than the native-born of native parentage, whom they most resemble in other respects. The Irish and Germans moved from place to place only until they gained a foothold. Then they set about extending that foothold into a small tenacious community of their own by helping kin and countrymen join them.

The process appears most clearly in the growing stability of first- and second-generation workers in particular occupations as they increased their proportion of the work force. At one extreme, the few German machinists who appeared at any census in Poughkeepsie rarely survived a decade. That trade continued to be dominated by native-born and British workers. At the other extreme, those Germans who became the large majority among the city's tailors and butchers persisted more frequently than the mass of their countrymen. Although the total work force in both these trades expanded during these years, the previously dominant ethnic groups tended to disappear more frequently as the German proportion rose.

In the labor force as a whole immigrant groups appeared with increasing frequency in occupations of higher status as they became a more stable element in the city. An index of their relative concentration in different occupational strata shows that whites of native parentage remained largely overrepresented in professional, proprietorial, and clerical and sales occupations compared to their proportion of the male labor force, but the immigrant Germans and British steadily advanced and by 1880 surpassed them in representation in proprietorial occupations.[32] In both the first and second generations, these groups concentrated disproportionately in skilled work throughout the period. The immigrant generation of the Irish remained underrepresented in the crafts but the second generation found work in them more often. The Irish in both generations concentrated disproportionately in semiskilled and especially in unskilled work, the immigrant generation being even more overrepresented in unskilled work in 1880 than it had been in 1850.

Whatever the influence of the influx of unskilled Irish in expanding opportunities for other ethnic groups and especially for natives in higher status occupations, an important minority of whites of native parentage continued to share the bottom of the city's occupational universe with the sons of Erin.

The native-born of both German and Irish parentage did find employment in the new consumer goods factories of the seventies, explaining their overrepresentation at semiskilled work in 1880. This increase in factory employment and decrease in ordinary labor among the second generation is the only significant evidence of leveling upward between generations in Poughkeepsie's manufacturing. As the overrepresentation of the immigrant generation at skilled work and ultimately in proprietorships suggests, the foreign-born set the pattern of self-employment in almost all of the manufacturing and also the construction crafts where their children had much success as shopowners or bosses. Only in the world of the professions, finance, and larger commercial enterprise where familiarity with the language, manners, and business practices of Americans counted for more than it did in manufacturing would the more assimilated second generation be the first to find frequent employment.

Their gradually improving position helps explain the lessening frequency of gross stereotypes of the newcomers in newspapers and in private diaries of natives. But the newcomers themselves helped by actions that suggested their identification with their new home, most notably by their patriotism in enlisting during the Civil War. Father Riordan, the pastor of St. Peter's, led the way with the dramatic gesture of a flag-raising ceremony in front of his church less than two months after Sumter.

Following the war Irish Catholics under Riordan's leadership joined in the battle against alcohol. No Protestant organization outshone St. Peter's Total Abstinence and Benevolent Society in numbers or local publicity. In the late sixties the parish also established a library association. By 1873 the separate parochial schools for boys and girls reported average attendance of 820 compared to only 1,671 for all of the city's public schools. C. N. Arnold, member of the Board of Education and owner of a chair factory, reported that 15 boys at the parochial school, all children of Catholic parents, were so far advanced that either they should be sent to the public high school or a new teacher should be hired for them.[33]

The board accommodated that progress by the controversial step of dispensing with the usual opening religious services at the high school. At the same time it took an even bolder action in response to a proposal from the pastor, trustees, and members of St. Peter's Church. The parish had informed the board that it intended to discontinue its two schools at the conclusion of the term, sending their children henceforth to neighborhood public schools, and inundating the unprepared system with an immediate 50 percent increase in students. The board noted that a large portion of the children resided "in the lower part of the city where the school buildings are already occupied to their full capacity."

The pastor, Dr. McSweeney, then proposed that the board lease for a dollar a year and maintain the two parochial schools. In the negotiations that led to acceptance of the proposal the parish conceded that no religious exercises nor instruction should occur during school hours. The board conceded that the teachers would be nominated by the pastor and that the parish would retain unrestricted control of use of the buildings outside regular school hours. The Poughkeepsie Plan, as it came to be known, remained in effect until 1898 when a resurgence of nativism led to its abandonment.[34]

In 1873 the plan together with the abandonment of Bible reading in the high school provoked a brief flurry of protest. One Protestant minister made an anguished appeal not for denominational education but for a secular education that "taught those moral principles which distinguish us as a nation." Religion, morality, and therefore the best citizenship required teaching of the Bible and so the state must furnish it in the public schools where "it is the foundation of usefulness — there are taught all the principles of thrift and enterprise."[35]

The local lodge of the American Protestant Association resolved that they would not send their children to any school where the Bible was not read. But the bitterest protest came from the historian, Benson Lossing. Lossing had been glad to speak at the flag-raising ceremony in front of St. Peter's Church soon after Sumter, encouraging patriotism among the Irish and other Catholic immigrants. But this was a different occasion. In a historical sketch of "Bible Societies and their Enemies," published in the *Eagle,* Lossing singled out the Jesuits with their "terrible oath to crush Protestantism." The Jesuits had concluded that the Bible "must no longer stand in the way of bringing this Republic under the control of our church," their command had gone forth and the "mandate has been obeyed in the High School of Poughkeepsie. What next?"[36]

Lossing's sounding of the alarm brought no change in policy. But after the public furor subsided the president of the Board of Education, a respected physician, wrote the historian explaining his private view of their disagreement. The mixture of prejudice, principle, and pragmatic consideration in that view nicely describes the reluctant but publicly relatively graceful accommodation by the city's Protestant establishment to this episode in which Catholic newcomers exerted some strength.

Dr. Bolton assured Lossing that the suspension of Bible reading in the high school was his personal act, "founded upon the principle for which Roger Williams contended many years ago, viz; a vindication of the rights of conscience." He also insisted that "the feeblest Roman Catholic child in that *common school* has rights which I, its committee-man, am bound to *protect* . . . Resistance to ecclesiastical tyranny is as much of an Americanism as is a desire to have the 'Bible in the Public Schools.' "[37]

Bolton confessed that he himself had opposed the Poughkeepsie Plan so long as it was in committee for two reasons. As "emphatically a *Bible* man" himself he had foreseen and warned the committee studying the proposal that the plan "would result in the exclusion of the Bible from the Schools (as it was not there by force of *law,* but only by *allowance,* and its use could not be maintained against a Catholic or Jewish protest.)" But Bolton also objected to the plan because it introduced an inferior element into the schools. "This was a *general* objection, and applies also to the *colored* race — all very well for the inferior, but depressing to the superior race." He concluded by urging that the plan had a higher motive than its opponents had recognized. It would bring the children of the immigrants "out from the prescriptions of sectarian influences, and into the glorious liberty of our American boys and girls . . . Hedge them in by Protestant prejudice — read them out of our Schools in a way which is offensive to them — and what have you got? an alien race, opposed to a government that will not protect them, denationalized by popular antipathy, and devotees of a hierarchy that satisfies all their wants both in life and death. But bring them out and scatter them among our own, and what will be the result? we will not proselytize them — oh no! but they will proselytize themselves."

Assimilation of the foreigners in their midst as quickly as possible had been the goal of the city's native Protestant establishment from the beginning, disagreement occurring only over means. The flexibility of the Board of Education had been preceded by ceremonial recognition of the representatives of the newcomers in public occasions as early as the outbreak of Civil War. That recognition would be vivid in the preparations for the city's celebration of the centennial of American independence. The seventeen-member organizing committee included not only editor Platt and other members of the Protestant establishment but also Michael Plunkett, John Dooley, and Andrew King, the German. More than one third of the officers of the fire and military companies marching were of Irish and German birth or parentage. In the line of march St. Peter's Total Abstinence and Benevolent Society under the leadership of Patrick Ward immediately preceded a lodge of the Knights of Pythias led by the German Jew, Adolph Ascher, Past Chancellor. The nativist Order of United American Mechanics brought up the rear.[38]

Conspicuous by their absence were any black citizens or organizations. The aspirations of that race for improvement and participation had never been in question; they protested the inferiority of their segregated education throughout the years of reconstruction. But despite the expressed support of prominent white abolitionists —some of whom vehemently opposed the accommodation with the Catholics of St. Peter's—it took the lonely action of one aggrieved mulatto parent to bring about the admission of the first black child to a previously all-white public school in the same year that the Board of Education approved the Poughkeepsie Plan. The end of segregation in education came by state law a year later. Members of a few black families prominent among their race took the opportunity to send their children to the high school.[39]

Blacks were too few and too poor in Poughkeepsie to achieve the recognition the Irish and Germans had won by the seventies. They found it difficult even to support the pastor of their Zion African Methodist Episcopal Church. Periodic appeals to sympathetic whites to contribute to his maintenance proclaimed their dependence just as the disproportionate numbers of blacks in the Alms House and on outdoor relief showed their race's vulnerability to loss of work in Poughkeepsie. As the church committee said in one advertisement, everyone knew that the "congregation are very poor which renders it impossible for them to meet [the pastor's] necessary wants at this time. All donors of money, dry goods and groceries will be received at the parsonage."

Rates of persistence for blacks in Poughkeepsie were sharply lower than those for any white group in the sixties and seventies. That fact is not explained by differences in skill distribution as comparison with the immigrant Irish shows. The most that can be said with certainty is that neither public policy nor private employment gave the city's blacks, many of them from families resident in the Hudson valley for generations, any reason to look upon this or any neighboring community as a place of opportunity for themselves or their children. Foreign immigrants, by contrast, could see clear evidence within the span of a generation that their children could find better jobs and more respectful treatment than they had found during the great influx of the forties and early fifties.

Because slow-growing Poughkeepsie continued to have a higher proportion of white wage-earners of native parentage, there was less occupational and residential segregation of immigrants and their children than in many of the more rapidly growing cities in the northeast. Although ethnic stratification in the river town conforms to the general pattern of advantage in this period, Poughkeepsie remained a less favorable environment for the emergence of a distinct working-class subculture. There was no counterpart during these years to a publicly recognized spokesman for workers' interests like J. P. McDonnell in Paterson. No individual or group of workers in Poughkeepsie won sufficient attention to provide an alternative through newspapers or public gatherings to the prevailing ethos of individual opportunity articulated by the city's businessmen, editors, and members of the professions.

2

Perspectives on Success

THE GOSPEL OF success had an untiring and flamboyant promoter in the president of Poughkeepsie's widely advertised business college, Harvey G. Eastman, himself the very personification of that gospel. He exulted that "the Mania for Money-Getting is growing stronger in this country every day" and told ambitious youth they could expect to succeed, since "nine out of ten of those who are assuming control of the country come from humbler walks of life, and start without money and friends . . . to begin life poor is to commence as nearly all great and successful men have."[1]

Most mobility studies have begun as ours did with the desire to discover how far America in the nineteenth century realized the promises of improvement made by men like Harvey Eastman. Increasingly, however, the very focus on vertical mobility has been questioned. Howard Chudacoff asks whether analysis of change in status illuminates an artificial structure—"an occupational elevator"—of the historian's making which bears little relation to contemporaries' perceptions, expectations, and aspirations. David Montgomery finds a self-confirming bias inherent in the problem of social mobility which tends to "rule out of consideration from the start any group cultures or values within the community other than those of the middle class."

Support for this kind of questioning comes from a variety of twentieth-century studies. Thus, for the Italians of Boston's North End in the 1950s, as Herbert Gans found, maintenance of close family ties took precedence over desires for individual mobility. For the same period Eli Chinoy showed that dreams of self-employment preoccupied many automobile workers—especially older men for whom that escape no longer was very plausible—much less than their ability to change jobs at the same level of skill and reward when their conditions of work or relations with supervisors became unsatisfactory.[2]

Our next chapter has the limitations of a narrow focus on the general dimensions of vertical occupational mobility. In the remaining chapters we probe the reality behind the abstractions in an attempt to describe as concretely as possible the opportunities available to nineteenth-century workers. That description will not tell us how workers defined opportunity. This chapter seeks to offset these limitations by identifying some of the more important perspectives on success available to Poughkeepsie's citizens at mid-century. It moves from more restrained versions of the success ethos to the values of artisan and immigrant subcultures with some consideration of the role of voluntary associations in expressing the values and satisfying the needs of both subcultures.

This discussion of alternatives is intended to show where our own judgments of the significance of mobility in subsequent chapters may be most questionable. Because of the paucity of direct testimony, the discussion must be speculative. Aspirations and expectations have to be inferred, since neither personal records nor newspapers provide more than scraps showing how men perceived their occupational and property mobility.

We assume that most men did not judge themselves by so extreme a standard of success as Eastman's vision of the poor boy rising to power and prosperity through pluck. In Poughkeepsie successful men of native parentage who shared that vision sometimes criticized the single-mindedness of the "Mania for Money-Getting" even when it was qualified by emphasis upon the responsibilities of riches—in Eastman's words, "Do all the good with your means you can." While the editor of the *Daily Press* preached the economic virtues insistently, he also expressed admiration of those less driven by their imperatives. The Puritans had "winter in their hearts always," this editor remarked in 1866; by contrast, "No people understand the true art of enjoyment better than the Germans. Now we grandsons of the Puritans ought to learn a lesson from our German cousins."[3]

Edmund Platt, son of the editor of the competing *Daily Eagle,* would never have entertained so direct a questioning of the emphasis on self-improvement and go-getting. During the depths of the depression of the seventies this merchant could speak on "Business Pluck" to the YMCA. His diary chronicles a staggering succession of activities—lectures, meetings of organizations, and church services, sometimes three services on one Sunday. Yet even such a paragon of the gospel of success and service as Platt had moments of uneasy reflection. Summing up 1875 in his diary, he commented, "To me it has been a busy year, days all devoted to business, evenings and Sundays to the Lord's work, scarcely any time to be called my own, but sleeping hours, hurrying to the store, hurrying to meals, hurrying here and there, no time to lose, almost neglecting my lovely wife and children who sometimes ask when I can give them a little time."[4]

We may surmise that other men, including many businessmen, felt the calls to do good and to do well less keenly. Occasionally fairly direct evidence appears. Credit reporters noted repeatedly that one young watchmaker who kept a variety store "would rather play the violin than attend to his shop." Described as "a good easy fellow and everybody's friend," he fiddled for dances whenever he could. He paid the price for his gregariousness and his relaxed approach to business; twenty years later "he had only a small repairing business, making about a living."[5]

Very often the manner in which a man conducted his business suggested that he had modest expectations for it. A credit reporter described one hatter in Poughkeepsie as a "good old-fashioned fellow . . . worth about as much as he was thirty years ago—does a little three cent trade, never buys over $25 at a time, manages to make a living." Of a grocer always described as honest, faithful, and prudent, another reporter observed, "One of the kind that grows poorer, the older they grow." Whatever the youthful fantasies of such retailers, they gave no sign of ever scrambling for wealth or position, apparently priding themselves instead upon their reputations for integrity and steady habits.[6]

Artisans who owned shops frequently won high praise from credit reporters for their craftsmanship but low marks for their lack of calculation and corresponding failure to make more than a living. Of an English cabinet maker, they said, "expert workman . . . temperate, industrious, but not successful in business . . . no calculation . . . a very old-fashioned man scarcely up to the times." Of a native edge tool maker, they commented, "a superior mechanic but is no financier and consequently has never been a successful businessman. Lacks the *head* to conduct a business . . . Would do well in a small way if he had someone with him competent to direct the business as his work sells well and he has a reputation in this section."[7]

Fortunately for such men another perspective on success still remained vital, predominating in the self-help books until the last quarter of the century. Pre-industrial and highly moralistic in outlook, it emphasized respectability and independence rather than riches, urging men to take up trades like blacksmithing and carpentry in which it was easiest to start your own business.[8] For self-employed artisans, in particular, the judgments of credit reporters about "old-fashioned" men lacking "the head" for business may be the misleading response of a more modern "go-getting" mentality to behavior which reflects a positive, continuing commitment to traditional rhythms of work in the crafts and to other customs of artisan culture.

Our evidence is insufficient to do more than indicate the possibility, but some fragments do suggest the presence in Poughkeepsie of a lively and not as yet defensive artisan culture until at least the Civil War. Even some of the larger employers during the fifties remained more wedded to the ideals of that tradition than to calculating business practices. The obituary of Egbert Killey, publisher of the *Telegraph,* noted that no apprentice of this printer "who had conducted himself creditably was ever discharged at the expiration of his time, but furnished with employment until an opportunity offered for good and permanent business, and the necessary aid in many cases furnished to enable them to go into business for themselves." Moreover, Killey's efforts "for the levelling up, as he used to say, of the masses" included successful campaigns to establish free public grammar schools, a free library for young mechanics and a program of adult education, the Poughkeepsie Lyceum.[9]

By the seventies the chances for artisans to start their own shops had diminished in economic significance and to a lesser extent in frequency. The argument for self-employment in a trade became less persuasive as the artisan shop became an anachronism or a specialized exception in many lines of manufacturing. The corollary emphasis on the fusion of manual and intellectual skills in the craftsman, idealized in the figure of Elihu Burritt, the learned blacksmith, also became less effective. The distinction between hand and brain labor sharpened and so did contrast between their attractiveness and respectability. To that extent, the modern division of the occupational universe between white collar and blue collar jobs seems much closer to the perception of Americans in 1870 than in 1850.

Despite this emerging contrast and the declining prospects for prosperity in small craft-related shops, journeymen continued to try self-employment. Furthermore, manual workers of every degree of skill frequently turned to petty retailing and service ventures — most often in their own neighborhoods — even when competition in these lines promised them a meager livelihood at best. We believe that the number of these shops throughout the closing decades of the century testifies more to the wish for independence through self-employment which twentieth-century surveys find so common among manual workers than to any aspirations to success or gentility suggested by the honorific designation of white collar. Desires to be free of control by others and to secure an income for the years of declining vigor seem more plausible as explanation for the numerous small groceries, cigar shops, saloons, and variety stores started by middle-aged manual workers than any ambition to become a successful merchant.

Whatever the level of ambition of workingmen and small shopkeepers we assume that men of different social classes usually judged their own achievement primarily by comparison with their immediate neighbors in work and residence and voluntary association. English-born Thomas Lumb may have preferred the independence of running a grocery in his home in one of the poorer districts of Poughkeepsie to his previous employment in Pelton's carpet factory. He also would have been aware that his fellow countryman and neighbor on Hoffman Street, railroad engineer John Ogden, had an annual income well above his own or that of most backstreet petty proprietors.

Beyond an immediate circle of acquaintance most men probably did not see very clearly. No man would have had so comprehensive a view as the historian's systematic tracing of occupation and property provides, specifying the patterns of opportunity for every level of the labor force in every neighborhood of the city. For the shoe factory operative living on the western edge of town the rich residents of the newly fashionable district more than a mile to the southeast must have been undifferentiated. When a banker lost so heavily by speculation that his fortune was reduced temporarily from half a million dollars to $30,000, men of his class noted his misfortune and his corresponding curtailment of family expenses. But to the factory operative he remained a bank president and one of the rich men in town.[10]

Newspaper editors in urging the more fortunate to charitable efforts sometimes testified to this social insulation. "There is more poverty and suffering through actual want in our city than one in a thousand of our citizens knows anything about." Usually, however, they talked in the stereotypical images that social distance breeds and followed respectable opinion everywhere in distinguishing between the deserving and the undeserving poor. Both remained faceless. The advent of summery weather in May brought a ritual lament about the number of men "loafing in the sunshine." Reporting the "crowds of idlers who, day and night, infest Main Street," the *Daily Press* typically lumped them all together as lazy. While transgressors against the law were carefully named, it was only to poke fun at their nationality and wayward ways.[11]

At the other extreme, in the rare instances when it emerged, the workingman's view of leading citizens indicates no greater discrimination. After watching the lottery for the draft in 1862, a farmer reported that the crowd roared its pleasure whenever a prominent name was drawn. A woman called on by the WCTU reflected the same generalized hostility to the more affluent when she remarked to her callers that "when the rich people stopped drinking, it would be time to speak to the poor about it."[12]

What remains unclear in retrospect is the extent to which generalizations about others at a social distance, especially their tendency to reduce social differences to grossly oversimplified distinctions, also represent a consistent self-identification. We assume that contemporaries did see themselves in such distinctions part of the time, notably when issues or events created a sense of group conflict. But we also assume that much of the time all workers, from professionals to ordinary laborers, were concerned with the much finer distinctions in position which they experienced in their immediate worlds of work, residence, and voluntary association and with the greater sense of possibility for change within that more limited range.

More important, we doubt that either the grosser or the finer distinctions were central to the self-definition of men early in their careers. For those still hopeful of improving their personal situation significantly, we assume that group identification served most often to reinforce a sense of fraternity with the group or of righteous indignation against injury from those outside it. By contrast, for men whose hopes of personal improvement had narrowed, we suspect that identification with others in the same situation became more profound. We do assume that the occupationally immobile in a society with a mobility ethos need some alternative or compensatory way of viewing their lives as important. For immigrants bringing with them a different ethos, the problem would develop with assimilation; for natives, even those still nourished by a less competitive, more fraternal artisan ethos, we believe the problem of compensation already existed by mid-century. It helps explain, for example, the appeal for workingmen of two different kinds of organization, trade unions and volunteer fire companies.

As the traditional difference between skilled craftsmen and unskilled laborers eroded through specialization and as the older sense of a fluid middle of society composed of shopowners and of craftsmen hoping to become shopowners disappeared, this latent class consciousness began to be expressed in the sporadic strikes and union activity mentioned in later chapters. Before 1880, however, Poughkeepsie had no strong unions outside the building trades. In 1868 representatives of the organized trades in the city did form a council which considered participation in the Eight Hour movement but no further mention of united action appears before 1880.[13]

Unorganized unskilled and semiskilled workers in the city sporadically struck over wages from at least the time of the construction of the Hudson River Railroad in the late forties. Sometimes these strikes acquired a bitterness that threatened to move beyond the specific grievances into a more generalized sense of conflict between haves and have nots. Correspondingly, the city's native establishment occasionally displayed some anxiety that battles between capital and labor elsewhere in the nation would be contagious locally. Local newspapers praised the calling up of the 21st Regiment in the county during the great railroad strikes of 1877. They stressed repeatedly that the city's railroad workers were "not turbulent men [despite] the severe reduction in pay" but also warned against the "idle, dissolute, and vagabond class . . . who prat most loudly, between drinks, about the wrongs of the laboring classes and seize upon an occasion like the present to commit acts of violence and place the well-disposed people of the community in terror." When Vanderbilt's employees in Poughkeepsie remained at work, the relief of newspapers and prominent citizens was audible.[14]

When galvanized by a local issue, workers could and did organize effectively to make the city government respond to their grievances. Thus, when open ponds owned by some of the city's larger manufacturers became acute public health problems, workingmen turned out en masse in 1870 to demand that they be drained and filled. John Kearney, an Irish laborer who served as spokesman, protested: "We have been lying sick over there by the dozens, yes hundreds . . . We want this dam down and we'll take it down and run the risk of the law." Another worker raised the issue of class: "There is an aristocratic party at work. The poor laboring man can die . . . If the Water Commissioners can't do this thing, we'll do it." The city government gave in and ordered the filling of the ponds.[15]

Reports of public expression of grievances by workingmen with overtones of class antagonism such as the pond fight were rare and the protests themselves seem to have been short-lived, however long resentments lingered. The unpopularity of the Civil War draft, particularly the hardship on workingmen who could not afford to pay for substitutes, did not lead to any public outbursts although the *Daily Press* reported in September 1863 that alarmists in town talked about the danger of draft riots. Rather in the hardest hit First Ward, small shopkeepers and workingmen organized a meeting at Michael Kelly's store to raise a fund to help out those unable to buy their way out. And with the unhappy example of New York City's recent riots before them, a number of prominent gentlemen spoke to a second and more general meeting in the city for the same purpose.[16]

This lack of rebelliousness among the city's workers does not necessarily imply any great respect for their betters; indeed, the occasional surfacing of anger and resentment warns against any notion of deference gladly given. Such passivity does argue for an expectation of marked differences in power and privilege and a tendency to avoid conflict over all but extreme grievances except where there seemed some reasonable chance of winning concessions. In so small a city as Poughkeepsie some men of very different social positions undoubtedly developed friendships, most often probably through shared religious work, but the composition of most voluntary associations indicates that the social life of the majority of men did not extend beyond their own class.

Social class does not lend itself to easy definition, certainly not at the boundaries between classes, but Poughkeepsie's clubs, fraternal orders, and other social organizations show too strong a clustering of members according to level of wealth and education to assume that consciousness of class differences did not shape their recruitment. Members of the city's upper and more comfortable middle classes founded literary societies, boat, driving, and horticultural clubs, civic organizations such as the YMCA, and charitable institutions such as the Home for the Friendless, St. Barnabas Hospital, the Old Ladies Home, and the SPCA. By contrast, a mixture of artisans and merchants of more modest prosperity peopled the fraternal orders, volunteer fire companies, military companies, and the rash of small social clubs that sprang up in the sixties and seventies. Even when fraternal orders like the Masons and the Odd Fellows appealed to both the more prosperous and the less substantial, the several lodges of each order in the city sorted themselves out largely by class and sometimes by ethnic group as well.

The volunteer fire companies offer the most important test for theories about the uses of voluntary associations for workingmen. Taken collectively, they do provide a striking example of membership drawn heavily from artisans and yet cutting across classes. At the same time they received a recognition and support from the city accorded no other associations. Their recreation and arrangements for mutual aid easily suggest a positive interpretation of the fire companies as promoting group solidarity without lessening prospects for individual mobility. Indeed, their behavior can suggest an expansive, optimistic outlook comparable to the boosters among the city's businessmen. On the other hand, the proliferation of voluntary associations of workingmen during the sixties and seventies, coupled with the increasingly social emphases of the fire companies, can be construed as a compensation for narrowing opportunities. They can be seen as a turning away of wage earners from expectations of substantial improvement in status and reward and a turning toward the satisfactions of a distinctive, insular style of living such as the emphasis on recreation and entertainment Gareth Stedman Jones finds among the working classes of London in the late nineteenth century or the premium on personal expression

Lee Rainwater finds among blacks in twentieth-century America.[17]

Our examination of Poughkeepsie's fire companies suggests that the latter interpretation may be closer to the truth than the former. The social life of the companies grew more intense as the class origin and prospects for mobility of members narrowed. Moreover, while the companies did provide mutual assistance in time of need, they did not push as the trade unions did for improvement in living conditions. Nor did they serve in the long run as a satisfactory substitute for the economic security that occupational mobility might have provided.

The history of the fire companies presents a curious spectacle. As they improved their equipment, built increasingly expensive fire houses, and developed an ever more elaborate social life around them in the late fifties and early sixties, the companies seem to have become more attractive to wage earners without a future of advancement and less attractive to the largest merchants and manufacturers. Moreover, the range of class representation in their collective membership as the city's fire department largely disappears when we examine the roster of the individual fire houses. As the city grew larger and neighborhoods became more sharply differentiated, so, too, did the companies. The two companies located nearest the central business district drew their members primarily from businessmen and from clerical and sales workers. Well over two thirds of the members of the five larger companies were skilled craftsmen. Unskilled workers, primarily boatmen, comprised a substantial minority of one company located near the river. Each of the five working-class companies had a sprinkling of small merchants and occasionally larger proprietors whose businesses happened to be located in that district.

Most of the wage earners in these companies were in their late twenties and early thirties, and for the most part, immobile in occupation. A comparison of artisans listed as members in 1867 with those who still remained in the city by 1880 reveals very few cases of a journeyman becoming a shopkeeper in his trade. Those who did become self-employed usually opened saloons or other petty retail ventures. The boatmen and ordinary laborers continued at unskilled work. The fire companies seem, therefore, to represent the stable — more accurately, the permanent — working class, men who had found their niche and stayed there.

What their members lacked in future prospects, they made up in present excitement. Companies frequently made excursions to other cities, occasions full of conviviality sure to be recounted in detail in local newspapers. One company made an excursion to New Haven where "bonfires lit their parade routes on every corner . . . and they were feasted and welcomed by the Mayor." The next day the entire fire department of that city escorted them to the steamer for New York. A delegation from the Firemen's Association met them in the metropolis, paraded them to Broadway, gave them breakfast, and took them to Central Park for a picnic. Poughkeepsie's fire houses returned the hospitality when their former hosts came to town. A letter to the *Daily Press* complained in 1868 about the extensive coverage of "firemen's visits abroad, including tar-barrels, torch-lights, collations, speeches, beautiful bouquets, pretty girls and all that sort of thing."[18]

For men whose working lives offered small reward and less promi-nence, leadership in a firehouse brought public attention. When he died of consumption at age 33, John Gildersleeve, a boatman, was foreman of one of the local companies. All the companies as well as two from other communities turned out for his funeral. Flags had been lowered and bells tolled as his cortege passed through the city. An unskilled worker on the river had achieved a kind of recognition rarely accorded laboring men. We cannot but suppose that his fellow firemen took pride in this recognition. Just five days later, however, the newspapers announced a subscription for his widow and four children, "a family now left destitute." Some of the city's wealthiest men signed the subscription, which alleviated but did not end the family's hardship. Five months later the fire company held a picnic to raise more funds for Mrs. Gildersleeve.[19]

Expectation of support from their co-workers in time of need gave firemen some sense of security in a very insecure existence. Such instances of help occurred regularly, and they did not depend upon popularity. When George Tyne lay dying in 1870, without friends or relatives in the city, fellow members of the Booth Hose Company took care of him.[20] But this kind of solidarity does not seem to have fostered efforts for any more general improvement of the condition of workers.

Participation in fire companies need not, in principle, have been incompatible with membership in trade unions. In practice, we find little overlapping in Poughkeepsie, strengthening our sense that the two kinds of association represented not only a difference in purpose but also in outlook.

Attempts to organize journeymen in most trades in Poughkeepsie during these years had only partial and temporary success, but two early unions showed some strength as well as stability. Both the carpenters' union and the masons' union conducted strikes and periodically advertised in the newspapers the names of bosses who paid union wages and hired union men. We have not been able to find complete lists of membership, but several times a year the newspapers reported activities of these unions and especially the election of officers.

From these accounts we compiled a list of 40 officers—20 each from the two unions—elected between 1866 and 1869. Of the 20 associated with the carpenters' union only three belonged to a volunteer fire company, yet the fire companies in 1867 listed 23 carpenters as members. Of the 20 leaders of the masons' union, only two also held membership in a fire house. This apparent lack of interest by union leaders does not seem to have been primarily a matter of lack of time for other activities. Jacob R. Kidney did serve in 1868 as foreman of his company as well as officer of the carpenters' union. Moreover, many officers of the heavily Irish masons' union also appear as officers of societies within St. Peter's Church and societies devoted to Irish causes. Our limited evidence can do no more than suggest that fire companies and unions generally represented different points of view among the working classes rather than different means of accomplishing the same ends. The question needs closer study in towns with a more active union movement and better union records.

Even more than working-class associations, foreign immigrants pose the question of competing perspectives on success. A man's ambition to improve his lot could conflict with his identification with his fellow countrymen and co-religionists. Alternatively, submersion within his own ethnic group could insulate a man from the larger society. Herbert Gans documented both these possibilities for the Italian-Americans in Boston's North End in the twentieth century.

While the ethnic communities in mid-century Poughkeepsie may have impeded structural assimilation, to use Milton Gordon's helpful distinction, they seem to have had little effect on behavioral

assimilation. In being "not a room but a corridor," they resemble
the later Slavic communities of the Mesabi range as Timothy Smith
has described their aspirations.[21] Because Poughkeepsie was a small
city, ghettos did not appear. There were concentrations of Irish and
Germans in some neighborhoods, but few streets belonged exclusively to one group. Ethnic diversity within neighborhoods contributed to the city's rather rapid acceptance of the newcomers. Few
voluntary associations were segregated rigidly by ethnicity and those
few sometimes cooperated with organizations not confined to their
ethnic group.

Of all the ethnic groups in Poughkeepsie, the German Catholics
most self-consciously attempted to preserve both a distinctive religion and culture, viewing the strength of one as dependent on the
strength of the other. If tendency to reside near their church and
fellow countrymen be any indication, then German Catholics in
Poughkeepsie showed more tendency than German Protestants to
insulate themselves from native Protestants. By 1880, 28 percent
of the German Protestants resided in predominantly native-born
neighborhoods to the east of the area where all German churches
and most of the German population concentrated, but only 17 percent of the Catholics did. Moreover, German Catholics founded
their own parochial schools and as late as 1896 their pastor cau-
tioned that parents "who send their children to public school thereby commit a major sin and cannot be absolved until they have taken
their children out of that school." Similarly he warned against societies that "are dangerous for a good Catholic because they further
too frequent intercourse with people of all religions"; to guard
against such fraternization, the church sponsored a host of associations to meet the needs of its parishioners.[22]

The pastor's admonitions fused the religious and the cultural. "In
your family German should be spoken; do not tolerate your children
speaking English to you, otherwise the sweetest family ties will
loosen, religion will be harmed and the respectfulness due to you
from your children and your power over them will be destroyed."
On their face, such admonitions seem to advocate a divorce of the
German Catholic from the larger society. But the pastor took a
more realistic position. "Count and calculate your dollars in English," he advised.

Such conflict as existed between individual aspiration and group
loyalty most affected those who struggled to establish a stable Ger-

man Catholic church. For some of them, the role of communal leader seems to have been more highly prized than any dream of individual success. Born in the Rhineland, Frank Hengstebeck began in Poughkeepsie as a locksmith in the late forties but within a decade had built up a flourishing business. He also branched out into real estate, erecting several brick stores. Credit reporters praised his industry yet worried about his generosity—laxness from their point of view—in guaranteeing other people's loans and credit. One remarked that he "does good business and makes money, but endorses the paper of everyone who asks him and has had to pay a good deal thereby." The worries proved to be justified. Hengstebeck failed during the depression having made some bad investments as well as continuing to go "security for most everybody." His family managed to stay in business but never recovered its former prosperity.[23]

Requests for endorsement would have been hard to turn down for this founder and patriarch of Poughkeepsie's German Catholic congregation, one of its few successful businessmen in the beginning. In 1855, at the first waxing of his own prosperity, Hengstebeck became the first president of a reorganized men's society for local Catholics of German nationality, preoccupied with creation of a German parish. All the surviving evidence suggests how central that project must have been to his sense of calling in life. On the occasion of the parish's fiftieth anniversary the pastor recalled, "When our large Saint Michael's bell was presented at the church, deeply moved, Mr. Frank Hengstebeck . . . told me, 'Now I can gladly die because I know the congregation is on a firm footing.'"[24]

For the most part, however, as the next chapter will document, German Catholics fared as well as German Protestants in their general occupational mobility and almost as well in their accumulation of property. While the German Catholic church maintained its own school, it is hard to find evidence that it inhibited the mobility of the second generation. It is true that a few Germans took advantage of the high school, but that was as true of German Protestants as of German Catholics.

For the most prosperous Germans, no matter what their religion, certain common practices emerged that reconciled their loyalties to their countrymen with their own self-interest. Protestant Jacob Blankenhorn and Catholic Peter Thielman served as moneylenders to their people. Thielman returned some of that money to his fellow

German Catholics by generous contributions to the parish. Moreover, while German Catholics had a full complement of fraternities
and societies—for Christian mothers, for youth, for adult men, for
ex-Civil War soldiers—the members of the parish were drawn into
organizations that emphasized a common German heritage. The
Germania Singing Society, the focal point of social activities for all
Germans in the city, included both Catholics and Protestants among
its members and officers. The Germania picnics and dances always
attracted a number of native Americans as well.[25] By the seventies
several Catholic organizations brought Irish and Germans together.

Admonitions to preserve their faith and national inheritance by
standing apart from American culture were not heeded by younger
members of the parish. As the pastor observed in 1897, "The rows of
the old are becoming thinner and not being replaced. Among the
young there are only a few who can become enthusiastic about the
preservation of specifically German attitudes and opinions."[26]

For the Irish Catholics, even the more successful, few signs can be
found of conflict between economic achievement and their loyalty
to their countrymen and church. Michael Kelly's role as communal
and religious leader nicely complemented his commercial endeavors. For him commercial success owed less to Harvey Eastman's
model than to the traditional communal role played by grocers,
pubkeepers, and other small businessmen in Ireland. Leaving
County Galway for America in the 1820s Kelly had run a grocery in
Albany before setting up in Poughkeepsie in 1835. By the time of
the famine migration a credit reporter called him "the king of the
Irish, right-hand man of the priest." The reporter also noted his
activities as moneylender and landlord to his countrymen. The
Kelly grocery never emulated the cash and carry provisioners of the
main business district and remained off the main business street in a
polyglot immigrant neighborhood, "a store of the old-fashioned sort
with a bar in the rear." Kelly mixed business with sociability and
especially with religious affairs. He always took an active role in St.
Peter's, the first Roman Catholic parish in the city. The priest celebrated masses in his house until the church was completed in 1837
and thereafter "to the end of his life he was regarded as a leader and
counselor by the men of his faith." His role seems very similar to the
leadership which Conrad Arensberg found Irish pubkeepers exer-
cising in the west of Ireland during the 1930s.[27]

Nevertheless, after his father's death, Kelly's son Timothy joined two native-born Protestants in the formation of a dry goods firm in the mid-seventies. Because of the competition from the newly emerging department stores, the firm did not last long. Timothy returned to running his father's grocery. But the father's deep involvement with the Irish Catholic community had not prevented his son from trying to move into the mainstream of the city's business life.[28]

Even those Irishmen who participated in the nationalistic Fenian movement did not insulate themselves from the larger society. On the contrary, the Fenian leaders were men who already exercised leadership in business and union affairs, reinforcing the common sense that men who exercise leadership in one sphere will transfer those talents to other endeavors. They also were active in St. Peter's Church.[29]

Some immigrants did feel more threatened by the second generations's adaptation to native culture especially when it involved intermarriage. The son of Patrick Costello, an Irish saloonkeeper, not only refused to fulfill his father's dream that he become a priest but compounded that transgression by marrying a non-Catholic native girl. When Costello died in 1868, leaving an estate of $30,000, he disinherited his son's child. Religious loyalty as well as patriarchal authority took precedence over any dream of economic mobility for his son.[30]

By the 1900s sons of Catholic saloonkeepers and grocers, many of whom began at ordinary labor, had moved out successfully into the larger community. The greater hardship of the first and second generation Irish in Poughkeepsie when compared to other immigrant groups seems to us more a reflection of the preponderance among them of unskilled laborers than of cultural or religious values. We cannot be sure, however, that those who remained at unskilled work longest may not also have clung hardest to old country ways, deliberately keeping as much distance as they could from Americans of native parentage and their mores.[31]

Because of their low occupational starting point, most of the immigrant Irish found it difficult to make the leap envisioned by Eastman or even to emulate the more successful of their countrymen. Their progress as a group was slow in escaping the most arduous and dirty work; a lack of skills and native doubts about their competence was compounded for some by problems of literacy and sometimes drunkenness and disorder. On the whole, however, they made substantial gains. A far larger proportion of Irish laborers than of any other unskilled group of workers achieved the ownership of a house and some land. Owners of real estate did not comprise more than one fifth of native-born, German, or British laborers in Poughkeepsie, yet in 1860 nearly one half of the Irish laborers reported property. We assume that for men who came from a society where ownership of land was both highly prized and forbidden them, this achievement was deeply gratifying even if the modest dwellings these laborers could afford initially were not much above shanties.

Moreover, Irish laborers in Poughkeepsie showed a desire for assimilation, education, and improvement. Unlike their counterparts in Newburyport, they sent their children to school—once the immigrant generation had settled down—as often as those of native parentage and more often than those of German parentage. The most numerous as well as distinctive organization of Irish laborers in the city was St. Peter's Total Abstinence and Benevolent Society, usually abbreviated as the TAB. The majority of its members were unskilled or semiskilled workers although it always had a substantial minority of skilled workers and a scattering of professionals and proprietors; collectively, they comprised more than one tenth of all men of Irish birth or parentage in 1880.[32]

While the current preoccupation of historians with social control encourages interpreting an organization like St. Peter's TAB Society as an effort by middle-class Catholics and the priesthood to force respectability upon their countrymen, it seems just as likely to us that such organizations expressed the aspirations of those members. In a small city like Poughkeepsie, the initial intermingling of classes within Catholic organizations, Irish or German, is notable. Thus, St. Peter's Library and Literary Association, founded for the "moral, intellectual and social improvement" of its members, included laborers among its officers as late as the eighties. Moreover, each of these organizations numbered some of the most spectacular Irish success stories. Peter Shields who was first reported in the census as a resident of the Alms House but who became Deputy Sheriff of Dutchess County served as president of the Library Association while still a laborer. William J. Leahey, the son of another laborer who first reported himself in the census as a tinsmith, joined the Total

Abstinence Society as a young man; Leahey subsequently became president of the Dutchess Manufacturing Company, founded by affluent natives.[33]

Just as typical of the membership of these "improving" societies were men who remained wage earners, accumulated some property, and served as active members of trade unions or of voluntary associations like the fire companies. Timothy Capper, organizer for the bricklayers, masons and plasterers and a leader of the Fenians, belonged to the TAB. So did his fellow unionist, Patrick Lamb. Thomas Tynan, successively reporting himself as carpenter and shoemaker, served as an officer of the Library Association and as a volunteer fireman.

We cannot know whether a Thomas Tynan judged himself unfavorably through comparison with economically successful men of his own ethnic group like William Leahey. We do find that as the Irish in Poughkeepsie developed their own professional and more prosperous business class, some tendency appears toward lesser representation of manual workers within their associational life, at least in the leadership. It may be that the less successful Irish increasingly relied upon the more private networks of kinship and friendship for their self-esteem. We do assume that working-class members of every ethnic group could limit the hurt of unfavorable comparison based upon the American success ethos by continuing to value as achievement among themselves what outsiders might deem insignificant. Such settling by wage earners into niches with a protected social life need not imply lack of ambition nor lack of awareness of how outsiders saw them and their jobs, especially employers and others with authority over them. It does suggest that many of them much of the time did not look at their own working lives from the perspective of the American success ethic, even its more modest versions.

3

Chances to Rise

By ANY STANDARD men changed occupations in nineteenth-century Poughkeepsie frequently. A young man's first job did not fix his career. Excluding shifts between such closely related occupations as tanner and currier, plumber and gasfitter, carter, carman, and teamster, in any one of the three decades after 1850 two out of every five men who remained in the city between federal censuses reported a shift in occupation. Such fluidity reinforces the picture given by commentators from Tocqueville to Daniel Boorstin of the restless American, forever giving up old callings, homes, and possessions for new ones. How much of this remarkable fluidity should be regarded as vertical mobility, that is, as significant improvement or decline in occupational status, and how much should be regarded as horizontal mobility may vary with the definitions of the investigators, but the most commonly used definitions have provided satisfactory and quite similar broad measurements for a number of cities.

This chapter describes the general dimensions of vertical mobility for the male labor force of Poughkeepsie between 1850 and 1880, the chances that workers and their sons would find occupations in the city superior or inferior to their first reported jobs there. It will show how the chances of sons varied according to their fathers' occupations and how both mobility within the individual career and between generations varied with race and nationality. The chapter will conclude with brief analyses of two less comprehensive indices of opportunity — wealth and education — to see how much they seem to reinforce, qualify, or question our interpretation of our frequencies of occupational mobility.

As aggregate analysis preparatory to our closer examination of opportunity within the context of specific occupations, this chapter sacrifices individual illustration. Its very abstraction underscores the limitations of aggregate analysis in the writing of social history. This essential but long neglected tool can obscure as much as it reveals unless its results be interpreted and vivified through historical particulars, both those it abstracts for quantification and those that do not lend themselves to quantification.

Occupation as a Surrogate for Social Status

We chose occupation as the focus for this study of Poughkeepsie because it alone seemed knowable for the entire labor force and capable of disclosing more than any other individual trait would about the various dimensions of opportunity. We agree entirely with Michael Katz's objection that occupational titles by themselves may tell us little, since they often prove to be ambiguous or misleading.[1] However, the titles given in the manuscript census can be clarified by a variety of means, some of which will be described shortly. We do not assume that the titles so clarified represent a man's social status with any exactness, but we do believe that they show the status of all members of a male labor force relative to each other more satisfactorily than any other single type of evidence. They also provide the best leads to other types of contemporary evidence about a man's probable earnings and chances of accumulating property, his education, his control over his job, where and how he lives, and with whom he associates.

Other traits employed as surrogates for social status seem to us liable to more serious objections either because of the quality or, more often, of the comprehensiveness of the evidence available to historians. The more usual choices like amount of income, property, or education and more recent proposals such as employment of servants or membership in voluntary associations can be determined at mid-century only for a minority of the male labor force in

any American city—ruling out any gradations in status among the
majority—or else, as in the case of census reportage of children in
school, the evidence is of dubious accuracy. For the same reasons,
no combination of traits seems feasible as a surrogate now even if we
could agree upon their relative importance.

Among the alternative criteria for ranking, income, and property—the most promising candidates because of their preciseness
—give us no means of distinguishing differences in status for three
fourths of the male labor force in Poughkeepsie and in other American cities at mid-century. During the ten years of federal income
taxation after 1863, the vast majority of citizens were exempted
from reporting. In 1866, the year of smallest exemption and therefore of largest reportage, less than one fifth of Poughkeepsie's male
workers claimed an income of $600 or more, the minimum amount
taxed.

Owners of real and personal property assessed for local taxation
comprised one fourth of the total male labor force, a slightly higher
proportion than for income. But the problems of comparing property mobility in different cities dwarf those of comparing occupational mobility. Moreover, crude as the comparison of occupational
mobility has had to be so far, the patterns and frequencies revealed
for widely divergent communities have had enough similarity to
focus further investigation more sharply, helping us distinguish the
more pervasive patterns from those which seem idiosyncratic to particular localities and regions. Stephan Thernstrom's preliminary
assessment offers reassurance that individual community mobility
studies do indeed contribute to the understanding of broader social
processes throughout urban America.[2]

Vertical Ranking of Occupations

Discussion of the difficulty of ranking occupational titles as they
are given in nineteenth-century sources was one of the earliest signs
that the historians developing this field were having troubles with
their collective borrowing from the pioneers in the study of social
mobility, twentieth-century sociologists. Discovering the deficiencies
of past enumerations of occupation and also the limitations of
modern schemes of occupational classification in ordering them is
much easier than correcting either, however. We believe that any
attempt now to substitute different conventions based on our still

primitive knowledge of nineteenth-century stratification would be to lose the usefulness of even crude comparison with contemporary studies of occupational mobility without sufficient compensating gain in ability to describe past fluidity and interpret its significance. Our emphasis on preserving the basis for comparison does, however, require constant attention to those points where modern nomenclature and classification distort our understanding of the past.

The very names that twentieth-century studies use for their primary vertical division of occupations — white-collar and blue-collar or, alternatively, manual and nonmanual — are a source of trouble for nineteenth-century studies.[3] The master craftsman employing several workers who continued to do some handwork himself does not fit comfortably with either the functional distinction of nonmanual or the honorific white-collar, but he clearly belonged to Poughkeepsie's middle class by most criteria — certainly before the sixties — and by no means always the least prosperous part of it. Twentieth-century labels inevitably convey a misleading impression of a middle class in which artisan proprietors played so large a role.

In the absence of a more adequate nomenclature, these labels remain the common coin of comparison between the nineteenth and twentieth centuries and so we employ them. The elaboration of the middle of the occupational hierarchy in the remainder of the book will show more fully the limitations entailed in their use in this chapter. Overlapping in reward and status between manual and nonmanual employment did not await the twentieth century. Eric Hobsbawm's description of tendencies in England during the nineteenth century applies to Poughkeepsie: "Socially speaking the best-paid stratum of the working class merged with what may be loosely called the 'lower middle class' . . . In the earlier part of the century this would mean mainly small shopkeepers, some independent masters, foremen, and managers (who were also generally promoted workers). Towards the end of the century it would also mean clerks and the like . . . skilled labor aristocrats, being, if anything, superior in social status to many white-collar workers."[4]

Recognizing that the definition and number of strata chosen by investigators determine the frequency of vertical mobility they find, we have paid more attention to a division of occupations into five strata — unskilled, semiskilled, and skilled manual and low and high nonmanual — because it reveals more with less distortion than the

simpler division of manual and nonmanual only. Our ranking deliberately follows Stephan Thernstrom's five strata scheme in *The
Other Bostonians*, itself a modification of the socio-economic ranking devised by census statistician Alba Edwards and followed by
most modern mobility studies.[5] We have erred on the side of comparability in the scheme as a whole although our assignment of individual occupations to strata sometimes differs, reflecting our perception of differences between the communities and eras studied.

This five strata hierarchy does not recognize finer gradations in
status and reward which we can find in some of our evidence, gradations which will be discussed in subsequent chapters. We
preferred not to build too much refinement into our scheme of
strata, however, because we soon discovered that the process of
refining definitions of status for particular moments in time
continues so long as the project does. The more we learned about
the changing organization of work and changing rewards in various
occupations, the more inadequate any finely graded ranking
scheme became for any extended period of time.[6] Moreover, even in
establishing a finer sense of hierarchy within our brief period, one of
the most useful clues to the changing situation of particular occupations turned out to be mobility frequencies between these five
broad strata. Thus, differences between the skilled trades in the frequencies with which their workers achieved proprietorships or appeared subsequently at unskilled work helped us define the progress
of skill dilution.

Regardless of the ranking system employed, the very focus on vertical mobility excludes from consideration some kinds of
occupational change which can tell us a great deal about the choices
available to various groups of workers. Thus, shifts of craftsmen
from one trade to another can point up the extent to which certain
skills found ready applicability in a variety of jobs, giving some
artisans a wider range of opportunities with a greater freedom of
choice and security against obsolescence. In subsequent chapters we
examine in detail some of the more important patterns of change
which our ranking system classifies as horizontal mobility.

Problems of Classification

Several features of our five vertical strata and of our assignment
of individual occupational titles to them need preliminary mention.

First, many of the titles given in the census required clarification before they could be assigned. The chief clarification was the differentiation of wage earners from proprietors where the title alone indicated a manual occupation. Self-employed workers in the crafts and in some services commonly reported themselves by the name of their trade or calling only. Thus, five local blacksmiths employed from two to four workers each in 1860; although several of these shopowners appear in three censuses, the enumerators never distinguished them from journeymen in their trade. Even the owners of the city's largest cooperages—employing between 20 and 80 men at various times—usually were enumerated simply as cooper and only rarely as master or boss cooper or as cooperage manufacturer.

We have used city directories to distinguish the self-employed. Beginning in 1862 the alphabetical section systematically specified whether the business was conducted at the owner's residence or at a separate address; in most years, all the self-employed in that section also appear as subscribers in the classified section, the great exception from 1874 through 1881 showing the local impact of the depression after 1873.[7]

Second, clarified occupational titles alone cannot differentiate small shopkeepers from the city's more substantial businessmen. For example, most dry goods merchants had larger capital than the average retailer in other lines, but a minority reporting that title and so advertising themselves in the classified section of the directory show no property in either census or tax list. Members of this minority almost always appear in credit reports with comments like that made on John Jacobs, "asked for as a peddler . . . small store . . . $200 would probably buy him out."[8] To classify such self-designated dry goods merchants as Jacobs with large dry goods proprietors would be as misleading as classifying the minority of large grocers in the city as petty proprietors along with the majority of small neighborhood shopowners in that line. Accordingly, we have used reported property in the census—$5,000 or more real estate or $3,000 or more personal property as the dividing line—to assign proprietors to the high and low nonmanual strata.[9] This simple division does not pretend to convey the range of prosperity among proprietors nor the distribution of individuals along that range; because its only purpose is to distinguish petty proprietors, the amount of property deliberately has been kept low.

Third, our general tabulations of vertical mobility in this chapter do not show the frequency of factory employment. Since occupational titles in the census usually indicated the work done rather than the place of employment, laborers as well as skilled artisans employed by factories often remain unidentified. For the censuses prior to 1880 most of the workers we have classified as semiskilled were service workers, not operatives. A fuller identification of factory workers for some years in city directories is analyzed in Chapter 9.

Measuring Occupational Careers in One Community

This chapter presents two kinds of measurement of upward and downward occupational mobility within a man's lifetime: mobility between censuses and mobility between first and last census enumerations in Poughkeepsie. Measurement by decade makes no pretense of describing the frequency of change in occupational status over the course of an entire working career. Its purpose is to show the magnitude of vertical mobility within the city for all male workers over identical periods of time to see how that magnitude varied according to the age as well as the occupation of workers at the earlier of the two censuses.

This kind of measurement has one important function for a study covering so short a period of time as thirty years; it permits comparison of frequencies of mobility for three successive decades to see whether changes in patterns of opportunity show any consistent trend. Because this analysis by decade looks for shifts in the avenues and in the short-run frequencies of advancement rather than for the prospects that an individual would change his status over a lifetime, it includes all persisting male workers. Refinement of this analysis to show differences in mobility according to age at the beginning of a decade shows the frequency with which different types of occupational change occurred at different times in the life cycle.

In the presentation of mobility for three decades we make one deviation from the wholly vertical ranking scheme which we use for career mobility. For the decadal analysis we employ a division of the white-collar occupations into the three functional groups of professionals, proprietors, and clerical workers rather than a vertical division based on amount of property.[10] By distinguishing clerical and sales workers from proprietors, whether large or petty, this functional division suggests the extent to which the jobs of these workers should be regarded as apprenticeships for business.

Our second kind of measurement does try to capture the occupational mobility of individuals over an entire working career within the limitations imposed by our 30 year period and by the 10 year intervals of the census.[11] This analysis is confined to workers who held jobs in Poughkeepsie both before and after 30 years of age. This common convention in career analysis serves the purpose of limiting the proportion of men whose vertical mobility did not appear in Poughkeepsie censuses but did occur in another locality or in the very transit between localities, often referred to as "shipboard mobility." The highest frequency of upward mobility consistently occurs among young men from their mid-twenties to early thirties; to include men who left the city before they reached 30 even if they already had been employed at two censuses there or to include men already older than 30 at the time of their first recorded employment in Poughkeepsie risks serious underestimation of a man's chances to rise.

Ideally, measurement of careers should compare first job as a full-time worker with last job before retirement or death. But that exactness in comparison eludes any nineteenth-century community study. Only that portion of their working lives which men spent in Poughkeepsie itself can be identified systematically; furthermore, the decadal intervals for census enumeration do not coincide precisely with first or last jobs even for men who never worked in any other community.[12] A Jeremiah Shook appears first in a Poughkeepsie census as a grocer and after failing at that as a clerk. But he had saved the money for his grocery by practicing the trade of coopering, a fact discoverable only by tracing him in city directories in the years prior to his first census listing.

For young workers first reported in the 1850 census who never emigrated from Poughkeepsie, our tracing through four censuses records a maximum career span of 30 years between first and last jobs. For any worker who first appeared in the 1870 census we have a maximum span of a decade; we could extend this span only by the less certain method of tracing in city directories after 1880 so that we have confined discussion of such extensions to the more specialized analyses of workers in particular occupations and occupational groups in subsequent chapters. In presenting both our general career and intergenerational analyses in this chapter, we consider

only men born between 1820 and 1849, the youngest of whom would
have been 31 and the oldest 60 years old in 1880. The majority of
the career cases analyzed, however, comprehend spans of time
longer than the peak years for occupational mobility, 59 percent of
the total being more than 41 years old at the last reported job in
Poughkeepsie.

The Mobility of Three Decades

Recognizing the limitations of decadal measurements, what general dimensions of occupational mobility do they exhibit? Considering first the simplest division between blue-collar and white-collar
work, Poughkeepsie shows more upward than downward mobility—
more than twice as much during the fifties and sixties but only half
again as much during the seventies, the decade with prolonged
depression. The percentages of upward mobility for the three successive decades were 17, 18, and 13 percent compared to downward
mobility of 7, 8, and 9 percent.

This general pattern resembles what Stephan Thernstrom found
before the 1930s in the cities he could compare with Boston, with
the single exception of Boston itself in the eighties when downward
mobility equaled upward mobility. The frequency of movement in
both directions in Poughkeepsie falls near the middle of the range in
mobility rates which Thernstrom presents for Boston, Atlanta,
Omaha, Los Angeles, and Norristown. The similarity in these rates
led him to conclude: "The striking [geographic] volatility of the
American people must have served as an equilibrating mechanism
that tended to iron out differences between local opportunity struc-
tures."[13]

Similar frequencies of mobility computed for broad occupational
strata may, however, disguise important differences between communities in the composition of strata and in the relative importance
of various avenues of mobility. A small city like Poughkeepsie with
much manufacturing, service, and retailing conducted in small
shops will be likely to show a higher proportion of its mobility to
white-collar work take the form of self-employment rather than
managerial and supervisory jobs or even clerical and sales work as a
permanent employment. In Poughkeepsie proprietors overwhelmingly account for the category "proprietors, managers, and offi-

cials." Blue-collar workers rarely moved into clerical and sales jobs, but a substantial minority became shopowners.

The variations in decadal mobility between broad occupational groups do conform generally to contemporary notions of careers for these groups. Thus, at one extreme professionals conceived of their work as lifetime callings and overwhelmingly they remained at the same occupation at the end of each decade (Table 3.1). Although proprietors change occupational status a little more frequently, nine out of ten remained at white-collar employment as might be expected of a group of men already in business for themselves at the start of the decade and therefore older than the labor force as a whole. By contrast, younger men predominated in clerical and sales jobs which they hoped would be apprenticeships for careers in business; only one third of these workers persisted at such jobs in any decade. Only in the fifties did as many as one fourth experience downward mobility to manual work; the remainder appeared next as proprietors or professionals.

Like professionals, men who devoted several years to learning skilled trades normally expected to pursue them for life, since most of these skills had limited transferability to other occupations. A minority, however, could be expected to make a change in occupational status from wage earner to self-employed worker. In each decade two thirds of all journeymen remained wage earners, one fourth achieved white-collar status, mostly as proprietors, and less than one tenth shifted to less skilled work except during the seventies. Jobs in the lowest manual strata offered little job security and required minimal training; correspondingly, half of the men employed in these jobs in any decade reported shifts of occupation during that period, but some of these shifts qualify as horizontal mobility. Thus, three fifths or more of the unskilled workers remained in that stratum each decade; less than one tenth achieved white-collar status, and slightly higher proportions reported skilled or semiskilled employments subsequently. Men at semiskilled jobs at the start of each decade, primarily service workers, rose above blue-collar status more often than unskilled workers, but had no advantage in entering the crafts. Moreover, between 15 and 22 percent of these men reported unskilled jobs by the end of the decade.

In every decade small steps predominated in both upward and downward mobility. Most changes occurred between adjacent oc-

TABLE 3.1. Occupational mobility for three decades

Occupation at start of decade	Decade	Professional	Proprietorial	Clerical	Skilled	Semi-skilled	Unskilled	Number of cases
		Occupation at end of decade (percent)						
Professional	1850–60	98	2	–	–	–	–	58
	1860–70	95	4	–	1	–	–	96
	1870–80	91	6	3	–	–	–	126
Proprietorial	1850–60	2	87	5	2	1	2	300
	1860–70	1	89	2	3	2	3	389
	1870–80	2	85	4	5	2	2	545
Clerical	1850–60	2	35	39	10	6	10	52
	1860–70	6	40	39	7	3	5	116
	1870–80	5	28	51	7	5	4	195
Skilled	1850–60	1	22	1	68	4	4	387
	1860–70	–	23	1	68	3	5	630
	1870–80	1	13	2	73	5	6	858
Semiskilled	1850–60	–	11	6	9	59	15	106
	1860–70	1	12	1	11	56	18	176
	1870–80	1	8	3	12	54	22	242
Unskilled	1850–60	–	5	–	18	17	60	265
	1860–70	–	7	1	11	12	69	366
	1870–80	–	8	2	12	18	61	562

cupational strata. Semiskilled workers achieved nonmanual employment more often than unskilled, but less often than skilled workers. This hierarchy in opportunity became less sharp during the period, however. As artisans became self-employed in their trades less frequently and laborers, gardeners, teamsters, and other less skilled workers more often opened small retail ventures, the advantage of the upper over the lower manual strata narrowed substantially. In the fifties four times as many artisans as unskilled workers achieved self-employment compared to only twice as many in the seventies. Poughkeepsie had moved toward but did not reach that convergence in opportunities between manual strata that characterized Boston after 1880.

In every decade, including the seventies, age groups show a consistent pattern in frequency of mobility (Table 3.2). The highest upward and the lowest downward movement occurs among those in their twenties at the start of each decade. Each successively older group diminishes in frequency of upward mobility, but even men in their fifties climb often enough to encourage a sense of chances to rise late in life. Thus, in both the fifties and the sixties about 15 percent of skilled workers at this older age achieved white-collar employment compared to 30 percent of craftsmen who were 21 to 30 years old at the start of the decade.

Downward mobility never varied much by age group with two exceptions. First, as might be expected, workers who were in their teens at the start of any decade climbed less often than men in their twenties and also suffered more often from apparent downward mobility. These tendencies emphasize the tentative nature of early occupational achievements and very often the limited character of the work performed, especially by comparison with older workers reporting the same occupation. The native-born son of a German tailor clerked in a store at age sixteen, but a decade later he appears near the waterfront as a fisherman and by his mid-thirties as a stevedore.

Second, among skilled craftsmen older workers consistently appear subsequently at less skilled designations much more often than the young or the middle-aged. In no decade did more than 7 percent of any younger age group move downward from skilled to semiskilled employment, but the percentages for those starting each decade at ages between ages 51 and 60 are 27, 11, and 24 percent.

TABLE 3.2. Occupational mobility of clerical, skilled, and unskilled workers by age group, 1860-70

Occupation at start	Age group at start (years)	Occupation at end of decade (percent)						Number of cases
		Professional	Proprietorial	Clerical	Skilled	Semi-skilled	Unskilled	
Clerical	11 – 20	10	29	43	14	2	2	42
	21 – 30	3	58	32	–	7	–	31
	31 – 40	5	43	33	5	5	10	21
	41 – 50	8	17	42	8	–	25	12
Skilled	11 – 20	–	13	1	76	7	2	88
	21 – 30	–	28	2	64	2	3	212
	31 – 40	–	26	–	66	1	7	165
	41 – 50	–	20	1	70	5	5	102
Unskilled	11 – 20	–	6	6	31	11	47	36
	21 – 30	–	8	3	15	15	60	89
	31 – 40	–	7	–	7	16	71	143
	41 – 50	–	6	–	6	8	80	63

The disparity between the older and younger workers in percentages shifting from skilled to unskilled designations is even greater. Apart from these artisans, occupational mobility by itself does not suggest greater precariousness in the situation of the old. Property mobility does change the picture as we will see, and income information, if we had it, presumably would make the situation of the old even more unfavorable.[14]

Three decades provide a slight basis for establishing trends, especially when the culminating decade also saw prolonged depression and the end of rapid growth in Poughkeepsie's population. What can be done is to isolate those shifts in frequency which seem significant, such as those which coincide with long-range trends in the nation or in other cities, and then explore them subsequently through more refined analysis of individual occupations.

The difficulty in separating the effect of depression from longer range trends in the economy can be seen at once in the sharpest change in frequency of mobility during the seventies, the reduction of achievement of nonmanual employment by manual workers. Old and young workers alike suffered reduced opportunities except for the most vulnerable group, the unskilled, whose opportunities for entering skilled as well as nonmanual work became a little better during the depression than they had been in the sixties through increased entry into the metal and building trades and into petty retailing ventures.

The great reduction, however, occurs in one group only, the skilled, and in one kind of mobility only, the achievement of proprietorship. During the fifties 22 percent and during the sixties 23 percent of the journeymen at the start of each decade had become self-employed by its end, but during the seventies that proportion almost halved to 13 percent, largely wiping out the great advantage which artisans previously had had over the semiskilled and the unskilled in becoming shopowners. The decline of artisan manufacture throughout the middle decades in the northeast suggests that this decline in achievement by the skilled, despite its suddenness, reflects more than a temporary setback.[15]

One other reduction in upward mobility poses a similar problem in separating the immediate effects of depression from the longer-run effects of increasing scale and specialization. The proportion of clerical and sales workers continuing at that level rather than going into business for themselves jumped during the seventies. This change comes in the wake of a slow but steady increase in the proportion of clerical and sales workers in the male labor force and of increased scale of firms in some lines of commerce. Taken together these changes suggest that a growing number of clerical and sales workers would remain employees in the future rather than achieve businesses of their own.

Downward mobility from white-collar and skilled work increased only slightly in the seventies. It did not contribute significantly to the labor forces of the new and larger factories opened in that decade. A few older artisans and clerks did seek employment in them, but they remained exceptional; a German shoemaker worked in the shirt factory at age 62 as did a 49 year old native, formerly a clerk. Local boys entering the labor force during the seventies and immigrants to the city account for most of the male workers at the shoe, shirt, skirt, silk, and glass factories in 1880.

The only consistent tendencies over the three decades emphasize the importance of exploring the apparent lessening of differences in opportunity between skilled, semiskilled, and unskilled workers. A small but steadily increasing proportion of unskilled workers achieved white-collar employment, primarily as proprietors. The proportion of all proprietors previously employed at unskilled work increased in a similar manner. The other consistent tendency over three decades also shows increasing fluidity but in a different direction. A progressively larger proportion of those reporting themselves at semiskilled jobs at the start of a decade appear at unskilled jobs by its end. This apparent increase in precariousness throws a different light on the situation of the unskilled, especially on the significance of some of their upward mobility, since semiskilled jobs provided their most frequent advances.

Career Mobility

Comparison of mobility for three decades can only suggest long-run tendencies and does so by making the changes of a decade serve as surrogate for full working careers, forgoing the heightened frequencies of both upward and downward mobility which career analysis yields. No more than 24 percent of the skilled workers at the start of any decade reported nonmanual employment by its end; of the 700 men who first reported skilled jobs and meet our criteria for career analysis, however, 33 percent had made that improvement by their last job. The same patterns of movement also characterized full careers, however. Change in occupational status usually consisted of small steps in either direction, but steps upward were far more frequent. In Poughkeepsie during these years a man was twice as likely to enjoy upward mobility within his lifetime as he was to suffer downward mobility. The less fortunate could improve their positions without seeming to be a serious threat to men who began their careers at or near the top.

The lower the stratum in which men began their careers in the city, the larger the proportion who moved on to better jobs. Thus, 43 percent of the unskilled ended in a higher stratum compared to 41 percent of the semiskilled, 32 percent of the skilled, and 29 percent of the petty white-collar beginners. Downward mobility reversed this pattern, however. With one significant exception, the higher the stratum in which you started your working career in Poughkeepsie, the lower the chances that you would report an inferior occupation there later. Thus, only 6 percent of the men beginning at high white-collar jobs failed to sustain their initial rank compared to 9 percent of the skilled and 16 percent of the semiskilled. The intervening rank of petty proprietors, clerical and supervisory workers forms the exception to the generalization, 12 percent ending their careers at blue-collar jobs.

Intergenerational Mobility

So far we have been talking only about men's chances of rising. Modern studies of mobility more often use another measure of opportunity, the inheritance of occupational status between generations. By comparing a son's occupational status with that of his father, this measure seeks to determine how such a son's social origin improved or hurt his chances to rise. Insofar as the father's occupational status can be regarded as a surrogate for social class, this measure describes how the class into which men were born influenced their own occupational mobility. We have preferred the more ambiguous term social origin here because it does not presume to represent dimensions of social class which occupational status alone cannot describe.

Inheritance of occupational rank between generations shows less continuity in rank than does analysis of careers. In mobility within careers 90 percent of the men who appeared first at white-collar jobs maintained that rank at their last reported jobs. By contrast, the sons of white-collar workers often did not start at their fathers' rank; moreover, regardless of their starting rank, only 74 percent of these sons appeared at white-collar work at their last reported jobs.[16] The fact that one fourth of these sons show slippage downward from their fathers' rank during the span of their careers which can be traced heightens the sense of social fluidity. But the fact that sons were not always as successful as their fathers did not mean that there was no positive relationship between superiority in the fathers' rank and their sons' prospects.

The proportion of the sons of white-collar workers who could expect to begin at that rank themselves was nearly six times as great as the proportion of sons of blue-collar workers beginning there. Social origin profoundly affected initial opportunities. Even the substantial minority of sons who started work below their fathers' occupational rank had a clear advantage in mobility within their careers over other men who shared the same starting level but whose fathers had inferior rank (Table 3.3). Thus, the sons of white-collar workers who began at skilled jobs had a better chance of obtaining white-collar employment subsequently than did the sons of skilled workers who began at skilled jobs. With the exception of the sons of unskilled workers, the chances of mobility for sons starting at the same level can be ranked according to their fathers' occupational status. This advantage, however, did not prevent some narrowing of the gap in occupational position between the sons of blue-collar and white-collar workers by the end of their careers.

The one exception to the general pattern of advantage in intergenerational mobility also emphasizes fluidity rather than continuity and challenges any notion of a pervasive culture of poverty at the bottom of the occupational hierarchy. The sons of unskilled workers showed no disadvantage compared to the sons of the semiskilled in the frequency with which they began their careers at skilled and nonmanual employments. Those sons of the unskilled who started at these higher levels also remained at them as often as the sons of both semiskilled and skilled workers starting there.

Whatever the situation of subgroups among the sons of the unskilled, collectively they were not trapped in menial labor. Of sons born between 1840 and 1849, half reported skilled or nonmanual jobs by 1880 when they were between 31 and 40 years old. Another 20 percent listed themselves at semiskilled jobs so that only 30 per-

TABLE 3.3. Occupational mobility of sons from first to last reported job by father's occupation

Son's first occupation	Father's occupation	Son's last occupation (percent)					Number of cases
		High white collar	Low white collar	Skilled	Semi-skilled	Un-skilled	
High white collar	High white collar	94	6	—	—	—	34
	Low white collar	83	17	—	—	—	6
Low white collar	High white collar	30	65	2	2	2	105
	Low white collar	19	68	8	—	5	63
	Skilled	12	65	15	3	6	34
	Semiskilled	8	54	23	8	8	13
	Unskilled	20	47	7	13	13	15
Skilled	High white collar	16	37	40	5	2	57
	Low white collar	6	31	57	—	6	67
	Skilled	3	19	67	6	5	170
	Semiskilled	—	12	21	55	12	38
	Unskilled	4	23	60	3	11	80
Semi-skilled	Low white collar	17	33	8	42	—	12
	Skilled	4	26	30	35	4	23
	Semiskilled	—	12	21	55	12	33
	Unskilled	5	5	40	40	10	20
Unskilled	High white collar	8	25	33	8	25	12
	Low white collar	6	22	22	11	39	18
	Skilled	3	15	31	18	33	39
	Semiskilled	—	15	35	40	10	20
	Unskilled	—	10	18	14	58	112

cent still followed their fathers in unskilled work. This record supports the plausibility of the common hope at mid-century that a man's children might find better jobs even if he could not.

Ethnic Differences in Mobility

The general frequencies of decadal, career, and intergenerational mobility which we have been describing so far average out differences between native whites and blacks and first and second generation Americans of Irish, German, British, and other national ancestries. The differences were large and conform broadly to contemporary perceptions. Although 36 percent of the persisting whites of native parentage appear first at nonmanual work, only 9 percent of the foreign-born and 15 percent of the native-born of foreign parentage do. Of those starting at nonmanual work, the percentages sustaining that position by last reported jobs are 91, 81, and 82 percent respectively.

Native advantage largely disappears in mobility from manual work at first job to nonmanual work at last job, the percentages making that improvement being 25 percent for the natives compared to 22 and 24 percent for the first and second generation newcomers. And in this gross comparison of both upward and downward mobility, the more favorable situation of the Germans and British is obscured by grouping them with the Irish. Only 5 percent of the Irish in the immigrant and 14 percent in the second generation began at nonmanual work; of those few, 25 and 28 percent failed to sustain the status. Of the overwhelming majority of the Irish who began at manual work, only 11 percent in the immigrant and 19 percent in the second generation had achieved nonmanual work by last report.

Attention to such gross distinctions as manual and nonmanual proves especially misleading for analysis of ethnic differences in mobility, however, because the groups concentrated at different levels within the occupational hierarchy, the Irish at unskilled and the Germans and British at skilled manual work. Native whites had a more even distribution but initially monopolized the forms of white-collar work that required formal education.

A mere 15 men of foreign birth began their census careers as professionals or as large proprietors and all but one of them sustained that rank at last reported job. Far more of the newcomers began at petty white-collar employments, primarily smaller proprietorships, and clerical and sales jobs, and they experienced downward mobility more often. By last reported job 11 percent of the men of native parentage who began at low white-collar employments reported blue-collar jobs compared to 22 percent for both first and second generation immigrants. The foreign-born, however, achieved high white-collar status by last reported job as often as native sons.

Native advantage largely disappeared among skilled manual workers (Table 3.4). Indeed, unless we presume that a larger proportion of native than of immigrant artisans actually were inexperienced hands, then mobility frequencies suggest that in some industries at least native craftsmen must have been at a disadvantage in the competition for jobs and customers. Craftsmen of each nationality in the immigrant and in the second generation did not report as much downward mobility by last job as craftsmen of native parentage. In the immigrant generation the upward mobility of British and especially of German artisans—overwhelmingly the achievement of shop ownership—far surpassed that of natives, the percentages climbing to low and high white-collar combined being 38, 49, and 28 percent respectively. Contrary to the stereotype that immigrant success came in the more assimilated second generation born in America, the foreign-born of these nationalities escaped the status of wage earners more frequently than the second generation. Once again the immigrant Irish lagged behind, only 18 percent of those starting at skilled trades improving their status by last job. Moreover, the proportion of natives starting at skilled work who subsequently achieved white-collar employment barely exceeded that among the second generation of both British and Irish Americans and fell below that of the native-born of German parentage.

No such distinctiveness appears in the occupational mobility of the British and the Germans who began their careers in Poughkeepsie at unskilled jobs. Men of native parentage starting at this level achieved skilled and white-collar employment slightly more often than the Germans starting there; few British immigrants reported unskilled first jobs in Poughkeepsie, but the careers of those who did resemble the Germans. The handicap of the immigrant Irish concentrated in unskilled work was extreme; a mere 15 percent reported skilled or white-collar employment by last job. The second generation of the Irish had shed that handicap, the proportion

TABLE 3.4. Career mobility of skilled and unskilled workers by nativity[a]

Nativity	Last reported occupation (percent)					Number of cases
	High white collar	Low white collar	Skilled	Semi-skilled	Unskilled	
	First occupation — skilled					
White of native parentage	8	20	60	6	7	420
Black	(1)	(2)	(2)	(1)	(1)	7
Native-born of foreign parentage						
Irish	4	20	67	6	4	54
German	2	30	61	4	4	54
British	7	20	73	—	—	41
Foreign-born						
Irish	5	13	70	3	9	94
German	12	37	48	1	3	111
British	12	26	52	2	7	42
	First occupation — unskilled					
White of native parentage	1	17	23	20	39	163
Black	—	3	3	29	65	34
Native-born of foreign parentage						
Irish	—	13	26	15	46	46
German	—	(1)	(2)	(2)	(3)	8
British	(1)	(2)	(2)	(4)	(1)	9
Foreign-born						
Irish	1	7	7	12	74	196
German	—	14	23	31	31	35
British	—	(2)	(1)	(1)	(3)	7

[a]Where the number of cases for a group is less than 30, the table gives the number (in parentheses) rather than the percentage in each category.

achieving semiskilled, skilled, and white-collar work being similar to that of men of native and of German parentage. The Irish do conform to the stereotype that occupational mobility was rare for the newcomers until the more assimilated second generation.

Mobility between generations confirms these general patterns of ethnic advantage. Sons of native white-collar workers more frequently inherited their fathers' occupational rank than did the sons of foreign-born parents but this native advantage largely disappeared among blue-collar workers and their sons. At the very highest rank the 53 sons of immigrant fathers had much greater difficulty sustaining high white-collar status than did the sons of native fathers. Even more striking, however, is the frequency with which the sons of immigrants at that rank ended their careers in blue-collar jobs. A mere 13 percent of the sons of native fathers with high white-collar status appeared at manual work at last job compared to a stunning 40 percent of the sons of immigrant fathers. This greater downward mobility points up the probable importance of differences in type of business or profession and in extent of wealth between the native and the immigrant fathers. Among the sons of low white-collar workers, 51 percent of the sons of immigrants sustained or improved upon their fathers' position compared to 61 percent of the sons of natives. At this level, the disadvantage of the immigrants' children diminished sharply; indeed, only 11 percent of them appeared at unskilled or semiskilled jobs by last report compared to 14 percent of the sons of native petty white-collar workers.

Intergenerational mobility among skilled workers reveals that the sons of immigrant artisans as a whole had a decided advantage over the sons of native artisans, reinforcing our belief that craftsmen were affected more seriously than other native workers by the coming of the immigrants (Table 3.5). Although the number of craftsmen's sons was not great for any single foreign nationality, the Irish made the best showing and the British, the next best. While the sons of German artisans achieved white-collar jobs as often as native sons, they did so far less often than the career mobility of immigrant craftsmen of that nationality would lead us to expect. The seemingly much greater initial success of the Germans compared to other newcomers did not extend to their children.

Among the sons of unskilled workers the advantage of the Irish and the Germans over native sons remained. Growing up in the New World quickly dissipated the initial sharp differences between Irish

TABLE 3.5. Intergenerational mobility of sons of skilled and unskilled workers by nativity[a]

Father's occupation	Father's nativity	Last occupation of son (percent)					Number of cases
		High white collar	Low white collar	Skilled	Semi-skilled	Un-skilled	
Skilled	White of native parentage	3	24	49	13	12	152
	Irish	10	33	47	–	10	30
	German	2	25	65	6	2	48
	British	6	29	51	11	3	35
Unskilled	White of native parentage	4	13	33	17	33	54
	Irish	3	14	34	10	41	116
	Sons born in Ireland	5	12	21	5	58	43
	Sons born in America	1	15	41	12	30	73
	German	3	29	35	9	24	34
	British	–	(2)	(8)	–	–	10

[a]Where the number of cases for a group is less than 30, this table gives the number (in parentheses) rather than the percentage in each category.

laborers and the unskilled of other nationalities. While their fathers for the most part remained trapped at unskilled work, the sons born in America to fathers at that rank rose to white-collar jobs as often and entered the skilled trades more often than the sons of native unskilled workers. German laborers' sons do appear more frequently at skilled and white-collar employments than either native sons or native-born sons of Irish parentage but these young men of German parentage comprised a much smaller proportion of all sons of unskilled workers.

Religion and Mobility

The more limited occupational advance of the Irish compared to that of other immigrants from northwestern Europe inevitably raises the question of how their religion influenced their mobility. Since such well-studied cities as Boston and neighboring Waltham received comparatively few Catholic immigrants in the nineteenth century who were not of Irish descent, the temptation is strong to regard the poor showing of the Irish as suggestive of the influence of Catholicism on occupational mobility. Resistance to that temptation comes first from the obvious peculiarity of Irish Catholicism itself, a church whose leadership as well as its membership shared both lower social status and antagonism to their Protestant governors of English descent. Furthermore, studies of ethnic diversity within European Catholicism and its New World representation offer a variety of cautions against any assumption that the economic behavior of one group may represent the whole. For example, Irish, German, and Italian Catholics describe not only a wide range in intensity of religious involvement as measured by parental church attendance and parochial school enrollment but also very different perspectives on relationships between religion and nationality, social class, and the economic virtues so often identified with Protestantism.[17]

Our evidence for Poughkeepsie cannot suggest an answer to the very complicated question of the influence of religious background upon occupational mobility; it can, however, suggest the danger of any simple claim that Catholics show less tendency toward economic rationalism, that Protestantism distinctively fostered the economic virtues of sobriety, industry, frugality, and ambition. In Poughkeepsie Germans not only comprised a substantial proportion of the labor force and began predominantly at skilled work but also show a less uneven balance between Protestant and Catholic than do the city's Irish, more than four fifths of whom appear to be Catholic throughout our period. Of the immigrant Germans who appear employed in the city in at least two censuses, at least 30 percent can be positively identified as members of Nativity parish, the German Catholic congregation, and another 8 percent can be identified from a variety of sources as Jews. We have not identified the religion of all the remaining 62 percent, but the evidence we have, direct and circumstantial, suggests that most of them had some association with local Protestant churches through members of their family, if not through personal membership, and no connection with either Catholicism or Judaism. This identification permits comparison of achievement according to religious background within an ethnic group which did not begin with the disadvantages of the overwhelmingly agrarian, unskilled, and propertyless Irish.

Comparison of occupational mobility does favor the German Protestants slightly but primarily in the frequency with which they began their careers in Poughkeepsie at a higher rank rather than in frequency of improvement thereafter (Table 3.6). Thus, first and second generation Protestants began a little more often than Catholics at nonmanual employment. Among the sons of manual workers, by contrast, the proportion of Catholics rising after beginning at manual work is higher.

The achievement of both Protestants and Catholics in the first

TABLE 3.6. Religion and career mobility: the Germans[a]

Origin	Start white collar (percent)	End white collar (percent)	Blue-collar starters climbing (percent)	White-collar starters falling (percent)	Number of cases
First generation					
Protestant	17	37	27	15	238
Catholic	15	35	27	18 (17)	113
Jewish	55 (29)	90 (29)	77 (13)	0	29
Second generation (white-collar father)					
Protestant	35	63	46	5 (20)	57
Catholic	41 (22)	55 (22)	31 (13)	11 (9)	22
Jewish	88 (8)	100 (8)	100 (1)	0	8
Second generation (blue-collar father)					
Protestant	14	23	10	9 (11)	80
Catholic	12	25	18	20 (5)	43
Jewish	–	–	–	– –	0

[a]For this comparison we have increased the size of the group and the length of many of the careers by using the 1890 city directory rather than the 1880 census as terminal. Where the number of cases on which the percentage is based is less than 30, the table gives the number in parentheses.

generation in escaping wage-earner status is identical. The one consistent difference for both generations appears in the greater tendency among Catholics beginning at nonmanual employments to shift subsequently to manual jobs, but the cases are few and the percentage differences not that large. Jews, whether of foreign birth or parentage, more often than not began their recorded careers in Poughkeepsie at nonmanual employment and three fourths of the minority who started at manual jobs in the immigrant generation had become shopkeepers at last report. As in other cities at midcentury, Jews stood out as a small but very successful group among immigrants.

Comparison of income reported in 1866 by the 42 German immigrants earning $600 or more that year does modify the picture given by occupational mobility. The proportion of Protestants and Catholics within this group is a little less than among the city's Germans who persisted for a decade — 60 and 26 percent respectively compared to 63 and 30 percent — but the proportion of Jews was higher — 14 compared to 7 percent. Protestants, however, comprised a larger proportion of the higher incomes, 68 percent of those reporting $1,000 or more compared to 16 percent each for Jews and Catholics. A similar picture emerges from comparison of accumulation of property among the persisting Germans. Taking the highest amounts reported in three censuses beginning with 1850, the Protestants do more frequently list larger amounts of real estate than the Catholics but not the Jews; the percentages of each group with $10,000 or more being 8, 4, and 21 percent respectively. But at the other extreme, the Protestants show a slightly higher proportion with no property. Catholics concentrate in the middle range, 30 percent of them reporting real estate between $1,000 and $5,000 in value compared to 21 percent of the Protestants.

The tax lists of 1880 and 1890 show a similar distribution. Taken together, the evidence on occupational mobility, income, and property suggests that while German Catholics set up in business for themselves and prospered sufficiently to own some property as often as German Protestants did, they did not as frequently join the ranks of the city's richer businessmen. As Chapter 2 suggested, the greater tendency of the Catholics to reside near their church may reflect a greater tendency to prefer communal satisfactions to moving out into the larger life of the city in search of individual advancement. To the extent that that may have been true, entrepreneurial vigor and success may have been blunted by comparison with German Protestants who more often socialized with and even married natives. But that remains speculation.

What German Catholics did share with German Protestants was more frequent achievement of the status of shopkeeper after a first job at manual work than either native or Irish Protestants, an important caution against any presumption that Catholicism inhibited the virtues needed for at least modest prosperity in business. This caution does not depend upon any quirk such as the city's Catholics having been educated in a predominantly Protestant region in Germany. On the contrary, the majority of the richest Protestants and Catholics and even a few of the city's richest Jews came from the south and west of Germany where Catholicism was stronger, especially Bavaria.

The example of the immigrant Germans suggests the limitation in any interpretation of the handicap of the Catholic Irish in occupational mobility which emphasizes their religion rather than the predominance among them of agricultural laborers with a history of deprivation and insecurity. While we have not identified the religious affiliation of a large enough proportion of the Irish-born to warrant statistical analysis of the relationship of their religion to their occupational mobility in Poughkeepsie, our evidence so far supports our expectation that Catholics made up the large majority of the Irish in Poughkeepsie and an even larger proportion of the unskilled workers of that nationality. The minority of Protestants account for a disproportionate share of Irish who appeared only at skilled or nonmanual occupations in the city. Of the 27 richest taxpayers of Irish birth or parentage on the 1870 and 1880 lists, only 13 were Catholics; these 13 do show a distribution by amount of assessment which seems slightly superior to that of the Protestants.

More important for the future, among young men of the second generation who first reported employment in the 1870 census and remained in Poughkeepsie for at least another decade, 21 of the 25 who had already opened their own businesses by 1880 or would do so by 1900 were Catholic. The role of the Catholic church in Poughkeepsie in encouraging emulation of Protestant respectability, especially temperance and literary cultivation, and the sharp improvement in the mobility of the second generation Irish suggest that religion imposed no bar to economic success.

Race and Mobility

Unlike religion, race visibly and unambiguously influenced mobility. Native white suspicion of both Catholics and Jews meant social and economic discrimination of varying duration, but only the immigrant Irish experienced anything like the constriction of opportunity faced by blacks in Poughkeepsie throughout the middle decades. Stephan Thernstrom has shown that newness to urban life does not explain the occupational disadvantage of black males in Boston after 1880; blacks born in Boston enjoyed no more mobility than blacks born in the South who immigrated there.[18] Poughkeepsie between 1850 and 1880 offers no more support for the view that blacks suffered the same handicap as immigrants and progressively would escape it as they adapted to a new urban environment. In 1870, 86 percent of the 178 black males of working age had been born in New York State and another 4 percent in Connecticut and Pennsylvania. Only 10 percent had been born in the South, primarily in Virginia. Of the majority born in New York State an important minority bore distinctive surnames common in the city and the county since the eighteenth century.

The frequency with which conventions of Poughkeepsie's blacks during the years of Reconstruction passed resolutions for schemes by which their children would escape inferior education in the city's "colored school" suggests no lack of aspiration. Yet only a handful of local blacks achieved either skilled or nonmanual employments between 1850 and 1880. This tiny minority of black businessmen and craftsmen suffered more defeats than advances during these years, whether through loss of property or of self-employment. Except for a tinsmith who later opened his own shop, younger blacks entering the labor force after the Civil War did not learn skilled trades.

Only two black workers reported real estate of $5,000 or more by 1870. Of the few blacks who achieved nonmanual status at any census, only six sustained that status for more than one listing. Of the few who appeared at skilled trades, several reported unskilled or service jobs subsequently. At every census about 90 percent of the blacks worked at occupations in the two lowest strata in our ranking scheme, but more often in service occupations than the Irish.

In the last decade of our study the number of black males in

Poughkeepsie's labor force dropped only slightly from 173 to 166; with the coming of age of the second generation of the Irish, however, the opportunities for blacks now looked much worse. Blacks in unskilled and semiskilled jobs show about the same rate of persistence in the city during the seventies as members of other ethnic groups but the similarity ends the moment we compare occupational mobility. Only one of the blacks in such low manual jobs rose above them by 1880; by contrast, half of the native-born of foreign parentage who reported unskilled or semiskilled work in 1870 now reported skilled or white-collar employment. In this small northern city at mid-century blacks had the unenviable distinction of being natives with less opportunity than any group of newcomers.

Relating Occupational and Property Mobility

Judging by the frequency with which men who began at the same occupational rank experienced upward or downward mobility, Poughkeepsie's immigrants in the first and second generation — except for the Irish-born — do not compare unfavorably with native whites except in ability to pass nonmanual status from father to son. But similarity in the mobility of individuals from the same starting point did not mean comparable group achievement for natives and newcomers because of the great and continuing advantage of natives in frequency of beginning their careers in nonmanual employments. The general prospects for the city's ethnic groups do show a very clear ordering from most to least favorable: native whites, British, Germans, Irish, and native blacks.

The same kind of difference between individual and group mobility appears in an examination of property accumulation, the most precise and inclusive means we have of assessing whether occupational mobility brought a corresponding change in possession of economic resources. For the minority of the male labor force who for varying portions of their careers owned real estate, we find little difference between ethnic groups in the frequencies with which those starting a decade with property experienced significant gain or loss by its end. Between 1870 and 1880, for example, the proportions of native white, Irish, German, and British taxpayers showing a substantial increase in assessment ranged between 31 and 40 percent and the proportions showing decrease ranged between 20 and 26 percent. Once again, however, the similarity in ethnic mobility from a common starting point does not convey group differences in command of resources because the native property owners at the start of any decade show a much more favorable distribution in amounts owned.

The likelihood that individual property mobility would soon result in a substantial change in the economic position of the group seems less even for the British and the Germans after consideration of the range and distribution of their amounts of property in any census or tax list during the period or— a more graphic demonstration—of the shares of total wealth in the city which they owned compared to their ratio in the male labor force. Thus, in 1880 when native whites comprised slightly less than half of the labor force, they accounted for a somewhat larger proportion of the resident individual taxpayers and for three fourths of the total value of real estate those taxpayers owned. To underscore their preeminence, native whites made up 83 percent of the richest tenth of the city's taxpayers.

By contrast, the British were slightly under-represented both in proportion of taxpayers and of valuation and the Germans a little more so, paralleling the occupational position of these two groups. Comprising 16 percent of male workers and 12 percent of taxpayers, the Germans owned 10 percent of the total value. Blacks owned a negligible share of the city's real estate. The Irish accounted for only 9 percent of the value despite being half again as numerous as the Germans in the labor force. But the Irish, alone among immigrants, were not under-represented in proportion of taxpayers. The small houses and lots in which the Irish invested so frequently may not have added up to a large share of the city's wealth, but they testify to the hunger for security among the immigrant group with the least occupational mobility.

Because Irish property owners so overwhelmingly had modest investments, loss in assessment for them generally meant total loss. For every ethnic group, including native whites, a significant proportion of the property owners at the start of any decade who persisted in the city also reported no property by its end. Thus, 18 percent of the owners of 1860 reported no real estate in 1870. This frequency of loss in so short an interval suggests the precariousness of investment for many, but does not convey the frequency of fluctuations in prosperity within individual careers, including those of the more affluent. As subsequent chapters on businessmen will show, many men who remained constant in occupational status after their twenties experienced at least one and frequently several sharp shifts in prosperity thereafter.

Analysis of change over a decade has severe limitations for attempts to relate property mobility to occupational mobility. Because men more often than not achieved partnership, proprietorship, or profession before they reached thirty years of age but frequently did not invest in real estate until their forties, a weak relationship can be anticipated in any correlation of the two kinds of mobility over a short span. And for those who already had property, the relationship between improvement or stability in occupational status and wealth is also weak. The only strong relationship we found in a comparison of the taxpayers of 1870 who persisted in the city in 1880 was between downward mobility in both occupation and property.

Education and Mobility

The majority of men assessed for real estate never owned anything more than their homes; their property did not become an instrument of further economic mobility. For the majority of male children, school attendance short of high school probably had little more relationship to their subsequent mobility in occupation or property. Although the city had a system of public schools from the early forties, it provided for only three pre-high school divisions: introductory, primary, and grammar. The school commissioners conducted in public the annual oral examinations for promotion between the last two grades. A general appraisal of county schools at this time found them "mechanistic and rudimentary, . . . only training in reading, writing, arithmetic, English grammar and spelling"; no evidence suggests that the city schools were much superior.[19]

Participation in formal education, whatever its quality, was widespread. During the floodtide of Irish and German immigration from 1847 to 1856, school reports show average attendance of less than half of the children enrolled. But from then until 1874, the proportion hovered around three fourths, rising to 80 percent or more thereafter. Census reportage by parents gives a complementary picture. In 1850 25 percent of the male children between eight and fourteen years were reported as not attending school. The proportion dropped to 15 percent by 1860 and to 12 percent by 1870. What influence this level of reported participation in formal education had upon individual mobility cannot be measured from our evidence because the census does not tell us the grade of each boy reported in school, let alone how many years of education and what examinations he would complete before leaving school for good. The tendency to drop out of school increased steadily at higher grades. Even by the nineties when elementary education in Poughkeepsie had been divided into grades, enrollment for grades 5 through 8 remained between one third and one half that of the total for grades 1 through 4. Enrollment for the four years of high school never reached one third of that for the upper elementary grades. Work required in each grade varied substantially from school to school, so that age seems even less satisfactory as a surrogate for level of educational achievement.

For the children of immigrants participation in public schooling may have been more important for whatever general encouragement it gave to wider participation in community life than for development of skills, beyond elementary literacy. The evidence for Poughkeepsie does suggest that the newcomers found its schools more acceptable than did immigrants in a community like Newburyport, Massachusetts.[20] In 1850 at the height of the famine influx nearly one half of the Irish households with boys between 8 and 14 years old reported at least one son in that age group not enrolled in school; by 1860 the percentage had fallen to 16 percent. The Germans and the British showed a much better record of school attendance in 1850, but improved it only slightly in 1860. The group with the highest proportion of sons not in school had the strongest reason for objecting to the education provided them. Until a State law in 1874 struck down segregation, the city maintained a "colored school."

While the blacks protested segregation in education during the years of Civil War and Reconstruction, Catholic immigrants moved to create separate schools for themselves. They escaped that financial burden in 1873, however, when the Poughkeepsie Board of Education accepted the proposal of the pastor of St. Peter's that two parochial schools be run in the future under public lease and supervision. Under this innovation, the two former parochial schools reported the highest attendance in the city notwithstanding the ensuing depression during which an increasing number of boys took employment to help their families.

In 1873 the high school gave up the practice of readings from the

King James Bible for the entire student body, easing the conscience of Catholic parents who wished to give their children education beyond the grammar school. How much the increasing number of Irish graduates owed to this symbolic accommodation and how much to the premium which the pastors of the city's Catholic parishes put upon formal education is less important than the increase itself. Even in 1860, a few years after the first opening of the high school, 7 percent of the Irish and 8 percent of the German households with school age children reported at least one boy in school who was more than 14 years old, compared to 23 percent for the native whites. The native percentage remained the same in 1870 and the German fell slightly, but the Irish percentage nearly doubled to 13 percent.

The roster of high school graduates reinforces the impression that the Irish, the poorest of the immigrants, took advantage of the accommodation by the school board to their fears of Protestant influence upon their children. Of the 34 male graduates in the classes of 1879 through 1882, 10 were sons of Irish immigrants compared to two sons each of German and of British parentage. The eight who remained in the city subsequently found higher occupational status than the vast majority of the native-born of Irish parentage, becoming lawyers, clerks, bookkeeper, civil engineer, street superintendent, and boss plumber.

Several of the immigrant fathers had begun work in Poughkeepsie as ordinary laborers, further dramatizing the improvement in status of their sons. But these same fathers also raise the question of whether education made their sons' status possible or whether the fathers' own economic achievements provided the necessary confidence for seizing the opportunity the high school offered and so consolidating and extending the fathers' mobility.[21] For most of the Irish fathers of male high school graduates represented the more enterprising element among their countrymen whether they were junk dealer, teamster and contractor, boss plumber, or laborer with some real estate.

Examination of all identifiable fathers of male high school graduates between 1873 and 1882 strongly suggests the conclusion that the benefits of longer formal education normally went to those who already had some advantage in occupation or property, however recently achieved. The large majority of fathers appear as professionals or proprietors at the time their sons entered the high school; the small minority of skilled and unskilled manual workers included fathers who already owned property or subsequently would achieve self-employment. Most of these professionals and proprietors fall within the middle range of success; their more affluent peers usually sent their children to private academies. The moderately comfortable but not wholly secure members of the middle class had the most to gain from the high school; an education there generally would ensure white-collar employment for their children.

The high school nicely exemplifies the dual character of opportunity in Poughkeepsie and other cities at mid-century. Students from the poorest homes in the poorest parts of the city, in theory, could make their way up the ladder of primary and grammar grades in their neighborhood public school or in the "colored school" and, simply by passing the necessary examinations, go on to the high school. But very few of them did. More often, the high school provided an easier avenue of ascent for the children of families already in the process of improving their position or helped preserve the advantages of families already established but not too firmly.

4

Men at the Top

WITHIN SEVEN YEARS of his arrival in Poughkeepsie, Harvey Eastman's business college earned him one of the four largest annual incomes in the city. Four years later in 1870, now 37 years old, he owned enough local real estate to place him among the 25 largest taxpayers. The next year he became mayor, an office occupied thus far only by rich men and — with the exception of his immediate predecessor — old residents.[1] Whether the apparent ease with which an Eastman achieved leadership accurately represents the openness of the city's economic elite to newcomers will be the focus of this chapter.

It will show that his career does indeed suggest the fluidity at the economic apex of this small city during the middle decades although not, of course, the prospects for ordinary citizens of achieving it. During these years of rapid growth, the infusion of new men and especially of newcomers to the city among its richest citizens is impressive. Outsiders made their way into positions of entrepreneurial, financial, and civic responsibility with too much speed to justify any picture of an entrenched elite successfully defending its privileges. Admittedly this generalization applies primarily to white men of native parentage; those immigrants, especially Germans, who became rich enough to qualify as members of the city's economic elite as defined by property did not achieve comparable positions in the city's civic and financial leadership, such as directorships in banks and in new promotional schemes like railroads.

This chapter does assume that for the study of communities in nineteenth-century America, the most useful and reliable criterion for an elite is an economic one. For Poughkeepsie and many other communities in our past we lack any precise data about how most economic and political decisions were made or any surveys of the status people attributed to the various occupations and social groups. Lists of officers and members of voluntary or business associations provide important clues about which individuals had sufficient reputation to warrant the use of their names, but such associations coalesced around specific interests or activities and include individuals who lent their prestige to only one or two endeavors, sometimes for quite idiosyncratic reasons. Attempts to use frequency of participation, even by assigning weights to memberships and positions held according to their apparent importance, is fraught with pitfalls. Such lists are perhaps better used, as they will be in this chapter, to assess the extent to which an economic elite exercised power in a variety of areas.

Since no one type of historical evidence measures all the economic holdings of all individuals in a community, problems also beset the determination of an economic elite. Comparison of property holdings over time probably provides the most accurate and convenient means in most communities for identifying the very rich and measuring their stability, as Edward Pessen and Frederic Jaher have done for New York and Boston. Despite the imperfections of tax lists — including gross under-assessment of personal property, the exclusion of income from securities and salaries, and even some under-assessment of real property — the imperfections, as Pessen notes, may at least be presumed to be consistent. The federal census does record real and personal property holdings but the census takers relied on self-reportage and did not gather information on property beyond 1870. The local tax rolls have the advantage of being a more objective appraisal and being available in Poughkeepsie for 1880 and 1900 as well as for earlier years.[2]

Accumulation of wealth in Poughkeepsie did not occur on the grandiose scale of Boston or New York. We have defined the rich in

Poughkeepsie in 1857 as those 52 individuals with real estate assessed at $10,000 or more, a group comprising 4 percent of the city's taxpayers that year. Assessments doubled on the average by the end of the seventies, so we have defined the rich in 1880 as the 78 individuals with holdings of $20,000 or more who also account for nearly 4 percent of the taxpayers. In 1900 the same percentage yields 93 individuals assessed at $16,000 or more.[3]

In both 1857 and 1880, the rich were mostly whites of native parentage, 90 and 83 percent respectively. By 1900 native whites comprised only 73 percent of the wealthy, reflecting the slow but steady progress of immigrant groups and their children. Among the first and second generation immigrants who replaced natives, Germans made the greatest gains, comprising 9 percent of the rich in 1880 and 15 percent in 1900. The Irish, who had no representation on the 1857 list, by 1880 accounted for 3 percent and by 1900, 4 percent.

The most dramatic changes between the 1857 and 1880 rich occurred in occupations. In both eras professional men, largely lawyers, accounted for roughly one quarter of the large real estate owners, and bankers accounted for about 5 percent. Gentlemen of leisure living off their fortunes constituted 33 percent of the economic elite in 1857 but only 15 percent in 1880. Individuals whose wealth derived from manufacturing enterprises increased from 14 to 19 percent but a much sharper change occurred in the proportion of individuals associated with mercantile enterprises, an increase of from 10 to 23 percent. Those whose wealth derived from trade or service enterprises such as freighting, restaurants, and butchering changed only from 12 to 14 percent. By 1900 the proportion of professionals among the rich had declined, the proportion of manufacturers and those engaged in trade and service enterprises increased slightly while the proportion of merchants continued to rise sharply and that of gentlemen with inherited incomes to decline.

Many of the gentlemen on the 1857 tax list had acquired their fortunes merely by being in the village early and owning real estate which appreciated in value as Poughkeepsie grew into a small city. Through land acquisition, especially around some ponds along the Fallkill Creek, which became prime manufacturing sites, a native harnessmaker gained a considerable fortune. Similarly, an English farmer numbered among the city's wealthiest in 1857 because property which he had bought on the outskirts of the village in 1825 now had become valuable. The decline of landed gentlemen and their replacement by a manufacturing and mercantile elite was a natural accompaniment of further growth and industrialization in a small city.[4]

Lists of real and personal property assessments do not, of course, measure a man's economic standing completely and in Poughkeepsie at least underestimate the prosperity of manufacturers. At best such lists only record those who have a propensity for investing in local real estate and even then they tell us nothing of a man's mortgage indebtedness nor any ownership of real estate and assets in other communities.

Fortunately another measure of economic standing exists for Poughkeepsie but unfortunately only for the middle of our period — a published list of incomes of $600 or more for the federal tax in 1866. An occupational breakdown of the richest 50 men on this list — those who paid taxes on incomes over $5,000 — revealed 29 percent of them to be manufacturers. Manufacturers comprised a far smaller proportion of the rich on all the real estate lists: 14 percent in 1857, 16 percent in 1865, and 19 percent in 1880, pointing up the fact that manufacturers' physical plants continued to be assessed at a relatively low valuation although they produced a good current income.[5]

The general shifts in the occupations of the wealthy need not have prevented the same families from continuing as the city's wealthiest citizens either through tenacity in real estate holdings, investment in manufacturing and mercantile enterprises, or domination of the professions. The tax lists of 1857 and 1880 span only one generation and provide a convenient means of assessing how well the wealthy and their sons adapted to the economic changes in Poughkeepsie or, conversely, how often the growing economy provided opportunities for newcomers to the city or for enterprising local citizens who were not among the wealthiest of 1857 to rise to the top.

Less than half of the 1857 rich and their descendants appeared among the wealthiest taxpayers of 1880. Or to reverse the perspective, 62 percent of the 1880 group had no family connection with the 1857 rich (Table 4.1). By comparison with the largest property owners in New York City, Philadelphia, and Boston, the 1857 rich in Poughkeepsie less often maintained their local economic preeminence. Since the biggest fortunes in this small city fall within the

TABLE 4.1. Continuity of the rich between tax rolls[a]

Tax roll	Number of rich	Percent Represented subsequently[b]	
1857	53	In 1880: 47	In 1900; 17
1880	78	In 1900: 41	
		Represented previously[b]	
1880	·78	In 1857: 38	
1900	93	In 1880: 49	In 1857: 12

[a]Defined as richest 4 percent of the taxpayers on each tax roll.
[b]Represented by themselves or by their ancestors or descendants.

lower range of the wealthiest taxpayers in our largest cities and so correspondingly provided less of a cushion against losses, this greater lack of continuity among Poughkeepsie's rich families seems only common sense. This vulnerability of the rich needs emphasis, however, since the very focus so far of studies of American urban stratification during the nineteenth century upon wealth in the three largest cities tends to suggest by default of qualification a greater degree of continuity in fortunes in most American cities than closer examination is likely to support.[6]

The decline of the 1857 rich did not occur through a process of displacing living residents. Rather death and the consequent division of estates made room at the top for a new elite by 1880. The next generation's inability or failure to seize upon local opportunities and so rebuild fortunes reinforced the leveling tendency of that distribution. Excluding nine men whose estates had not been probated by 1880, 26 of the deceased or departed 1857 rich had reported sons or relatives living with them on the 1850 and 1860 census returns who would be of age in 1880. An examination of the fate of the 46 sons helps explain the decline of the 1857 rich.

The 22 sons who left the city by 1880 may have attained prominence elsewhere, but they did not take advantage of their families' position locally. Since a quarter of these sons reported themselves before emigrating without any occupation or alternatively as gentlemen, one cannot safely assume that all of them found careers to rival those of their fathers.

Of the 24 sons who remained in the city, only nine appeared

among the top real estate holders in 1880. Only five of these nine pursued active business careers but four of the five found themselves in financial trouble by the eighties or associated with declining businesses. George Innis had used the money left to him by his father, a freighter, to invest in a successful dye wood mill characterized by R. G. Dun and Company as the leading firm in its line in the United States. By the early eighties Innis was heavily in debt and at the end of the nineties the dye wood mill closed, no longer able to compete with the newer chemical dyes. William A. Davies, son of a gentleman farmer, pursued an active banking career and had been estimated as worth $500,000 in 1870. He lost heavily through stock speculation, however, dropping that estimate temporarily to $40,000 in the early eighties. By the end of the decade Davies' fortune remained less than half of his worth in 1870.[7]

Fifteen sons of the 1857 rich who remained in the city never approximated their fathers' positions. Nine of these sons either did not work at all or engaged in dubious businesses. Part at least of the failure of the 1857 rich to maintain their positions seems due to the incompetence or lack of interest in money-making in the next generation. One lawyer, for example, had three sons living in Poughkeepsie in 1880, ranging in ages from 40 to 29. The middle son worked as a bookkeeper at a local bank but the other two reported no occupations and presumably had retired on their inheritances. A successful New York dry goods merchant who had retired to Poughkeepsie had an only son who at one point tried to engage in the manufacture of patent springs for buggies. A credit reporter described the business as a white elephant and it survived only five years.[8]

A successful doctor and druggist set his sons up in business in Hartford where they failed. One of the sons then returned to take over his father's business but his "habits as to intemperance" forced the father's executors to sell out after two years. Young Elias never recouped. He ended up at the poor house in 1877; the admitting officer commented, "Well brought up; his father was one of the best citizens of Poughkeepsie and his family was considered one of the first in the city. The use of strong drink has brought Elias here." Three years earlier his wife had appeared before the local Women's Christian Temperance Union to tell of her "sufferings during the past winter." Her sympathetic audience gave her a collection.[9]

While no other family suffered the reversal in fortunes

experienced by this druggist's son, death, departure, and the incompetence of the next generation left ample room at the top in Poughkeepsie. Three fifths of the 1880 rich had acquired their wealth since 1857 and 42 percent of these new men of wealth in 1880 also were newcomers to the city, with Harvey Eastman foremost. They had not been present nor owned real estate in 1857.

Like Eastman, some of these newcomers had made their money in Poughkeepsie in the years after 1857. William Johnston served for many years as a captain in the New York City police force until the opening of the Hudson River Railroad in 1851 enabled him to secure a position as a stationmaster and then as a conductor on the railroad. Spotting the opportunity provided by the regular delay in Poughkeepsie for change of engines, Johnston, in partnership with his brothers, opened a restaurant at the Poughkeepsie depot. By 1870 they had opened additional restaurants in Albany and Syracuse and, as the R. G. Dun and Company report noted, were "making money all the time."[10]

Many of the other newcomers to town after 1857, however, had made money elsewhere before investing in enterprises in Poughkeepsie. Born on a New Hampshire farm, John O. Whitehouse migrated to New York City in his teens and at age 22 established a boot and shoe business in Brooklyn, becoming a leader in the manufacture and wholesaling of shoes. In 1860 at age 43 he sold his Brooklyn business and came to Poughkeepsie, ostensibly to retire. A decade later, however, he opened a shoe factory which became Poughkeepsie's largest employer.[11]

Another newcomer, German-born Charles Kirchner, had spent some time in Poughkeepsie as a young man but achieved his first success in business in Newark, New Jersey. Arriving from Germany in 1854 he worked for six months as a clerk in the butcher shop of his countryman and future father-in-law, Jacob Petillon. He then migrated to Newark where he opened his own meat market two years later. Returning to the Hudson valley city in 1862 he continued in butchering but used the proceeds for shrewd investments in local real estate, erecting Poughkeepsie's first modern building block. By 1900 Kirchner had become the largest owner of real estate in the city.[12]

More typical of the new 1880 elite, however, were the men who not only had been in Poughkeepsie before 1857 but also had made all of their money there through businesses which expanded as the local economy grew. Of the 64 men — 82 percent of the 1880 rich — for whom there is sufficient data, 75 percent had spent most of their business careers in the city and 44 percent were largely self-made. Their more gradual and largely local rise to the top exemplifies career patterns among the city's self-made rich men better than Eastman or Whitehouse. James Collingwood, for example, came to the United States from England at age eighteen. He worked first as a shoemaker in Newburgh, then tried housebuilding in near-by Fishkill and farming across the river in Ulster County and finally settled in Poughkeepsie where he began what became a very successful coal and lumber business. A growing city needed new houses and fuel to heat them.[13] Another immigrant came first from Germany to Albany where he had practiced his trade of tailoring. Although he began as a tailor in Poughkeepsie, he moved quickly into the liquor business investing his considerable profits in that line in local real estate.[14]

During its rapid expansion after 1850 Poughkeepsie offered opportunities for both newcomers and older, but previously less affluent, residents to become members of the city's economic elite. Between 1880 and 1900, however, Poughkeepsie's rates of both population and industrial growth declined sharply. An examination of the top real estate holders from the 1900 tax rolls shows an even greater attrition of the wealthy individuals of an earlier generation. Only 17 percent of the 1857 rich had descendants among the largest real estate holders in 1900 and only 41 percent of the 1880 rich or their descendants were still represented in that year.

Yet some significant differences did appear in the character of the rich in 1900. While 42 percent of the new 1880 rich immigrated to the city after 1857, only 13 percent of the 1900 rich had come into the city after 1880. In a period of population stagnation, the dynamic and successful newcomer became a comparative rarity. The decline of entrepreneurial talent from outside also appears in the higher proportion of the 1900 rich who owed their fortunes to the 1880 rich. More striking, 27 percent of the 1900 rich were women, largely widows and daughters of the successful entrepreneurs of 1880. While it undoubtedly reflects a greater willingness to leave estates to wives and daughters, the much greater proportion of women on the 1900 tax list also suggests that older money did not face the same challenge to its position in the community that the 1857 rich had faced during a period of rapid expansion. By the end of the century a fortune once made seems to have offered more stability in economic preeminence. Moreover, by 1900 a high proportion of the sons of the 1880 rich had left town reinforcing the suspicion that Poughkeepsie's slower growth after the depression of the seventies not only discouraged newcomers but also encouraged emigration among those born there. Of the 57 sons of the 1880 rich whose fathers had died or left the city, almost two thirds of the sons also had left the city compared to about one half of the sons of the 1857 rich during a similar period of time.

To be sure, death and declining fortunes accounted for some of the disappearance of the 1880 rich as it had for those of 1857. The son of a rich furniture dealer committed suicide as did the son-in-law of a German butcher and moneylender. A successful flour merchant who appeared on both the 1857 and 1880 lists turned over his business first to his oldest and then to his youngest son, both of whom ran it in partnership with an able cousin. By 1879 the oldest son was "busted" and thought to be trying to get into business in the West, forcing his father temporarily to return to the business. By 1887 the firm, now under the control of the younger son and the cousin, went bankrupt and hurt many creditors; the principals disappeared from Poughkeepsie soon afterward.[15]

Of the 22 sons of the 1880 rich, 9 appeared among the 1900 rich. All but one of these wealthy sons continued to run enterprises founded by their fathers. Of the other 13 sons who remained in the city but who had lost their fathers' economic preeminence, half reported no occupation.[16]

With two exceptions the newly rich of 1900 made their money in enterprises producing only for a local or a regional market. They contrast with earlier entrepreneurs like Whitehouse, Adriance, Tower, and even Eastman, the educator, who had served national and—in the case of Adriance—international markets. Thus, three of the native-born men among the 1900 rich, all Dutchess County boys, had founded and built up Luckey, Platt & Co., the largest department store in the mid-Hudson region. One new arrival began in the hotel business but switched to real estate and insurance. The considerable entrepreneurial talents of another focused on local street railways and a newspaper.[17]

The increasing dependence of the successful on local or regional markets eased the progress of Poughkeepsie's immigrants. First or second generation immigrants who had been in town most of their

adult lives comprised almost half of the newly rich men of 1900.
George Lumb, son of an English carpet weaver who became a
neighborhood grocer, began as a factory hand in Pelton's carpet
factory. Later George learned the sash and blind trade and with
two partners including his brother opened a factory in that trade
after the Civil War. By the end of the eighties he and his brother ran
separate shops, both prospering on regional demand. William
Smith's Scottish father had started a small candy store in the fifties
which later expanded into a restaurant and confectionery. Later
Smith and his brothers began the manufacture of cough drops
which soon received national reputation and distribution.[18]

William R. Maloney perhaps best exemplifies the opportunities
for immigrants to become rich with a purely local clientele, a clientele largely drawn at first from his fellow countrymen. Maloney's
Irish father appeared in the 1860 census as a laborer owning real estate worth $1,000. William first reported himself as a machinist
but by 1870 he had acquired a fancy goods store, specializing in the
furnishing of regalia to fraternal societies. A decade later he owned
real estate himself assessed at $9,600, and by the nineties had pur-
chased *The Evening Star,* a local newspaper. Maloney's son married
the granddaughter of Robert Thorn, whose estate had been assessed
for more than $100,000 in 1880 and who belonged to one of Dutch-
ess County's oldest and most aristocratic families.[19]

Despite the relative fluidity of Poughkeepsie's economic elite and
the failure of so many members to confer their economic preeminence upon their descendants, the majority of the rich at any
particular moment during the last half of the nineteenth century
operated as a fairly closely knit group for certain purposes, and
especially in new promotional schemes. As in many nineteenth-
century cities, Poughkeepsie's businessmen, politicians, and local
editors believed that the development of external and internal
railroad linkages would result in rapid, lasting economic growth for
their city as well as handsome profits for themselves. In particular,
they sought an east-to-west railroad linkage, which of necessity included construction of a railroad bridge spanning the Hudson River
at Poughkeepsie.

Almost two thirds of the incorporators of the Poughkeepsie
Bridge Co. in 1872 came from the city's economic elite. Similarly, all
but one of the founding officers of the Poughkeepsie and Eastern
Railroad Co. came from the same group of men and so did the ma-

jority of officers of the Poughkeepsie, Boston and Hartford. Locally the Street Railway Co. had less representation among the rich, but the incorporators were substantial merchants and lawyers, all of whom also served as bank directors and had invested in other enterprises. Although the Board of Trade, organized in 1871, included many lesser merchants among its board of directors, its executive committee and officers always included a number of the very rich.[20]

None of the ventures promoted by the elite had much financial success, however; when the rich invested together, they often also lost money together. The Poughkeepsie and Eastern went into receivership; the Street Railway Co. had to be reorganized in 1877; the Poughkeepsie Bridge Co. always remained in marginal financial condition although it completed the bridge seventeen years after its chartering. Furthermore, investors outside the city owned the two largest new factories of the eighties and nineties. While the old Innis dye wood mill, the Vassar brewery and even the newer Whitehouse shoe factory declined, the Poughkeepsie Glass Co. and the DeLaval Separator Co. flourished. DeLaval was a Swedish firm; a group of investors from England and Rochester, New York, founded the glass works. Only the Adriances at Buckeye and the Towers at the Poughkeepsie Iron Co., themselves newcomers in the fifties, continued to head up the city's largest industries by the turn of the century.[21]

The elite did dominate the town's banking structure and so controlled local loans and mortgages. Throughout the period all the presidents of the major banks ranked among Poughkeepsie's fifty richest men. In any given year, well over half of the bank directors came from this same group. Moreover, the same man might serve as an officer or director of rival banks over the course of our three decades and members of the same family served simultaneously on the boards of rival banks. Thus, William A. Davies acted as president of the Farmers and Manufacturers Bank while his brother Thomas presided over the Poughkeepsie National Bank. George Innis served as president of the Fallkill Bank and his brother Aaron as chief executive of the City Bank.[22]

None of the German and Irish immigrants who achieved success in these years ever appeared on bank boards. While few immigrants invested in bank stock, some did have more substantial holdings than natives who sat on the boards. Only two immigrants appeared among the incorporators of the bridge company, and although immigrants had become prominent among proprietors of the city's retail and craft stores by the seventies, no German or Irish merchant appeared among the directors of the Poughkeepsie Board of Trade founded in 1871. By contrast, native-born newcomers to the city like John Whitehouse and Harvey Eastman soon took their seats on bank boards and the Board of Trade and joined in the leadership of promotional schemes.

In some ways, the exclusion of Irish and German immigrants from the leadership of the city's banks may have helped the further rise of successful individuals within those ethnic communities. As early as 1867 a credit reporter described Peter Thielman as a "monied man, loans much of it." Lending to his countrymen enabled Thielman to achieve a success beyond what his shoe store alone made possible. On the other hand, exclusion from the local financial community also denied immigrant businessmen some of the special consideration the native-born rich received from their own kind. When one of the city's leading entrepreneurs who had been a bank president himself overextended himself in the early eighties, creditor banks showed themselves very sympathetic to his plight. A credit reporter commented in 1880 on the policy of the bank of which this entrepreneur had once been president: "He has strong friends on the board of directors and there is no disposition to push for a settlement." Although his indebtedness exceeded $100,000, he had paid very little of it by 1883. One of the banks became sufficiently nervous to press for a settlement on the $86,000 he still owed them, but even they stood ready to grant a generous extension of time on the bulk of the debt. The R.G. Dun and Company reporter concluded assessment of his position by saying, "His friends stand by him."[23]

To sum up, the elite in Poughkeepsie — measured by income or by property holdings — did not form a self-perpetuating or closed class. The children of wealthy men usually did not succeed to their fathers' economic preeminence in the community. As the economy expanded, an older generation of wealth was displaced. When the expansion slowed, there was more continuity at the top but also more frequency of local men, including immigrants and their children, among the city's rich.

No entire occupational group belonged to the economic elite, but one group, professional workers, were represented in the elite out of all proportion to their numbers and those who were not rich themselves more often associated closely with the rich than members of other occupational groups. They also were unusually stable and homogeneous. Overwhelmingly native-born at every census, lawyers, doctors, teachers, and clergymen rarely listed themselves at other occupations; neither did members of less well-established or emerging professions like dentistry, architecture, and civil engineering. Less than 7 percent of Poughkeepsie's professionals in any decade shifted to a nonprofessional occupational designation and many of the reported shifts prove to be spurious. Some lawyers, for example, spent various portions of their careers in finance and government and listed themselves accordingly; others, especially those who managed their own inherited estates, preferred in some censuses to call themselves gentlemen. In short, professions once achieved offered insurance against downward mobility.

In reward and recruitment, the professions did differ markedly. By the criteria of income or of property accumulated, lawyers garnered the greatest rewards but their superior earning power partially reflected the frequency with which they came from rich families and themselves participated in business. Just as the rich ministers in town owed their property to inheritance rather than to salary, so many of the richest lawyers came from wealthy families. Of the 37 lawyers practicing by 1880 whose fathers' occupations can be identified, almost half were sons of farmers, usually of the variety descended from old county families who owned substantial acreage. About the same proportion had fathers who were professionals, especially lawyers and ministers. Only five of these lawyers could claim a distinctly humble origin; two of them were unusual also in having had a common school education.[24]

Of the 33 lawyers whose secondary educational background could be traced, only two had attended public schools; the rest graduated from private academies. It seems likely that another eight who reported a college education but did not detail their secondary schooling also attended academies. In a day of few public high schools, the prevalence of academy education does not surprise but it does suggest that the choice of the legal profession as a career became closed practically to many men at a young age by default of an adequate secondary education.

The most common route to the bar after completing private secondary education was the reading of law in a local office. Twenty-six of the 35 lawyers whose legal training can be determined followed this route. Only 13 had gone to college and only nine to law school; only four attended both. In contrast to the twentieth century when college education has become the prerequisite, in the nineteenth century the minimum would seem to have been an academy education and good connections with the right law firms.

The ability of lawyers to obtain professional competence locally eventually enabled more men of lower class origin to become attorneys, especially after the establishment of the public high school. Since we lack systematic biographical or census information for the period after 1880, the following evidence is suggestive rather than definitive. At least seven of the 51 male graduates of Poughkeepsie High School between 1873 and 1883 became lawyers. Some of these graduates did go on to college or law school. The son of a black gardener attended Williams College and studied law in a local office. The son of an Irish grocer graduated from Albany Law School as did the son of an Irish harnessmaker.

Just as typical, however, were the high school graduates who read law in local offices immediately after graduation. One of the twelve children of an Irish wheelwright had just such an education; he subsequently served as city judge, corporation counsel, and mayor, having also married into one of the wealthiest families in town. Similarly, John E. Mack attended parochial school and the public high school before reading law locally. Mack combined a lucrative practice with local politics, serving for many years as Democratic chairman of Dutchess County. Sons of native parentage often took the same route. One father had been successively a clerk in the post office, a printer, and a salesman and the mother a dressmaker; a high school education and local legal apprenticeship enabled their son to become an attorney.[25]

Admission to the bar did not guarantee financial success, but at the least it provided a secure and respectable career. Three quarters of the lawyers over 30 years old reported incomes of $600 or more in 1866, but the largest proportion fell in the middle range between $1,500 and $2,500. The richest lawyers were either well-born, well-married or pursued business and banking careers beyond their practice of law; nine of the ten lawyers reporting annual incomes of more than $2,000 in 1866 shared one or all of these characteristics. Charles Swift earned the largest income of any lawyer in that year and his estate in 1880 bore the highest assessment of any individual taxpayer; son of a prominent lawyer, he descended from one of the major landowning families in southern Dutchess. Swift participated in most of the railroad promotions of his day, served as president of the Dutchess Turnpike Co., an officer of a local bank, the Dutchess County Mutual Insurance Co., and the Poughkeepsie Gas Co., mayor of the city, and a trustee of Vassar College. But his financial success also rested on his role as a private moneylender. The R.G. Dun and Company reports mention him more frequently than any other citizen as a holder of real estate and chattel mortgages.[26]

James Emott, the lawyer with the third largest income in 1866 as well as substantial real estate, also combined an elite background with extensive entrepreneurial activity. Son of a Supreme Court judge and son-in-law of a rich freighter, Emott organized and served as president of the Merchant's Bank as well as of a chair manufacturing company in which he had an interest. When Edward Bech had to withdraw from ownership of the Poughkeepsie Iron Works because of the failure of the Cunard Steamship Co., in which he was a partner, Emott and Charles Swift together with William Davies supplied the capital and controlled the firm until Albert Tower could afford to take over a large interest. In 1860 Emott joined with Tower and Bech to form another company, the Fallkill Iron Works, serving as its president until a consolidation with the Poughkeepsie Iron Works in 1875.[27]

While the combination of inherited wealth and entrepreneurship occurred frequently among the richer lawyers, some relied upon one or the other for their economic standing. Phillip Hamilton, son of Alexander and the second richest attorney in the city, does not seem to have pursued an active legal career; after holding minor posts in New York City, he lived in semi-retirement in Poughkeepsie. Joseph Barnard, who became a Supreme Court judge in the state, devoted himself to his profession; he made a point throughout his career of taking poorer clients who could not pay as well as serving the more affluent. But Barnard's father, a retired sea captain from Nantucket who owned extensive lands in the county, had been a member of the 1857 economic elite in Poughkeepsie.[28]

Except at the highest rank, the medical profession in Poughkeepsie reported incomes roughly similar to those of the legal profession. Only 4 percent of the doctors reported incomes of $5,000 or more whereas 19 percent of the lawyers did. Doctors attended college no more often than lawyers, but a far greater proportion received formal training in their calling. Twenty-eight of the 39 doctors whose medical training is known had attended medical schools, almost all of them reputable; graduates of the College of Physicians and Surgeons in New York accounted for half of the 28. Of those without formal medical training, three had attended college and three were licentiates of local medical societies; all of them were older men who had apprenticed with doctors before the burgeoning of medical schools in the forties. The remaining five studied medicine with doctors of the dissenting variety. Four were homeopathic physicians and the fifth had studied locally with a practitioner of the Thomsonian school of medicine. While homeopathic physicians often did not attend formal medical schools, at least two of those in Poughkeepsie in these years had graduated from the Homeopathic Medical College of New York. Younger homeopathists in the community after 1880 also attended that school.[29]

With one exception, the five doctors receiving the largest incomes in 1866 did not owe their prosperity just to their practices in Poughkeepsie. Two of them had settled in the city after successful careers in New York City, one coming because of ill health and the other after his wife inherited a large fortune. Two others combined medical practice with prosperous drug firms suggesting, as was true of lawyers, that the largest rewards lay beyond the profession itself.

For both the legal and medical professions upward mobility into their ranks from manual work rarely occurred during one man's career. Two lawyers had that distinction, one of them gaining regional notoriety as "The Poughkeepsie Blacksmith." Although William H. Van Wagner, Jr., abandoned his craft in his early forties to set up as an attorney, he spent much of his time during the later fifties and early sixties traveling around with a big tent giving lectures upon temperance and other subjects. A more frequent presence in local courtrooms, but no less unusual in manner than Van Wagner, had begun in even humbler circumstances as a gardener employed by one of Poughkeepsie's most eminent attorneys. The historian of the county bar said that Irish-born John Moore somehow gained admission without any apparent course of study in a law office but by 1870 in his mid-thirties had numerous clients. "With a hazy idea of the more intricate paths of law, he had naturally a keen intellect, and this coupled with native Irish wit, made him an effective trial lawyer where the issues were of fact only." In later years, clients dropped away and finally "the poor, battered, unsuccessful hulk drifted into port," run over at a railroad crossing.[30]

The two men who reported other occupations in Poughkeepsie

prior to claiming to be physicians probably were quacks, since the supposed change in calling occurred after they were fifty years old. One of them, a New Jerseyan of Scottish parentage first appeared in Poughkeepsie as a foundryman and then as a shoemaker with his own shop before reporting himself as a cancer doctor. What cure he offered for cancer cannot be determined for he left no advertisements.[31]

The teaching profession depended on business enterprise for economic success even more than other professions. With one exception, all of the surprising number of educators reporting large incomes in 1866 owned private academies, most of them having started out as teachers. The other better-rewarded teachers on the income list were music teachers or dancing masters whose reward depended upon their ability to attract a clientele. Most of the remaining teachers with $600 or more income in 1866 belonged to the faculty of Eastman's business college and they tended to move into business careers. One gave up his position that same year to engage in business in Watkins, New York, and another emigrated to San Francisco for the same purpose.[32]

Most of the male instructors at the private academies for boys did not earn as much as $600. Some of these teachers would one day become school proprietors themselves. Few who did not achieve that goal stayed in Poughkeepsie very long and some of these soon found other employment. By their early thirties one had left teaching to become a photographer and another, to become a carpenter. The marginality of these teachers in the world of Poughkeepsie's professionals appears in the frequency with which they shift occupations and the relative ease with which former manual workers could find positions. A native tinsmith and an English-born iron moulder — who later adopted the monicker "Colonel" — both left Poughkeepsie for varying periods of time and both found teaching positions upon returning to the city.

Like teaching the newer professional callings, notably in architecture and in engineering and its developing specializations, offered more opportunity for upward mobility for men who started at manual work. Self-study and informal apprenticeship provided an even more usual path to success in these emerging professions than it did in law, medicine, or the ministry. When Arnout Cannon, Jr., sought in 1860 to go beyond the skills he could acquire through apprenticeship as a builder with his father, the first architectural school in the United States was still four years in the future. So Cannon spent two years studying in the office of a New York architect.[33]

An established Poughkeepsie builder, James Post, apparently educated himself for the same calling. This "man of first class ability," as credit reporters described him, advertised by the seventies that he now offered clients the services of the architect as well as the builder. Post was in his early forties at the time. Another man in his forties made a more unusual shift into a professional practice. John Faust was one of three brothers, all journeymen coopers from the German state of Hesse, who first came to New York City in 1852 and then went to Poughkeepsie in 1859, setting up their own business a year later. John left the firm in 1875 and the next year listed himself in the city directory as a veterinary surgeon although he did not take the examination for that degree from the New York Veterinary Society until 1881. Subsequently he joined national professional societies, wrote several treatises on his specializations and served as state inspector for inoculation of cattle against tuberculosis. His son became a doctor, graduating from the Homeopathic Medical College of New York one year after his father passed his examination.[34]

Faust remained the exception among Poughkeepsie's tiny minority of German and Irish professionals during the middle decades both in the ethnic inclusiveness of his clientele and in his state and national professional relationships. Clergymen predominated and the handful of doctors and teachers depended upon their fellow countrymen. Doctor Haidlauf lived and practiced in the heart of the largest German residential concentration. John O'Donnell taught in St. Peter's parochial school before becoming proprietor of a Catholic bookstore and serving as parish librarian.

With the exception of O'Donnell, Haidlauf, lawyer John Moore, and the pastors of St. Peter's Church, foreign-born professionals before 1880 did not remain in the city as long as a decade. Not until the second generation did the Irish in Poughkeepsie begin to have a stable group of lawyers and doctors of their own. In 1900 Irish-Americans account for ten of the 71 attorneys advertising in the city directory, most of them born in Poughkeepsie. Five of the 34 doctors advertising that year claimed Irish descent but, like local doctors generally, had not grown up in the city. Two of these listed themselves as clairvoyant and electromedical specialist respectively. The

Germans in 1900 had yet to develop a stable professional element in the city, being represented by only one lawyer and one doctor.

For the Irish the emergence of their own professional class represented not only a gain in respectability—after years of being identified with the heavier and dirtier forms of manual work—but also an articulate leadership. Symptomatically, when the Knights of Columbus organized in Poughkeepsie in 1898, four lawyers and a doctor account for five of the 14 officers, all Irish-Americans who had grown up in the city. The importance of these professionals in advancing the status of the ethnic group within the city becomes apparent by contrast with the remaining officers whose occupations can be identified: a newspaper publisher, a furniture dealer, a plumber, and two confectioners, all self-employed, and a teacher of penmanship. Still lacking bankers, manufacturers, or more than a handful of prosperous merchants, the Irish in Poughkeepsie at the turn of the century depended far more heavily than citizens of native ancestry upon the opportunities the professions, especially law, now offered the second generation.

5

The Precariousness of Enterprise

THE AMERICAN SELF-HELP creed made the happy assumption that business enterprise would bring both stability and progress not only to the individuals who pursued it but also to the communities in which they lived. Growth and innovation could be achieved without any sacrifice of order and continuity in the community. This premise pervaded nineteenth-century boosterism. The advertisements for small towns and cities such as Poughkeepsie noted with pride the native sons among the leading businessmen and citizens. They often recorded the origins of newcomers but emphasized wherever possible how long those citizens had been in business locally. Old timers suggested reliability; by their presence newcomers among businessmen testified to the attractiveness of the community, but boosterism presumed they had settled for life in their new home and had identified themselves with its interests.

Historians have long since pointed out that the creed arose at the very time when corporate organization, increase in the size and specialization of firms, mass marketing, and all the changes associated with the rise of big business made it harder for a man to compete successfully without capital resources and help from his family and friends. But we have only begun to pursue close examination of the careers of businessmen in firms of every size and type in one locality, and especially where modest scale in enterprise was prevalent, to see whether they support the assumptions of boosterism.[1] This chapter examines opportunity for individuals to rise through business ventures in Poughkeepsie and its relation to stability in the business community. The next chapter will describe opportunity for different ethnic groups in various types of commercial enterprise and in clerical and sales jobs.

Poughkeepsians behaved as if they believed that business offered them opportunity. Using the listings of firms in the classified section of the city directory, in most lines the number of firms increased more rapidly than the population between 1859 and 1870. Between 1870 and 1900, a period of much slower population growth, there was a decrease or slower growth in the number of firms in many lines.[2]

This rush to start up a business for oneself attests to a desire for self-employment, but the reality of business life contradicted the idea that business would bring security. The high proportion of proprietors in the census who remained proprietors for a decade is very misleading because the census, taken every ten years, does not capture numerous businessmen whose firms only lasted a few years. Of the 1,530 firms reported on by R. G. Dun and Company between 1845 and 1880, 32 percent lasted three years or less and only 14 percent lasted twenty years or more. The credit reports, furthermore, by no means include all small businesses nor do they list all firms throughout their existence. A comparison of grocery stores reported on by R. G. Dun and Company between 1845 and 1880 with all those listed in the main body of the directory during those same years reveals that credit reporters only assessed 37 percent of the groceries in the fifties, 65 percent in the sixties and 80 percent in the seventies. A more inclusive tracing of firms in all lines from city directories by the Hutchinsons and Newcomer found that for the period between 1843 and 1873, 60 percent of the firms lasted less than three years although that figure counted all changes in partnerships as new firms and included some artisans who were not self-employed.[3]

Not only did most businesses fade rapidly but also only a minority were very promising ventures at the outset. Business enterprise in any community encompassed a tremendous diversity of firms and individuals. The shoe trade in Poughkeepsie, for example, included

John Whitehouse, the manufacturer, Daniel Heaton, a large retail shoe dealer, and James Bradley, who "has been a shoemaker here in a small way, cobbling mostly, had small shop and moved a short time ago." The majority of businessmen resembled struggling proprietors like Bradley rather than a Whitehouse or Heaton. Of the 1,317 firms whose worth was estimated by credit reporters, 42 percent were worth less than $1,000, 38 percent were worth between $1,001 and $10,000, and only 20 percent rated above $10,000.[4]

Reflecting changes in the national economy, the nature of small business in Poughkeepsie altered in the years after the Civil War. These years saw a decline of small craft-related shops and toward the end of the period a proliferation of small retail and service businesses. From 1859 until 1870, the number of firms in almost all lines increased at a faster rate than the population. From 1870 to 1900, however, only businesses catering primarily to a local clientele, such as saloons, groceries, confectioneries, bakeries, and barbershops increased at a rate faster than the population as a whole. Other lines were more seriously affected by the introduction of ready-made goods produced elsewhere. Brewers, cigarmakers, carriage shops, tailoring and clothing firms, shoemakers, and shoe dealers all declined, reflecting the decreasing viability of artisan manufacture. The decline might have come sooner but for the influx of German artisans who initially engaged in small shop manufacture in many of these lines. Moreover, even in some craft-related businesses, such as tailoring establishments, there was a greater emphasis on the sale of ready-made clothing among those proprietors who had started out with a custom trade.[5]

The recruitment of proprietors reflected the decline of the artisan businessman. The proportion of proprietors who started out as skilled workers had decreased by 1880. A slight and temporary increase in the proportion of proprietors drawn from the ranks of the skilled during the sixties reflected the attempts of immigrant artisans to set up shops as well as the tendency of rapid population growth to stimulate the founding of new businesses, many of which faded quickly. The drop during the seventies in the proportion of proprietors who had previously been artisans was too dramatic to attribute solely to the depression; the proportion who had previously been unskilled workers continued to rise in that same decade.

Moreover, clerical and sales workers increasingly became the source of new proprietorships as compared to skilled workers.

Among men already in the city who became proprietors during the fifties, those who held clerical and sales jobs at the start of the decade were only one fifth as numerous as those who had been at skilled work; the ratio changed to one third in the sixties and one half in the seventies. At the end of the period, the business class still drew more of its new members from skilled than from clerical and sales workers but the differences had narrowed dramatically. First and second generation immigrant businessmen were still twice as likely to be drawn from skilled work, but in the recruitment of new businessmen of native parentage the skilled no longer had any superiority during the seventies (Table 5.1).

Analysis of the recruitment of proprietors from the census alone, however, underestimates the attempts of skilled and unskilled workers to set up small businesses. More than one tenth of the owners of firms on which R.G. Dun and Company reported never appeared in the census as proprietors. An Irishman who listed himself in the census respectively as a laborer and iron weigher opened a grocery in 1870 which lasted until 1879. A native designated in the census as a butcher owned a small shoe store in 1873-74, and a cabinetmaker and carpenter operated a confectionery for five years in the sixties. Such enterprises usually lasted only a few years, often between the years when the census was taken. Moreover, since Dun missed many small firms and since many proprietors on whom they did report could not be identified in the census, the number of business starts among manual workers undoubtedly was even greater.[6]

Manual workers frequently engaged in businesses unrelated to their skills or previous experience. Of the grocers in 1860 and 1870 who had been in the community a decade earlier, 16 and 19 percent had been skilled workers. In any census year slightly over 10 percent of the grocers who had been employed in the community at the preceding census had been unskilled workers. Saloon keepers were recruited even more heavily from blue collar ranks. In 1880 over half the saloon keepers who had appeared in the census in 1870 were previously blue-collar workers, skilled craftsmen accounting for 25 percent. Similarly, the Hutchinsons and Newcomer, using directory listings for selected years, found that manual workers comprised 39 percent of the owners of grocery stores, meat markets, saloons, and confectionery and cigar stores. Since many of these small enterprises operated out of their proprietors' homes, they had a natural attrac-

TABLE 5.1. Previous occupations of men achieving proprietorships during a decade

Nativity	Decade	Number of cases	Professional (percent)	Proprietorial (percent)	Clerical (percent)	Skilled (percent)	Semi-skilled (percent)	Unskilled (percent)
White of native parentage	1850–60	301	—	71	6	18	2	3
	1860–70	381	1	66	11	17	3	2
	1870–80	398	2	72	11	11	2	3
British	1850–60	31	—	52	—	32	13	3
	1860–70	40	—	65	3	25	8	—
	1870–80	36	—	78	—	22	—	—
Native of British parentage	1870–80	18	—	40	17	33	11	—
German	1850–60	30	—	60	—	33	3	3
	1860–70	93	—	44	2	47	3	3
	1870–80	120	—	70	2	21	3	5
Native of German parentage	1870–80	28	—	32	11	50	4	4
Irish	1850–60	25	—	44	4	44	4	4
	1860–70	47	2	45	—	26	2	26
	1870–80	59	—	54	2	7	9	29
Native of Irish parentage	1870–80	26	—	27	15	35	4	20
All	1850–60	392	—	67	5	22	3	4
	1860–70	583	1	59	8	24	4	4
	1870–80	698	1	66	8	16	3	6

tion for workers with little capital. Of the saloons, groceries, and confectioneries listed in the directory between 1873 and 1876, 86, 54, and 60 percent respectively were located at their owner's residential addresses.[7]

If the self-help creed did not suggest the marginality of most proprietors, the notion that the business community consisted of individuals who came almost entirely from the ranks of local citizens was similarly misleading. Of the proprietors in 1870 almost half had not been in the community ten years earlier and in 1880 about one third were newcomers. The large influx of new proprietors during the sixties indicates that a community which was prospering and expanding readily attracted outside businessmen from other places. Similarly, proprietors persisted in the community so long as times were good but left in greater numbers when the expansion slowed. Thus, of the proprietors listed in the census in 1860, 58 percent remained in town in 1870 but by 1880 the proportion of 1870 proprietors still in the community had dropped to 48 percent.

Many left a few years after their arrival. Two brothers moved up from New York City where they had been in business to open a grocery and feed store in Poughkeepsie. Perhaps because they did not have "the confidence of the people" and because "there was always a mystery about them," their store did not prosper. One brother within a year had moved upstate and the other, after several failures during his ten years in Poughkeepsie, opened a small grocery in a nearby rural village. An upstate man opened a large shoe store in Poughkeepsie in 1869; nine years later he had sold out and returned to his native county.[8]

Other proprietors moved in and out of the city several times. A German sold out his shoe store in Poughkeepsie in 1864 and continued the same business in Philadelphia before opening still another shoe store in Poughkeepsie in 1866. By 1868 he disappeared permanently from the community. A native first appeared in the 1870 census as the owner of a carriage shop. In 1872 he operated a carriage factory in Uniontown, Pennsylvania, but by 1880 had returned to Poughkeepsie as a travel agent.[9]

Many new proprietors to the community, however, did settle down, finally becoming old merchants to whom the community could point with pride. In every decade almost half the proprietors listed in the census remained in the community ten years later although not all continued as proprietors. Many of those men who chose to remain in Poughkeepsie also had had extensive business experience elsewhere before establishing their long-lived businesses, pointing up the tendency of young men in the nineteenth century to experiment with different businesses and locations before choosing a permanent career in one place. While the origins of the majority of new proprietors cannot be traced, a large number came in from rural areas but often with intervening clerical or business experience in other towns and cities, especially New York City.

Sylvester Andrus, for example, appeared in all four censuses as a lumber merchant, reflecting his long partnership with the Arnolds in that business. In fact, he had started out as a tanner in the Catskills, came to Poughkeepsie in the thirties, and entered the employ of a captain. He set up his own coal and lumber business but soon gave it up and went to New York City first in the stove and hardware business and then in the lumber business before returning to Poughkeepsie in 1841 when he permanently joined the Arnolds.[10]

Merchants like Andrus explain the high proportion of proprietors in the census who had been at that designation ten years earlier. At every decade about two thirds of the proprietors who had been in the city at the start of the decade had reported themselves as proprietors then. Moreover, over 80 percent of the proprietors who remained in Poughkeepsie ten years later continued to so report themselves. Our classification exaggerates the continuity in occupation of the residentially stable members of this class, however, because it does not show shifts between different types of business. Thus, although a native appears in the census successively as a merchant tailor and furniture dealer and a German Jew appears first as a merchant tailor and then as owner of a cigar store, these men appear only as proprietors in our tables.

Even the census designations themselves overstate stability in type of business among proprietors because they do not record the many cases where men carried on several businesses simultaneously or shifted businesses several times during the course of a decade. Listing in two censuses as a stove merchant did not record one Quaker's ventures into dry goods, a country store proprietorship, and a confectionery. While his son's listings as a dentist, harness merchant, and undertaker reflected his peripatetic career in business, they missed his stints as a clerk, city chamberlain, and insurance agent. An Irish Catholic's listings as a merchant and lumber merchant fail utterly to convey the multiplicity of his ventures;

credit reporters described him variously as "a trading kind of man" and "in too many kinds of business," including ice, grain, liquor, groceries, a steam saw mill, a dry dock, and a lime kiln as well as extensive real estate speculation.[11]

Despite these qualifications, a majority of the largest proprietors, distinguished by amount of property reported in the census, did continue in the same businesses. A native who had emigrated from New York City had his own saddlery and harness shop in Pough-keepsie for fifty-two years and at the same location for forty-three years.[12] For such men business did bring an increase in wealth or at least a modicum of economic security. An examination of the property mobility of those proprietors who owned real estate in the city in 1870 and remained as proprietors in 1880 reveals that 40 percent increased their real estate holdings substantially, 35 percent owned approximately the same amount, and 25 percent experienced a significant loss. Because this analysis eliminates those proprietors who left the city, who owned no real property in 1870, or who did not remain proprietors in 1880, it only includes the most stable and prosperous businessmen.

The R. G. Dun and Co. reports confirm that, in general, the richer a firm the longer its life. Thus, 50 percent of the firms that received reports for twenty years or more had a maximum worth during their lifetime of $10,000 or more but only 4 percent of the firms lasting three years or less and 22 percent of the firms lasting between 10 and 19 years ever achieved a worth of $10,000. Conversely, a majority of businesses with an estimated worth of $1,000 or less lasted three years or less while a near majority of those who at any time had an estimated worth of over $25,000, continued for more than twenty years (Table 5.2).

On the other hand, longevity did not guarantee prosperity. Just as nearly a quarter of the proprietors on the tax list of 1870 recorded a loss of value by 1880, an even higher proportion of the firms reported on by R.G. Dun and Company for more than twenty years ended up in serious trouble, one third slipping into a COD rating and another one tenth experiencing fluctuations and reversals during their existence. Firms lasting between ten and nineteen years had an even greater tendency to decline, 40 percent ending up with a COD credit rating.

A native who ran a grocery from 1844 to 1875 was one of those businessmen whose firms were marginal for a large part of their long

TABLE 5.2. Highest estimated worth of firms by number of years reported by R. G. Dun and Co.

Years reported	Not estimated	Highest estimated worth (percent)			Number of firms
		$1,000 or less	$1,001-$10,000	$10,001 +	
1 – 3	27	55	15	4	490
4 – 9	11	40	38	11	407
10 – 19	7	25	47	22	419
20 +	3	8	38	50	214

lives. In 1844 the credit reporter characterized his grocery as a "small safe business," a judgment immediately reversed when he failed the next year. In the early sixties he was estimated to be worth $10,000, but by 1866, after another failure, his credit rating fell to COD. In 1870 he had recovered enough to earn the designation of "old grocer, good store and stock" but by 1873 was "generally hard up," an observation confirmed by his third and final failure in 1875.[13]

A proprietor of one of the foundries, by contrast, experienced a long, slow decline from 1852 to 1883. As late as 1872 his worth was estimated at $25,000 although the previous year a reporter had warned that "he gets help but always manages to wiggle through." He failed in 1877. From then until he retired from business in 1883 he was characterized as "not worth a cent" and, unforgivably, as not having paid his creditors anything.[14]

Proprietors of the largest and best-financed firms suffered less from reversals. Even when confronted with misfortunes, they often had the capital resources to recoup or to transfer their investments elsewhere. Nevertheless, fires, changing conditions in the national market and overextension in real estate investments temporarily injured even the most affluent and long-lived proprietors. The Pelton carpet factory, the Whitehouse shoe factory, and M. Shwartz, the clothing manufacturer, to name a few of the strongest firms, all suffered fires that interrupted their production schedules and forced them to rebuild.

Even so successful a proprietor as Harvey Eastman was not immune to reversals. Characterized as worth over $100,000 in the late sixties and possessing both a large income and extensive real

estate holdings, by 1873 Eastman was faced with declining enroll-
ments in his school, which was "greatly run down." Moreover, his
speculative development of suburban homes proved unprofitable,
and he sold many at a loss. In the mid-seventies a reporter noted
that "he must make about $20,000 a year but expenses such that he
is in hot water constantly, lets notes go to protest but manages to pay
when pressed." When Eastman died in 1882, the school had recovered; it continued under the ownership of his wife until after the
turn of the century.[15]

Eastman was not alone in suffering from speculative real estate
investments. While credit reporters normally considered the ownership of real estate as the safest guarantee of a man's ability to pay
his debts, they also noted the hazards of depreciation during depression years. Since merchants frequently raised capital by mort-
gaging their real estate, a downward fall in values could spell disas-
ter.[16]

If even the larger and better-financed businesses faced disloca-
tions and reversals, for the more marginal businessmen self-employment meant almost constant precariousness. The majority of businesses folded in less than three years. Although business failures
could occur at any time, depressions aggravated an already uncertain existence. During 1859-60 and 1875-79, the number of businesses that closed and the number of bankruptcies increased sharply.
Given this volatility, many businessmen could not sustain self-
employment. The more fortunate among them remained on the
fringes of the commercial world by shifting to clerical and sales
occupations. Twenty-three of the proprietors of 1870 — 4 percent of
those persisting in the city — had done so by 1880. Substantial or
long established businessmen who fell on hard times usually did not
take manual jobs, but their downward mobility to clerical and sales
work was no less visible to their peers and so presumably no less
painful a blow to their self-esteem.

One native started out in business at age nineteen, engaging both
in the dry goods and in the grocery businesses; at age 56 he became a
salesman for a cracker factory. By age 46 another native operated a
coal business inherited from his father and was reported as "a man
of property, considered good for a considerable sum . . . very honor-
able and upright." To the surprise of everyone, except the banks
that held judgments against him, he failed in 1871. The next year
found him running a small butcher shop as agent for his wife; in

1876 he had resumed the coal business but by 1879 he had given up that business and taken a position as second bookkeeper for a commission merchant and then appeared as a clerk for a livery stable. In 1880 this once comfortable merchant owned no property and his children had taken even less satisfactory jobs; one son in his mid-thirties had established his own flour and feed business but two younger sons worked as laborers and a fourth at the shoe factory.[17]

Other proprietors—and they were slightly more numerous in each succeeding decade—slipped back into manual jobs. Younger, less well-established shopkeepers proved more vulnerable to downward mobility to blue collar work, but with the exception of the very young, the difference in frequency was small. One fifth to one third of those appearing in business in their teens, largely as small vendors, did appear at manual jobs a decade later. But in the sixties and seventies only 10 percent of proprietors in their twenties at the start of a decade compared to 5 percent of men over 50 suffered that change by the next census.

Saloonkeepers, grocers, and other owners of small shops, especially ventures run at home in residential neighborhoods, comprised almost all those who reported manual work late in life; almost invariably they had pursued it previously. A credit reporter said of a 55 year old grocer, "a new beginner, knows little about business . . . formerly a farmer, lately a livery stable keeper." The grocery never did well and ten years later he was "not in any business other than selling and doctoring horses," listing himself in the census as a horse farrier. A journeyman tanner opened a small grocery for a few years, subsequently kept a drinking saloon, went to Troy for two years, returned to open a "kind of oyster cellar and saloon" and then in his fifties listed himself in city directories for more than a decade as a wool dealer without any shop while reporting himself in the 1880 census as a tanner again.[18]

Many businessmen confronted with adversity closed up their businesses after selling out their stock and then took other jobs or left the community, but numerous others faced the stigma—or the challenge—of bankruptcy proceedings as their creditors pressed for settlement. Not all bankrupts, however, immediately closed their doors. It is a testimony to the ingenuity of small businessmen in Poughkeepsie that, of those for whom R.G. Dun and Company received reports, 40 percent managed to survive three years or more after failure and 20 percent remained in business for twenty years after their initial failure. Businessmen devised a variety of maneuvers — some of dubious legality — to avoid their creditors and survive.

Easiest of all was to leave in the night. A boot and shoe dealer from Boston sold out his stock to a local purchaser but when the buyer went to take possession of the goods he discovered, as the newspaper noted with appropriate indignation, that "most had been taken away the night before." Two grocers "undertook to cheat their creditors in a rather bare-faced manner and, in order to do so, they secretly disposed of a large stock of goods by hiding it in various parts of the city, though able at the time to pay twice the amount of outstanding debts. When their little game was discovered, paid all they owed for fear of being prosecuted."[19]

The more common and complicated manner of avoiding creditors was to transfer assets and real estate to another party. A grocer assigned his assets in 1876 and offered to pay his creditors 20 percent. When his creditors refused the settlement, the assignee sold the assets to the grocer's clerk. The clerk then sold the assets back to the grocer and his new partner. In this case as in the case of three brothers who failed in the clothing business the credit reporter implied that by going into bankruptcy "they paid their debts that way."[20]

In such complicated legal maneuverings, family members most often were used to avoid payment of debts. The Married Women's Property Act of 1848 and the subsequent act of 1860, which gave wives control of their premarital and inherited property as well as property acquired during marriage, proved a boon to harried businessmen struggling to survive in the Darwinian jungle of small business enterprise. They could put their dwellings, land, bank stocks, and other assets not involved in their businesses in their wives' names and therefore beyond the reach of creditors. Moreover, faced with the prospect of insolvency, many businessmen transferred even their business assets to their wives or children through hastily arranged chattel mortgages or bills of sale covering merchandise, fixtures, and equipment. When failure came, a member of the family who had not contracted for the goods would hold title to them and so not be liable to creditors. Such transfers could be declared illegal by the courts if too obviously fraudulent and made too close to the time of failure, but more often than not they succeeded.[21]

A brewer gave a real estate mortgage to his wife in 1879 which the local correspondent suspected of being a bluff. In 1882 with the business doing poorly, his wife was found to own all of his stock, security for the mortgage. When it turned out that a grocer's wife owned everything after his failure, the grocer claimed she had inherited the property she owned. An investigation by the local correspondent, however, disclosed a deed conveying the property to her shortly before he got into trouble.[22]

Wives, and less commonly parents, also made it possible for men to continue in business when they had been declared bankrupt but had not been discharged from their former debts by their creditors. Men resumed business as agents for their wives, usually having transferred their property to the wives before their failure. The wives as principals would now be liable for the debts of the firm but their property could not be seized to pay off their husbands' old debts. A treatise on credit generalized about this kind of agency: "The logical conclusion in regard to this stamp of individuals is that the acquisition of property by any means, and the comfort of their families, at all hazards, is the chief aim before them, and they do not scruple to attain these results, even at the loss of character and name."[23]

While Poughkeepsie did offer many examples which credit reporters never tired of praising of the small dealer who paid every debt regardless of the burden to himself and his family, such scrupulousness and preoccupation with family honor did not predominate. More typically, family members demonstrated their inventiveness by frustrating the attempts of credit reporters to fix responsibility within their enterprises. To the wonder and chagrin of local correspondents, a hardware dealer and his family managed by frequent shifting of ownership to keep their once prosperous hardware store afloat after the father's failure in 1875, continuing to do a fair business and to earn more than a bare livelihood despite a wholly adverse credit rating. In 1880 the correspondent observed that the family "have turned over several times in the past few years in order to evade creditors and the stock of goods is now claimed by a son who is running the business as his own . . . The style is changed whenever the one in charge becomes unable to pay his bills." Six years later the situation remained unchanged: "If you see the father, the business belongs to the mother; if you see her, it belongs to the father; if you see both, it belongs to the son."[24]

While family members could aid each other in times of crisis,

families rarely succeeded in founding firms that would provide
security for future generations. Given the struggles of so many proprietors, it is not surprising to find that few businesses in Poughkeepsie passed from one generation to the next. Of the 1,530 firms
reported on by R. G. Dun and Company, 106 at some time included
fathers and sons as partners, but in only 45 of these firms did the
sons finally succeed to the business. In another 44 cases, sons inherited their fathers' businesses without ever having been partners,
making a total of 89 firms that passed from one generation to the
next within the same family.

Since these firms tended to be among the most economically prosperous in the city, sons had an obvious economic inducement to
continue the business. Adriances, Towers, and relatives of Matthew
Vassar all inherited flourishing enterprises. No immigrant father
compared to these natives in what they could pass on, but some did
lay a strong foundation for their sons to build upon. A German
Methodist first reported himself in the 1850 census as a tailor, already employing 6 men and 18 women. In 1860 he employed 20
workers and had invested in land as well as having "money loaned
out, independent of his business." When he died in the mid-sixties,
he left an estate worth $20,000. His son who started out as a peddler
in 1860, undoubtedly drumming for his father, inherited the business. By 1880 he paid taxes on real estate assessed at $10,700 and
personalty of $10,000. In the eighties his clothing business con-
tinued to flourish and he also had "good investments outside his
business"; in 1900 he ranked among the richest taxpayers in the
city.[25]

Just as frequently, sons pursued different careers. A fifth of the
sons who had been taken into partnerships with their fathers
spurned the opportunity and left the business. Moreover, only about
one third of grocers' sons listed in the census became grocers and
only a slightly higher proportion of the sons of large merchants in
lumber, dry goods, and the like continued businesses in those lines.

Sometimes fathers furnished their sons with capital to set up in
different lines of business. The owner of the mower and reaper
works twice enabled one of his sons to buy into local bookselling
firms as a partner. A rich dry goods merchant financed two of his
sons in different businesses, one in a partnership in drugs and another in an unsuccessful coal yard. In many such cases, the sons,
despite help from their fathers, failed at their independent ventures.

While one of the successful German butchers in town did admit two of his sons to partnership with him, he financed the third in a retail shoe store. The son proved to be a "not reliable or good business-man, sells at any price, drinks . . ." A successful native-born merchant tailor stocked a drug store for his son before he was even of age. The son had "little knowledge of business" and his first partner ended up in an insane asylum; even with a new partner, the firm never did well.[26]

Whether they were ultimately successful or not, the sons of many proprietors at least sustained white-collar work beyond the age of 30. Their ability to do so, however, varied with their fathers' type of business. Sons of large merchants and big manufacturers, for example, rarely fell back to manual work, 90 and 83 percent respectively remaining at nonmanual occupations past age 30. Grocers' sons experienced more downward mobility but even among them, 75 percent stayed in white-collar jobs. By contrast, only 10 percent of the sons of saloonkeepers sustained nonmanual jobs past age 30.

The varying fortunes of the sons of proprietors emphasize the stratification within the business world. If the self-help creed did not suggest the marginality and instability that a career in business so often entailed, it also did not assume that men's chances for success would vary according to their fathers' fortunes. In the nation's age of freest enterprise, men believed officially that while competition in any line often would be fierce, merit alone would determine the degree of success. A man of ability could start up for himself and a free market would not stack the cards in favor of any of his competitors. Yet, as we shall see in the next chapter, a man's chances for success in business varied sharply both with his ethnic origin and accordingly with the type of business he could pursue.

6

Stratification in Business

IN 1872 A newcomer to Poughkeepsie, Irishman William Hanlon, opened a fancy goods store on lower Main Street, down the hill from the central business district in an area catering to working-class customers. He lived upstairs over his store. The following year a credit reporter commented, "He is barely making a living, keeps cheap line of goods." Hanlon's business suffered during the depression. He allowed his insurance to run out, dated his checks ahead, and paid his rent late. Only the help of his brother-in-law enabled him to continue in business. By 1886 he had recovered enough to employ three clerks, and though his capital remained small he was "favorably thought of as a citizen." His stock and credit received the rating of "fair" in 1890; his business continued until after 1900.[1]

Three years after Hanlon opened his small store, three other newcomers to Poughkeepsie opened a dry goods store in the central business district. Two of these former clerks from Connecticut were native-born and one was a Scotsman. They had saved enough from their clerks' salaries to start the business with a capital of $8,000. The credit reporter, noting their "medium stock, large rent and great competition," deemed their prospects unfavorable. Quick to adapt their business methods to the exigencies of the times — and

perhaps also because they were "mean, close, penurious men" —
these new merchants defied that gloomy prediction. Advertising a
one-price store and stressing bargain prices, they also took advantage of all discounts and paid cash as well as requiring their customers to pay cash. By 1886 the credit reporter concluded that they
were "making money very fast" and estimated the worth of the firm
at over $100,000. The business continued to prosper, becoming one
of the two leading department stores in Poughkeepsie.[2]

Both Hanlon and the dry goods merchants started businesses on
the eve of depression and both survived. As this chapter will show,
the differences between their nationalities, kinds of retail businesses,
locations, and amounts of capital typified stratification within
Poughkeepsie's business community.

The advantage of natives over newcomers in retailing reflected
initially their easier access to capital or credit and a wider clientele.
But the timing and the very magnitude of the immigrant influx at
mid-century also contributed to ethnic stratification in business.
The simultaneous increase in the scale of commercial as well as
manufacturing enterprises in the nation in response to expanded
demand had its local reflection in this small city. Non-British immigrants in Poughkeepsie did not compete successfully in those types
of retailing where large firms with costly inventories had a strong
advantage. The customary apprenticeship for proprietorship of
substantial businesses outside the crafts also contributed to ethnic
stratification. The second generation immigrants found clerical and
sales jobs in proportion to their numbers in the labor force by 1880,
but whites of native parentage still accounted for 73 percent of the
total in that year.

Although ultimate success within the business world varied
sharply with ethnic origins, the proportion of foreign-born proprietors advanced steadily after 1850. Considering only the more stable
element among the city's businessmen — proprietors who worked in
the city at the beginning of the previous decade — the proportion of
men of native parentage dropped from 77 percent in 1860, to 67
percent in 1870, and to 58 percent in 1880.

Natives owned almost all the larger, better-financed firms, accounting for 85 percent of the proprietors of firms ever listed by
R. G. Dun and Company as worth $25,000 or more. First and
second generation newcomers appear more often as owners of small
shops. Immigrants also were more often downwardly mobile in

occupation than native-born proprietors but the differences, except for the Irish, were not large. In any decade between 1850 and 1880 no more than 10 percent of the Germans, 14 percent of the British, and 25 percent of the Irish fell back to manual employment compared to 7 percent of the native-born. A higher proportion of downwardly mobile native-born proprietors found employment in clerical and sales jobs, and the Irish most often subsequently appeared at unskilled jobs. The Germans showed no clearly defined pattern of subsequent employment when they lost their shops (Table 6.1).

Irish shopkeepers concentrated more heavily than those of any other nationality in neighborhood groceries and saloons catering to their countrymen. Outside retail and service ventures, the Irish most often found self-employment in the building trades, primarily as boss masons and plumbers, and as florists or nurserymen; unlike the Germans they did not open many businesses in the manufacturing

TABLE 6.1. Occupational mobility of proprietors by decade and by nativity

Nativity	Decade	Remain proprietor (percent)	Clerical and professional (percent)	Skilled (percent)	Low manual (percent)	Number of Cases
White of native parentage	1850 – 60	88	8	2	2	245
	1860 – 70	90	4	4	3	279
	1870 – 80	87	8	3	2	333
British[a]	1850 – 60	94	6	—	—	17
	1860 – 70	87	—	3	10	30
	1870 – 80	85	—	12	3	33
German	1850 – 60	90	—	—	10	20
	1860 – 70	95	2	—	2	43
	1870 – 80	88	3	4	5	96
Irish	1850 – 60	69	6	6	19	16
	1860 – 70	75	—	7	18	28
	1870 – 80	73	2	9	16	44

[a]This table includes the immigrant generation only for each of the three nationalities; the persisting native-born of foreign parentage who already were proprietors at the start of any decade are too few for generalization.

crafts. Irish manual workers achieved proprietorships of any kind less often than manual workers of any other group—less than one tenth doing so in any decade; their unusually high downward mobility thereafter eroded a limited gain. Although between 750 and 1,000 Irish-born males reported employment in the city at the 1850, 1860, and 1870 censuses, the numbers of Irish proprietors who would still remain in the city ten years later were 16, 28, and 44 respectively and of those few, one quarter at the end of each decade would report manual work.

While Germans also opened small retail businesses, the great German successes occurred in firms that engaged in craft-related manufacture, such as tailoring, butchering, and brewing. Of the 15 German proprietors whose firms had an estimated worth of over $25,000 in the R. G. Dun and Company records, 11 had risen from skilled work. And, with one exception, all the Germans who had accumulated enough property by 1880 to make them among the richest in the city had started out as practicing artisans. The butcher Charles Kirchner, the largest property owner in the city in 1900, could still outdistance all his competitors in a meat cutting contest in 1866.[3] Because so many German proprietorships like Kirchner's so often depended upon self-employment in various skilled trades, the meaning of the German success in craft-related enterprises will be analyzed in subsequent chapters on artisans.

Among German businessmen, Jews were the least tied to artisan manufacture. Even if they had pursued a trade, most often tailoring, they increasingly engaged in retailing rather than in custom work. Moreover, they specialized in certain lines of retailing. Clothing, dry goods, and fancy goods stores and peddling accounted for two thirds of the Jewish enterprises listed in credit agency reports.

Jewish tailors soon dominated the clothing business. Of the eight tailoring or clothing firms estimated at $25,000 or more, six had Jewish proprietors, and clothing merchants constituted a third of all Jewish businessmen. Clothiers frequently listed themselves as tailors or merchant tailors, but by 1880 most of them dealt in ready-made clothing. Herman Hart always gave his occupation as a tailor or merchant tailor but had kept a boarding house and been a partner in a commission business before joining Benjamin Joseph in the clothing business; in 1870, Hart, now alone, "kept a small ready-made clothing store."[4]

Even Mark Shwartz, who in 1880 employed 60 hands in the

manufacture of clothing, increasingly emphasized retailing. In 1881 his store offered a "large, well assorted stock of ready-made goods besides considerable piece goods." By 1888 he had opened three branch stores in Newburgh, Rondout, and Albany. Benjamin Joseph established a branch of his store in Catskill, New York.[5]

A Shwartz's or a Joseph's success became so visible that credit reporters had no difficulty recommending a top credit rating or estimating the worth of the firm. While most Jewish merchants seem to have prospered—only 15 had an estimated worth of $1,000 or less—one third of the 75 Jewish firms defied evaluation. Credit reporters frequently commented on the difficulty of finding out accurate information about Jewish firms because they "keep their matters close," "no one can tell anything about a Jew's means," and "we can't give worth of the firm as Jewish merchants as a class don't make any display although really prosperous."[6]

Although such comments may have reflected accurately a reluctance on the part of the Jewish businessman to expose himself to what he perceived as a prying and hostile Gentile world, another favorite theory of credit reporters—that Jews avoided investment in real estate—was gainsaid time and again in their own reports. Credit reporters chastised Adolf Wimpelberg, to name one among many, for buying too much real estate and similarly attributed Samuel Jonas's assignment in 1875 to his "investing in real estate money which he should have retained in his business."[7]

Moreover, despite yet another common stereotype—that of the wandering Jew—the Jewish firms evaluated by R. G. Dun and Company showed a greater stability than most, 44 percent lasting ten years or more. While some Jews had had business experience elsewhere, often as peddlers in the South and West, even peddlers settled down. Some made the transition to a retail store. When Isaac Heyman started out as a small peddler with little means, a credit reporter recommended against extension of credit. By 1866 he operated a ready-made clothing store—"nice store and nice goods" —and was reported worth $20,000. Others continued their itinerant way of business but still remained settled in Poughkeepsie. One man peddled with his horse and wagon for 22 years despite the fact that "he has nothing visible and if credited, it must be on the honor of a Jew, which is below par here."[8]

The stability and wealth of many Jewish firms did not affect substantially the general distrust of Jews. Until a Jewish businessman succeeded, credit reporters suspected the worst. Judgments like "sharp bargainer" or "Jew, very tricky" reflected popular stereotypes.[9] When a Jewish businessman became too stable and prosperous to ignore, credit reporters usually regarded him as an exception that did not disprove the rule. As a saloon keeper's property increased to an estimated worth of $20,000, he won the commendation of "a Jew, but among the very few honest ones," and Isaac Heyman as he prospered became "a fair man for a Jew." In evaluating a Jewish dry goods firm, a reporter found "a certain distrust of them in some quarters because they are Jews but seem good enough to us . . . They are worth about $3,000 and would like to be considered 'White Jews' in the trade."[10]

Jews — especially those regarded as White Jews — succeeded despite the prejudice against them. Black businessmen received no such derogatory comments from credit reporters, but the dearth of black businesses suggests the difficulties black men faced in achieving self-employment. They specialized as much as German Jews but in less profitable lines. Only nine of the blacks reported in four censuses achieved self-employment. R. G. Dun and Company evaluated just seven black businessmen — three in barbering and hairdressing and three in cleaning and dyeing. One "reputable colored citizen" and the exception to this homogeneous pattern opened a clothing store in 1845 but had failed by 1849 "to the astonishment of all" and subsequently left town.[11]

None of the other black businessmen reported on by the Dun agency fared much better. Although Joseph Rhodes' Eagle Dyeing Establishment started out as a "good business, making a little money," by 1877 "all his effects" were mortgaged to the bank. Another black, who listed himself in the 1860 and 1870 censuses as a gardener and in the 1880 census as a missionary agent, only operated his dyeing business for a few years in the seventies and ended his career as a night watchman at the city reservoir.[12] Significantly, the richest black in Poughkeepsie in these years succeeded in a business closely related to the occupational specialization of blacks as waiters. This steward, associated with the People's Line of Steamers, presumably operated a concession although R. G. Dun and Company never reported on him. When he died in 1874 a newspaper estimated his worth at over $20,000; in 1880 his estate was still assessed for $5,500 of real estate.[13]

The differing opportunities for various ethnic groups as well as the divergent rewards available to businessmen can be seen even more sharply in specific retailing lines. Natives dominated businesses which required a large capital, such as dry goods or coal and lumber (Table 6.2). Their initial preeminence reflected advantages of long residence and capital accumulation that few immigrants had. By 1880, however, disparities between larger and smaller firms had increased, and a few large firms received the lion's share of the trade. Correspondingly, new entrants into these lines fell off, and opportunities for everyone — native or newcomer — declined.

In other retail lines such as groceries, which remained hospitable to new enterprises, the larger firms, many of which also operated as wholesalers, belonged to men of native parentage, but the immigrants made significant progress. Only at the bottom of the business world in marginal enterprises such as saloons, small hotels,

TABLE 6.2. Estimated worth of firms in selected lines of business[a]

	Estimated worth (percent)				
Type of firm	$5,001 +	$1,001 – 5,000	$1,000 or less	Not estimated	Total number of firms
All	29	21	35	15	1572
Dry goods	55	12	10	23	60
Lumber and coal	72	0	17	11	18
Fancy goods	22	16	35	27	36
Groceries	26	27	35	11	205

Percentage of firms owned by foreign proprietors
or natives of foreign parentage

					Percentage of all owned by foreign-born
Dry goods	24	29	33	38	28
Lumber and coal	8	0	50	11	11
Fancy goods	50	67	54	67	58
Groceries	38	42	30	45	41

[a]This table uses the *highest* estimated worth given for each firm in the R.G. Dun and Company reports.

and peddling did stratification disappear and immigrants appear at times to have a decided advantage. But such businesses were often so precarious that the immigrant advantage seems a hollow one.

Ownership of dry goods stores and fancy goods shops clearly illustrates the native advantage in retailing. Dry goods firms ranked among the wealthiest in the city, and their proprietors had the reputation of being "the safest class of businessmen in the city."[14] Credit reporters estimated 41 percent of Poughkeepsie's sixty firms in this line between 1843 and 1880 to be worth more than $10,000, and over half of the dry goods merchants who reported incomes in 1866 had annual incomes over $2,500. Once established, these firms also lasted longer than the average business; half of those listed in credit reports survived at least ten years. Native-born whites owned two thirds of the firms and immigrant Jews owned one fifth. The Jewish firms prospered less; only three of them had an estimated worth of over $10,000 and lasted more than ten years.

Native advantage rested on access to credit and capital and on the training in established dry goods firms of clerks who would become future proprietors. Because a complete line of dry goods required a large investment, native sons frequently relied upon family members to give them a start in the business, a support rare for first generation immigrants. Editor Isaac Platt loaned his son $4,500 when he entered his first partnership but cancelled the debt one year later. One merchant received help from his uncle, a brother in New York supplied another, and a third benefited from the endorsements of both his father-in-law and his daughter-in-law. Others inherited already flourishing businesses. Just six years after they had taken over their father's firm, two brothers were considered "safe as the bank" and worth $30,000 each.[15]

Whether or not they received family aid, most dry goods merchants learned the business by clerking for local firms. The formation of Luckey, Platt & Co., the largest firm in the city, illustrates the advantages of clerkships and the prevalence of shifting partnerships. Charles P. Luckey began his career in 1849, without any family advantages, as a clerk for Robert P. Slee. He received $250 a year but left a part of his salary with his employer each year until by 1857 "the sum had grown so large that Mr. Slee took him in as a partner." When Slee retired in 1866, Luckey formed a new partnership with two men who had clerked in dry goods firms in Poughkeepsie. In 1868 the first man left the firm, and the following year Edmund

Platt, who had clerked for another local dry goods firm, bought out the second man's interest. Finally, in 1872, Luckey and Platt admitted to partnership a third man who also had served as a clerk in a Poughkeepsie dry goods firm before becoming a salesman for Luckey and Platt.[16]

Clerking in local firms helped prospective proprietors by giving them familiarity with the local clientele. When George Cornwell and Josiah Elting dissolved their partnership with George Van Kleeck in order to open their own firm, the credit reporter speculated that "they will take with them many of Van Kleeck's old customers." Van Kleeck's troubles did not end, for in 1875 his head clerk also joined Cornwell and Elting. Van Kleeck lost still another head clerk, William Reed, who went into business for himself in 1889 and "will draw considerably on Van Kleeck's trade."[17]

Testifying to this advantage of local acquaintance, most dry goods firms run by outsiders did not last long. In 1861 a former clerk for Lord & Taylor in New York City opened a dry goods store but closed after a year. Two men tried to open branches of New York City stores but also closed quickly. Another firm lasted nine years but never overcame local suspicion of their being "strangers, New York men . . . all of their business transactions are in NYC can't know anything of them."[18]

Immigrants appeared far more often as owners of fancy goods stores. Natives owned four of the eight firms worth $5,000 or more, but a majority of the male fancy goods merchants were foreign-born. Although they stocked some of the same merchandise, fancy goods dealers did not sell a complete line of dry goods, specializing instead in varying combinations of hoop skirts, hosiery, corsets, ribbons, laces, and other sundries for ladies. Correspondingly, their estimated worth fell far below that of dry goods stores, only 8 percent being worth over $10,000 and only one firm being worth over $25,000.[19]

The most spectacular success belonged to a man of Irish parentage, William R. Maloney. Maloney, a moulder by trade, opened his store in 1867 with a few hundred dollars; by 1886 his worth was estimated as between $30,000 and $40,000. In a field in which "the competition is very strong" and "overdone here," Maloney catered to a special clientele; he concentrated upon "furnishing regalia to the different societies and his regalia pays good profit."[20]

Unlike dry goods merchants who usually reported clerkships as their first occupation, male proprietors of fancy goods stores often came from the ranks of skilled workers and in many cases operated the small stores as an adjunct to their trades. A German Catholic reported himself as a chairmaker at two censuses and continued to work at that trade while his wife operated the store. A German Jew who conducted a string band that played for local dances also left the running of the store to his wife. Others like a native shoemaker and the son of an English tailor, formerly a machinist, became full time proprietors although the shoemaker subsequently failed and took a position as a cutter in the shirt factory.[21]

The gradual immigrant progress in fancy goods might eventually have enabled them to expand into dry goods proprietorships if retailing methods had remained as before. But by the eighties the rise of the multi-purpose department store, best exemplified in Poughkeepsie by Luckey, Platt & Co., had diminished opportunities in dry goods not just for immigrants but for natives as well. Luckey's expansion into a department store, however, did not depend entirely on superior capital resources—other dry goods merchants had equally large stocks and capital—but upon innovation in merchandising methods and aggressive advertising.

The firm had a history of innovation. As early as 1860 the prior partnership of Slee and Luckey had installed the first plate glass window in town and prominently displayed merchandise with a price tag affixed. "'Lets people see your merchandise,' says Luckey, 'Lets them get close to your signs and price tags.'"[22]

In 1879 Luckey's advertised 15 departments, including notions, hosiery, gents' furnishing goods, cloaks, and carpets and employed 20 clerks. The firm's largest competitor only had nine clerks and the more traditional dry goods firms listed three or four each. By 1886 Luckey's boasted telephones, electricity, and other modern conveniences and had 50 attendants. Customers throughout Dutchess and surrounding counties could order by mail with the firm delivering its merchandise. It also instituted annual sales and dotted the countryside with 300 mileposts pointing the way to the store.

The expansion of Luckey, Platt & Co. and of Donald, Converse and Maynard, which also evolved into a department store, proved devastating to other dry goods firms. In the extreme case, the "wealthiest dry goods firm in Poughkeepsie" in 1872, which did not approve "of the modern style of business," saw its business shrink drastically as it continued to sell a very fine class of goods at high

prices; by the eighties the estimated worth of the firm had dropped
to half its former value.[23] Although Poughkeepsie's population
continued to grow, the number of dry goods firms declined after the
seventies. The business directory listed only 13 dry goods firms in
1900 compared to a high of 23 in 1873. Moreover, few new firms appeared. From a directory tracing of all firms, only four new dry
goods stores opened in the seventies, contrasted with 12 in the fifties
and 11 in the sixties.

Many dry goods merchants in the seventies began to adjust not
just to the new competition from the department stores but also to
the decreased demand for cloth and trimmings caused by the rise of
ready-made clothing. Charles Bowne gave up his general dry goods
trade and began to specialize in carpets. George M. Van Kleeck and
his son abandoned dry goods entirely in 1879 for the new field of
insurance. Several other merchants switched to clothing and
tailoring, a natural transition for men used to dealing in cloth.[24]

Fancy goods stores also declined, since many of their specialties
could be bought at the new department stores. The business
directory listed 21 in 1870 but only nine in 1900. Perhaps Benjamin
Vail's career best illustrates some of the consequences of the new
competition in this field. Vail began as a partner in the dry goods
firm of Luckey, Vail and Mandeville but soon left to found his own
fancy goods store. He ended his career employed by his former partner as a clerk in charge of the notions department of Luckey, Platt
& Co.[25]

Preemption of the market by a few large firms happened sooner
in the retailing and wholesaling of coal and lumber and confirmed
the advantages of those who had established themselves early. Two
of the three major lumber dealers and the leading coal merchant
were native-born, the other major lumber dealer being the self-
made Englishman James Collingwood. R. G. Dun and Company
estimated all these firms as worth well over $25,000 and two of them
at over $100,000. All of them established their businesses before
1850 except Collingwood, who began in 1851. During the fifties and
sixties others, largely native-born, tried to establish themselves in the
field, but in the seventies only five new firms opened as compared
with eleven in each of the preceding decades. The new entrants in
any decade usually lasted under five years, and ones that lasted
beyond that time specialized in the less profitable kindling wood
and charcoal.

Unlike dry goods this dominance of a few large firms depended less on innovative methods than on the large capital required to meet the changing supply conditions in the trade. Until mid-century supplies of white pine and hemlock abounded in lower New York State. With these supplies exhausted, lumber merchants needed sufficient capital to purchase forests elsewhere as Collingwood did in Pennsylvania or to import lumber in large quantities, pay the freight rates, and erect storage facilities. Furthermore, the large wholesale business in this line to carpenters and builders was on a credit rather than a cash basis; small dealers could not bear financially the slowness in payment or outright defaults that accompanied hard times in the construction industry.[26]

Coal required a similar capital investment. Until the completion of the railroad bridge across the Hudson in the eighties, most of Poughkeepsie's coal came from Pennsylvania by barge, through the Delaware and Hudson Canal to Rondout and then down the river. Merchants had to lay in their supplies for the winter before the canals and river froze, but sales were not completed until spring. Only men of some financial means could become coal dealers. A civil engineer from Brooklyn, received his start in the business because "in winter when he has to lay in stock, his father guarantees the bills" and two brothers inherited a "nice property" from their father, which enabled them to "carry a good stock of coal in winter." Two large lumber dealers, accustomed to transporting materials, dominated the coal business together with the Reynolds firm, which specialized only in coal and was worth $40,000.[27]

The need for capital and credit made the coal and lumber business almost exclusively native-born. Of the 42 coal and lumber dealers ever listed in the directories between 1843 and 1880, only five were foreign-born or the sons of immigrants and none of them survived for very long except Collingwood, the Englishman. In addition, however, to capital resources and proven reliability, the native dominance resulted from their prior monopoly of the river trade. Many coal and lumber dealers had been steamboat captains or proprietors of freighting firms—all four in the 1860 manufacturing census reporting capital of $25,000 or more—or received the backing of such men.[28]

By contrast with heavily capitalized businesses such as dry goods or coal and lumber, immigrants made far more rapid progress in the grocery trade. First, the capital needed to start a grocery remained modest. Credit reporters estimated only one tenth of the 205 groceries as having a worth of over $10,000, while nearly two thirds were estimated at $5,000 or less. Although the grocer who only ordered $75 worth of goods three times a year was poorer than most, manual workers could save enough from their wages to stock a small initial supply. Moreover, since local wholesalers in groceries and flour and feed were more numerous than wholesalers in any other line, it was less often necessary to establish credit in New York City, an advantage for a man of good local reputation but no business experience.[29]

Second, because grocers served a neighborhood clientele, immigrant proprietors could attract the patronage of their countrymen. Credit reporters noted this appeal, be it "a small Dutch grocery" or "an Irish trade and similar location." Groceries run by immigrants usually did not locate within the central business district as did the large native-born provisioners but remained instead within ethnic neighborhoods. Attesting to their social importance, many immigrant grocers served as aldermen and supervisors.[30]

Given these favorable circumstances, immigrants made substantial progress as grocers. Although natives owned the large wholesaling firms and most of the groceries worth over $10,000, the foreign-born owned half of all groceries worth between $5,000 and $10,000. For the Irish in particular groceries served as an important avenue of mobility. Of the 20 foreign-born proprietors worth over $5,000, 11 were Irish or native sons of Irish parents. John Corcoran's father appeared as a laborer with no property in the 1850 census and died in 1853. At age 13 John began working in the brass foundry but by 1860 reported himself as a gardener. He subsequently ran a florist business in Norwalk, Connecticut, before returning to Poughkeepsie to open a grocery store in 1869. While his store initially was "a small grocery on a cross street" with an estimated worth of $1,000, by 1877 it had a "safe, steady trade." In 1880 when he took in a fellow countryman, John T. Nevins, as a partner, the estimate had climbed to $5,000. By the late eighties Corcoran and Nevins employed three clerks and engaged in wholesaling as well. Corcoran eventually became an alderman, a vice-president of the Board of Trade, a member of the Retail Merchants' Association and of the Board of Water Commissioners as well as a leader in St. Peter's Church and the Catholic Benevolent Society.[31]

Credit reporters expressed doubts about two Irish Protestant brothers because they sold "considerable rum and most of the grocers who sell Rum in our city do not seem to go ahead much as most of them are in the business part of the city." The grocery was described as "rather a rough place." By 1880 another brother had joined them, and each had real estate assessed at over $5,000. Credit reporters found them worthy of all necessary credit. Still in business in 1906, the firm employed five clerks, kept two delivery wagons, and had expanded into wholesaling feed grains as well as groceries. None of the Irish grocers, however, could hope to compete seriously with the native W. T. Reynolds and Co., the largest commission merchants in the county. In the late eighties Reynolds had expanded its flourishing flour and feed business to include the wholesaling of groceries and by the turn of the century were the largest wholesaling and commission business between New York and Albany.[32]

The grocery trade had its hazards. Most groceries also sold liquors, and the temptation to indulge proved unfortunate for a number of proprietors, native as well as immigrant.[33] Profits in the line generally were small. The practice of granting credit to their customers increased the vulnerability of grocers. Unlike dry goods few grocers had adopted the cash principle by the late eighties. R. G. Dun and Company characterized "one of the smartest grocers we have in the city" as "the only man who has succeeded on the cash plan here." More typical was the grocer who reported sales of $300 to $400 weekly, but "his customers are mostly laboring men and he lets them have during the week what they want and they pay him on payday." The financial statement to a credit reporter in 1880 by a grocer of German parentage illustrates the problem of liquidity. He reported having a stock of $2,000, fixtures, a horse and wagon worth $700, good book accounts of $1,913, and cash of $150. On the debit side he reported owing $2,111 in bills in addition to a note of $250 plus borrowed money of $250. The latter was a loan from his uncle and was taken out in groceries. Clearly, if a number of his customers did not pay promptly, he would be forced to reduce his stock.[34]

As early as 1868 some of the grocers moved to protect themselves from nonpaying customers by forming a union. Members furnished each other with a list of delinquents on their books in an attempt to identify customers who ran up bills at a number of stores. Such a union, however, could not protect grocers from delinquencies on the part of normally reliable customers when lay-offs occurred or hard times came. Outdoor relief during depressed times did enable many customers to continue to patronize their neighborhood groceries, albeit at a reduced level of consumption. Immigrant grocers in particular benefited from outdoor relief. In 1879 nine of the twelve grocers reimbursed by the Alms House were foreign-born.[35]

The constant proliferation of small groceries meant rigorous competition both for established firms and for those desiring to enter the business. New entrants into the grocery trade did not decline markedly even during the depression decade of the seventies. A directory tracing reveals that 80 new firms started in that decade as compared to 78 in the fifties and 86 in the sixties. From 1880 to 1900 groceries increased slightly faster than the increase in the population as a whole. But, reflecting the marginal character of many of the firms throughout the period, almost half traced in the directories disappeared within two years and only one fourth lasted over ten years.

For the immigrant generation, business reversals could be devastating to the proprietors' careers. A brass moulder of Irish parentage had acquired real estate worth about $6,000 by the time he and his brother opened a grocery in 1869. Although they made some money initially, the depression of the seventies bankrupted them. The brass moulder went back to his trade, but his brother found less desirable employment, reporting himself at age 40 as an attendant at the nearby state asylum for the insane.[36]

Despite the hazards, retail lines like groceries provided the best avenue to improvement for unskilled immigrants; the expanding white-collar world of clerical and sales workers held opportunities for their children. In 1850 only 5 percent of the male labor force reported such occupations, but by 1880 the proportion had climbed to 11 percent. More significant, while the foreign-born comprised less than 10 percent of all clerical and sales workers at any census after 1850, in 1870 the second generation emerged suddenly as 17 percent of the total and in 1880 as 22 percent. By 1880 the children of the "old" immigration had taken a major step forward toward an occupational distribution similar to natives, being over-represented in those white-collar jobs in about the same ratios.

Natives still retained a significant advantage, however. By 1880 27 percent of the young native-born men of foreign parentage who had begun as clerical and sales workers in 1870 appeared at manual employment compared to only 14 percent of those of native parentage. Natives monopolized the most rewarding jobs such as agents, bookkeepers, dry goods and bank clerks. Moreover, the expansion of these more desirable specializations within white collar work meant a corresponding advantage, at least in the short run, for the sons of the native middle class. For example, the number of men designated as bookkeepers in the census grew steadily between 1850 and 1880: 14, 23, 52, and 73 respectively. This increase was not simply a result of greater specificity in census reportage; directory listings of bookkeepers grew similarly.

Since bookkeepers normally worked for banks or the larger firms operated by native men, proprietors' favoritism toward their own kind as well as superior educational training probably accounted for the overwhelming proportion of men of native parentage among bookkeepers. In 1870, 90 percent of the men listed as bookkeepers were natives and in 1880, 89 percent. Unlike clerks, 23 percent of whom fell back to blue-collar jobs, none of the persisting bookkeepers suffered that reversal, indicating that this native-dominated occupation did offer special advantages. In the 1870 census 35 percent of the bookkeepers compared to only 5 percent of the clerks reported real property.[37]

While bookkeepers generally enjoyed superior rewards, they rose no more often to proprietorships than those listed as clerks between 1870 and 1880. Indeed, the stability of bookkeeping as an occupation suggests that it became increasingly a bureaucratic career; 61 percent of the persisting bookkeepers in the census remained at the same occupation between 1870 and 1880 and some did so for life. One man had held a series of clerical jobs in the post office and county clerk's office before becoming a bookkeeper for the Reynolds' commission house at age 42. He did not retire from that job until he was seventy. Although he had accumulated some property, he never became self-employed. Another man first appeared in the directory as a bookkeeper in the mid-sixties; in 1890 he continued in that job at Hudson River State Hospital, a position he had held since at least 1869.[38]

Clerks remained at their occupation far less often than bookkeepers. At every decade only one third of the clerks who stayed in town were still clerks ten years later. While bookkeepers rarely fell to manual occupations, clerks did not enjoy a similar security. Almost one fourth of the 1870 clerks reported manual jobs in 1880, a slight increase in the proportion who made that shift between 1860 and 1870.

The youthfulness of clerks partially explains their frequent downward mobility. Throughout the period, more than two thirds of the clerks at each census were less than 30 years old. Teenage clerks shifted to manual jobs most often; nearly two fifths did so in the fifties, one fifth in the sixties, and one fourth in the seventies. A clerk at 16 appeared successively as laborer, night policeman, and in his mid-forties as laborer again. In 1850 the brothers of another clerk worked at ordinary labor and chair making, and he appeared as a corker in a bottling establishment at the next census.

Older clerical and sales workers did not fall to manual work as often as teenagers, but, in almost every decade, at least one fifth of those in their thirties and forties did so. After reporting himself as a clerk at two censuses, one native by age 60 worked in a lumber yard and a decade later listed himself as a laborer. Two men who reported themselves as clerks in their forties and bakers in their fifties were probably employed at the semi-automated cracker bakery. One of them apparently continued to work at the bakery, reporting himself as a driver later, whereas the other said he was a painter at the next two censuses.

The census did not specify place or type of work for clerks often enough to be more than suggestive about how much responsibility the downwardly mobile had been given. Of the clerks of native parentage who dropped to manual employment during the seventies, only one held so promising a position as apprentice bank clerk. The largest number with specific designations clerked in groceries. Of those reported in their teens, some probably did not wait on customers, much less keep accounts but rather spent their time filling shelves, carrying bundles, and cleaning up the store.

The businesses in which immigrants clerked more often were precarious and their work a poorer preparation for better white-collar jobs than those that employed native clerks. A listing of clerks by place of employment in the 1879 county directory permits a closer examination of clerks in different lines of retailing. Tracing in subsequent directories through 1900, for example, revealed that the 44 dry goods clerks, mostly natives, had clear advantages over the 47 grocery clerks, about half of whom were first and second generation newcomers. The most dramatic difference between the two types of clerk occurred in the rate of downward mobility to blue-collar work; 28 percent of the grocery clerks subsequently reported manual employment compared to 2 percent of the dry goods clerks. While dry goods clerks did not leave the community or achieve proprietorships much more often than grocery clerks, they maintained their position more frequently. The proportions of both reporting the same occupation twenty years later were 41 and 28 percent respectively.

The high proportion of dry goods clerks making a career of that position signified the decline of the versatile clerk who had learned all parts of a business in preparation for partnership. Between 1870 and 1880 far fewer clerical and sales workers became proprietors, only 28 percent doing so compared to 40 percent in the previous decade. An increasing proportion stayed in clerical and sales jobs, 51 percent so remaining between 1870 and 1880 compared to 39 percent between 1860 and 1870. Moreover, clerks often continued at the same place of business throughout their careers. Of the 18 clerks listed at Luckey, Platt & Co. in 1879, one third still worked there twenty years later. In 1919, Luckey's could point to 16 clerks who had joined them before the turn of the century and 40 who had served them for over ten years.

Whether stability of employment in the same firm, or at least in white-collar occupation, reconciled men to the loss of proprietorships and the diminished stature of a clerk cannot be known. Certainly the replacement of bargaining over price by a fixed price tag lessened a clerk's responsibility. Luckey's often advertised that, since their "goods are sold at one price to everyone, a small child can deal as well as the oldest shopper." By inference, although the advertisements did not say so, a relatively untrained, mediocre clerk could sell to that child.[39]

Moreover, admonitions by newspaper editors to employers suggest that clerks' working hours and conditions were becoming more rigid. A newspaper editorial in 1868, for example, complained of employers' reluctance to allow their clerks to participate in sports: "Baseball is forbidden the employees of many establishments, cricket is declared the enemy of business habits and boating decidedly immoral. Clerks who confess a weakness in either of these particulars are likely to be discharged." Similarly, in 1877 when the National Guard called up its members for strike duty, the newspapers observed that many merchants threatened to dismiss employees who obeyed the call.[40]

By contrast when Edmund Platt clerked for the Candee brothers'
dry goods firm in the early sixties, he took time off to attend weddings, visit relatives, and organize church meetings in addition to
his regular two week vacation. Although he received a salary of only
$550 in 1866 at age 23, Platt expected to become a proprietor and
knew himself to be the social equal of his employers. He attended
Candee family weddings, collaborated in religious work with John
and YMCA work with Will and made New Year's Day social calls
with Will. By the time Platt became proprietor of his department
store, such social contacts between employers and employees were
diminishing. Although Platt sent wedding presents to his clerks, he
usually did not attend their weddings, and his diary, a remarkably
full chronicle of his daily activities and contacts, records no occasion
of his socializing with his clerks after hours.[41]

On the other hand, while clerks stood more apart from their
employers, and less frequently achieved proprietorships, the expansion of clerical and sales work did provide a cushion for men who
failed in business, giving them respectable white-collar employment. When a 22 year old joined his father in a partnership in hats,
caps, and furs in 1860, the father had already been in that business
for thirty years. In 1866, however, the firm failed for the first of four
times. The last failure occurred not long before the father died in
1879, and soon afterward the son became a postal clerk. A crockery
salesman started his own crockery business at age 29; sold out by the
sheriff to satisfy creditors three years later, he returned to clerking
and a decade later still appeared as a salesman for another crockery
merchant.[42] Some men even returned to their former employers
after failing in their own businesses. When a dry goods store closed
in 1875, one partner returned to his old clerkship at another dry
goods firm.[43]

The increase in scale and specialization in local business which
stimulated the specialization in clerical and sales work also brought
an accompanying elaboration of local business and financial
services, especially insurance and real estate agencies, run largely by
men of native parentage. Native predominance in this expanding
field rested not only upon literacy but also upon acquaintance with
a potential clientele, many of whom could be expected to be natives.
In the 1880 census only 11 of 66 agents of every description were
foreign-born.

A German listed himself as an agent in both real estate and insurance in the 1860 directory and R. G. Dun and Company described him in the seventies as an insurance agent who sold drafts on Europe, noting that he also dealt in cigars. He never reported himself in the census as an agent but rather as a cigar maker in 1860, a life-line maker in 1870, and a tobacco salesman in 1880. A French teacher of that nationality at the Dutchess Academy sold insurance as a sideline in the sixties but quickly gave it up. Among the foreign-born only Andrew King, a German who first reported himself as a box manufacturer in 1870, succeeded in either line. King invested heavily in real estate, partly in collaboration with the very successful Corlies brothers, and described himself in 1880 as a real estate agent in both census and city directory although he did not advertise.[44] More often than not, men who became real estate and insurance agents in Poughkeepsie had had substantial business experience in the city previously. Three former grocers and three dry goods merchants as well as a former clothier, carriage manufacturer, and two lawyers shifted into the field during the seventies and eighties.

For some of these former merchants the shift represented an attempt to start over after doing poorly in other lines; these men rarely prospered through their agencies. One had failed in the dry goods business in 1862, then opened a small merchant tailoring firm, and finally became an insurance agent in 1870. He was not "doing much at it," however, so by 1873 he took a position as clerk in a county supervisor's office and continued to sell insurance as a sideline.[45]

For still affluent merchants caught in declining lines of business or unwilling to adapt to new methods of competition, real estate and insurance represented a promising new field. One father and son abandoned their 41 year old dry goods firm to open an insurance agency in 1879 which prospered into the twentieth century. A middle-aged clothier with large property holdings started up as an agent in real estate and in insurance. In 1875, in his mid-fifties, he failed because of speculations in real estate but continued his agency. His son, a lawyer, joined him in the early eighties and they also ventured into the manufacture of shirts in a small way so that by the time of the father's death the firm was worth a comfortable $10,000.[46]

The benefits of the elaboration of business and financial services during the middle decades accrued almost entirely to men of native parentage and usually men with prior business experience in the city. But that benefit often was less substantial or less certain than the continuity in occupational status suggests. With prosperity so fickle, the native advantage in seizing new white-collar opportunities created by the advance of specialization seems a little less like the solid stepping-stone to success which the imputation of advantage or privilege sometimes suggests. Ethnic stratification characterized Poughkeepsie's business community throughout the middle decades, but the continued preeminence of native proprietors as a group over immigrant and second generation businessmen did not prevent precariousness in the situation of individual native proprietors, with frequent shifts in fortune. The native advantage for the future rested on their establishing themselves as large proprietors at a time when, in many lines, a few large firms were coming to dominate the local trade even as nationally large corporations gained increased shares of the market.

7

Opportunity for Artisans during Industrialization

THE INDUSTRIAL FUTURE took shape all at once in the new textile towns in New England. The factory system dominated them from their foundations, casting the traditional crafts in an auxiliary role. The break with older methods of manufacturing would be much less quick and clear in most American towns and cities. The inertia of traditions of small shop artisan production coupled with differences between industries in division of labor and mechanization meant that the progress of industrialization in cities with diversified manufacturing would be slower and more complicated than in Lowell, Lawrence, and other mill towns. Opportunities for men trained in the skilled crafts differed correspondingly.

The erosion of craft manufacture in the middle decades which looms so large retrospectively received almost no public mention in Poughkeepsie. The city had no labor unions with more than temporary strength outside the building trades before 1880. Local newspapers sometimes reported strikes and occasionally organizing activities but otherwise paid no attention to mechanics beyond describing accidents on the job, interruptions of work, emigration, and demands for workers, most often in the building trades or other seasonal employments like ice harvesting and farm labor.[1] In the absence of local discussion about the impact of industrialization upon the crafts, the occupational and geographic mobility of their work forces help to describe that impact.

This chapter will first discuss general patterns of opportunity among skilled workers and then examine in detail the changing opportunities in four trades—those of cabinet maker, shoemaker, cooper, and carriage maker—to point up important differences in the progress of skill dilution and in the response of artisans to it. The sharpest contrast in opportunities appears between crafts expanding in work force and those contracting, excluding the building trades which followed fluctuations in demand for new construction.

Contraction occurred most often when local firms which previously had manufactured for themselves turned to ordering from firms outside the locality. The process of contraction did not vary much from trade to trade. Sometimes the early years would be marked by more frequent emigration of craftsmen from the city, but the largest loss invariably occurred through reduction in newcomers finding jobs in the industry. As contraction progressed, the trade gives the paradoxical impression of becoming both more stable and more prosperous. The proportion of propertied workers with long careers in the city increases.

Older craftsmen tended to linger in the trade and in the city. Although some had already saved enough to acquire property and had no compelling need to search for other jobs, others found themselves trapped by inability to learn or find employment in a new trade. As increasing acceptance of ready-made goods narrowed the demand for custom work in trades like cabinet making and shoemaking, for example, artisans who stayed at those trades either became retailers or found themselves reduced largely to a repairing business. Where wages for the repairing and for the dwindling custom work did not fall off much as in cabinet making and in carriage making, older craftsmen suffered least. Where journeymen faced very low wages as in shoemaking the plight could be extreme.

In most contracting trades where training in the craft remained useful, employers did not turn to green hands. Old hands had the advantage not only of experience in the firm's ways but also of the reluctance of employers to turn them out. The sons of old hands often accounted for most of the small number of young men entering the shrinking work force. Thus, of the twelve newcomers among the cabinet makers of 1880, three were sons of John Coxhead who learned the trade with their father. Those who followed their fathers would be a small minority of all the sons of old hands, however.

The pattern of opportunities in expanding trades normally reversed that in contracting trades: the more rapid the expansion the more pronounced the contrast. Newcomers to the trade and to the city predominated; the increase in job opportunities attracted craftsmen not only from the immediate hinterland but also from towns at some distance. New England-born machinists helped swell that trade in Poughkeepsie. When expansion of the trade was general throughout a region, then the trade had to recruit large numbers of men with no previous relation to it, personal or familial. As the demand for machinists increased in Poughkeepsie so did the proportion of apprentices whose fathers had not pursued the trade.

Rapid expansion also resulted in more frequent recruitment of workers previously employed at other occupations. The on-the-job training received by these latecomers does not seem to have handicapped their survival in the craft. Whereas green hands in contracting or relatively stable trades often moved on again to other occupations, men who came late to an expanding craft usually reported it thereafter. Neither expansion nor contraction bore a simple relation to the progress of skill dilution. Even expanding industrial trades like the machinists and moulders did not escape the increasing division of labor and use of machinery common to all crafts in the late nineteenth century.

Traditional differences between the artisan and ordinary laborers narrowed and distinctions between the artisan and the emerging class of factory operatives became less clear as division of labor increased. Since some tasks involved far more skill and responsibility than others, this lessening of differences between many artisans and less skilled workers was accompanied by increasing differences among craftsmen within particular trades. Thus, those tailors who specialized in cutting cloth became the aristocrats of the trade earning more than small shopkeepers in most lines of business.

Symptoms of the obsolescence of artisan manufacture appeared in some handicrafts in the fifties but by the seventies they multiplied and intensified. If he had remained prosperous, the master worker who combined manufacturing and retailing in his shop long since had adapted to selling more ready-made work from other shops or factories. Now men trained to retailing, not to the craft, replaced him in the city's hardware, furniture, boot and shoe, clothing, and other craft-related stores.

The organization of manufacturing also shifted visibly; men who had begun as merchants launched Poughkeepsie's new shoe and garment factories in the seventies and recruited women, children, and men who had not apprenticed in shoemaking or tailoring as operatives. The bigger firms both in retailing and in manufacturing continued to coexist with a much larger number of small shops, most of them run by artisans, but the bare livelihood earned by so many of these shops and their increasing dependence upon repairing rather than manufacturing reinforces the sense that the day had passed when artisan shopowners could hope to be part of the city's comfortable middle class.

To emphasize the multiplying signs of deterioration in the seventies, however, runs the risk of distorting the process of change during the middle decades. Old and new in organization, methods, and outlook coexisted through much of the period in many manufacturing crafts. More important, change in individual crafts in Poughkeepsie as in other localities sometimes reversed national patterns. Regression to smaller scale and less specialization in methods of manufacture occurred when local firms began buying ready-made goods produced elsewhere and limited their own manufacturing to the remaining local market for custom work.

Immigration at mid-century also increased the prevalence of pre-industrial organization and methods in a number of crafts in Poughkeepsie. Newcomers accustomed to small-shop craft manufacture rushed into business for themselves often with no assistant and rarely with more than two or three. They did so despite the presence of older and larger firms owned by men of native parentage who employed women and children as well as men with corresponding division of tasks. Finally, throughout the period some craftsmen of every nationality found it profitable to start small businesses with little or no division of labor to manufacture new specialties in well-established industries. Matthew Vassar's big, mechanized brewery had no competition in the manufacture of ale and porterhouse in Poughkeepsie, but it did not discourage the mushrooming of small lager breweries accompanying the influx of German immigrants at mid-century.

Some craftsmen continued to receive extended initiations into

their trades even at mid-century. In 1897 craftsmen in Poughkeepsie who had become successful enough to want recognition in a biographical encyclopedia specified the periods of their apprenticeship; in this very small and biased sample the most common number
of years reported by men entering trades as late as the fifties and sixties was five, regardless of trade, nationality, and place of apprenticeship. Most of these men also reported periods of employment as
journeymen, sometimes in several cities; one native marble worker
and one German tailor explicitly mentioned traveling for the purpose of perfecting their mastery of the craft.[2]

On the other hand, a variety of evidence points to growing infor-
mality in the training of young men in the trades. Moreover, greater
casualness and less paternalism on the part of employers had its
match — some contemporaries said its cause — in the restlessness of
apprentices, their eagerness to get their training over with as soon as
possible without any sense of obligation to the craft or to the master
worker.[3] The only systematic evidence available on the relations of
teenage workers and employers in the trades in Poughkeepsie is
purely external but it does strengthen the sense of diminishing likelihood of paternalism among masters. By 1850 a majority of teenagers in the trades did not live with their employers and by 1880
almost none did.

Skilled workers who shifted from one craft to another remained a
small minority in Poughkeepsie. They comprised only 7 or 8 percent
of all persisting artisans in any decade; moreover, one third of those
shifting trades in the fifties and seventies and one fourth in the sixties entered closely related crafts where their previous skill might
have immediate applicability without much adaptation. Census
tracing does miss some teenage workers who began an apprenticeship in one trade only to abandon it quickly for another. Annual
directory traces will not overcome this limitation, since they rarely
list men less than twenty years old. Poughkeepsie's directories do
not, for example, record any of Thomas McWhinnie's occupations
during his teens. This Poughkeepsie-born-and-educated son of a
Scottish weaver already had worked for nine months in the cotton
mills at nearby Wappingers Falls when he began employment in a
local bakery at age thirteen. Two years later he decided to try learning the tinner's trade instead but left that also after serving more
than a year. By age 18 he had entered the chair factory.[4]

At each census less than 8 percent of all craftsmen also employed in the city a decade earlier had worked at another trade; an additional 12 to 18 percent had been employed previously at unskilled, semiskilled or nonmanual jobs. Analysis by age shows a somewhat larger recruitment from occupations other than skilled trades among younger craftsmen, but these latecomers to crafts never comprised as much as one third of those previously employed in the city (Table 7.1). In every decade more than two thirds of all journeymen less than 30 years old who had been listed in a previous census with an occupation had identified themselves with a skilled trade; between 6 and 11 percent had reported nonmanual jobs previously and between 19 and 26 percent reported unskilled or semiskilled work.

As might be expected the proportion of older journeymen who had reported other kinds of occupations a decade before was even lower. The fact that one tenth of these older workers in every decade had been at less skilled jobs does suggest, however, some continuing recruitment of relatively green hands with no expectation that they would learn the whole craft. Thus, a native who appears as a carpenter at age 61 had reported himself in previous censuses at laboring and a decade later would describe himself as a gardener.

The biographies of mechanics with varied occupational careers catch the eye; there were enough of them throughout the nineteenth century to nurture the image of the American as jack of all trades. The reality among the whole body of artisans is less colorful. However often they experienced changes in residence, prosperity, employer or employee status, the majority of skilled workers who stayed in one community for a decade or more do not appear at any other occupation.

Downward mobility from skilled work was only 8 percent in the fifties and sixties and only 11 percent in the seventies (Table 7.2). Some green hands, only temporarily at skilled designations, returned to less skilled work. The least downward mobility occurred among skilled workers who were in their twenties and thirties at the beginning of a decade; teenagers, predominantly apprentices, and older workers show slightly higher rates. A majority of the older workers had reported themselves at their trades in more than one previous census. While unskilled jobs predominated, a number of older workers did find less strenuous service work, especially as watchmen, sextons, and janitors.

TABLE 7.1. Occupations at the previous census of workers reported skilled at the end of a decade

Age when reported skilled	Decade	Occupation at previous census (percent)						Number of cases
		Profes-sional	Proprie-torial	Clerical	Skilled	Semi-skilled	Un-skilled	
21–30	1850–60	—	2	9	70	7	13	46
	1860–70	—	1	7	74	7	12	91
	1870–80	—	1	4	68	6	21	145
31–40	1850–60	—	2	—	78	2	18	105
	1860–70	1	3	—	85	4	8	161
	1870–80	—	3	2	84	5	7	195
41–50	1850–60	—	3	1	80	2	14	104
	1860–70	—	2	1	86	3	7	125
	1870–80	—	4	2	86	4	5	185
51–60	1850–60	—	2	—	89	4	6	52
	1860–70	—	4	1	88	3	5	81
	1870–80	—	6	—	85	2	7	127

TABLE 7.2. Occupational mobility of workers by decade and by age at start of decade

Age of skilled at start of decade	Decade	Professional (percent)	Proprietorial (percent)	Clerical (percent)	Skilled (percent)	Semi-skilled (percent)	Un-skilled (percent)	Number of cases
All ages	1850–60	1	22	1	68	4	4	387
	1860–70	—	23	1	68	3	5	630
	1870–80	1	13	2	73	5	6	858
11–20	1850–60	—	16	—	74	7	2	43
	1860–70	—	13	1	76	7	2	88
	1870–80	2	11	5	66	6	9	149
21–30	1850–60	1	28	2	62	4	5	133
	1860–70	—	28	2	64	2	3	212
	1870–80	2	20	3	65	6	6	253
31–40	1850–60	2	22	1	69	4	3	120
	1860–70	—	26	—	66	1	7	165
	1870–80	2	12	2	76	4	3	208
41–50	1850–60	2	16	—	73	2	8	63
	1860–70	—	20	1	70	5	5	102
	1870–80	—	8	1	79	4	7	137
51–60	1850–60	—	14	—	76	—	10	21
	1860–70	—	13	2	78	4	2	45
	1870–80	—	5	—	86	1	8	79

In the fifties and sixties three times as many skilled workers experienced upward mobility as took less skilled jobs. The difference narrowed to only half again as many during the decade of depression. Proprietorships account almost entirely for this upward mobility; artisans rarely shifted into clerical and sales jobs. Whatever the type of business, the frequency of achievement of self-employment by skilled workers declined with age but not sharply. In the first two decades 16 and 20 percent of all journeymen in their forties at the start of the decade and only a slighly lesser proportion of those in their fifties had opened their own businesses by the next census. This compares with 22 and 26 percent of journeymen in their thirties and slightly more of those in their twenties. More of the businesses started by artisans later in life remained modest affairs, but at every age small shops predominated.

So long as custom manufacture remained competitive, initial capital requirements remained small in many trades. A German had been employed as a journeyman upholsterer by one of his fellow countrymen for nearly a decade before he opened a partnership at age 37 with another German. The two had no more than $1,500 in the business at the outset, but by hard work increased their capital to more than $5,000 by 1873.[5]

In industries where parts of the manufacture often were subcontracted, as in carriage making and chair making, self-employment often began at a young age. The son of a native shipbuilder at Haverstraw down river had apprenticed as a young man in carriage trimming at Rahway, New Jersey. He bought up the time remaining on his indenture at age 19 and set up for himself in New York City as a trimmer. When he came to Poughkeepsie in his twenties, he apparently pursued his craft by jobbing in his backyard shed before opening a partnership in carriage making at age 35.[6]

Throughout the middle decades small retail and service businesses provided an alternative means of self-employment for artisans. Craftsmen had no monopoly on this alternative, but so long as the skilled trades offered better reward than less skilled work including factory employment, artisans found it easier than other manual workers to save money to start up for themselves. Groceries, saloons, cigar shops, variety stores, and other petty enterprises of this kind had two advantages over craft-related shops, especially for men trying to achieve security for their old age. These ventures did not require the keenness of eye or the strength important in many crafts and they could be run by wives and other relatives if hard times forced owners to take outside employment temporarily.

Men in crafts threatened by factory competition, such as the contracting woodworking trades, found this alternative especially attractive. Two German-born wood carvers who first appeared in 1860 in their twenties abandoned their trade by 1880 for saloon-keeping. One of them invested about $500 in his small venture. Although a credit reporter described him as "doing fairly well," his 14 year old son and 12 year old daughter supplemented the family income in 1880 by working at the wheelbarrow and silk factories respectively.[7]

A negligible proportion of artisans found clerical and sales jobs during the middle decades, about 1 percent doing so in the fifties and sixties and little more than 2 percent in the seventies. Most shifts to white-collar employment occurred among young workers who had begun a trade in their teens but left it within a decade. A 17 year old reported himself in 1870 at blacksmithing, but ten years later clerked in a carpet store; he became a carpet dealer himself by 1890.

In the world of artisans at mid-century there was much more occupational mobility between generations than within the individual career. One third of all men born during the forties who started at skilled work appear at a different rank by last reported job, but one half of all the sons of artisans born during that decade appear at a rank other than skilled by their last reported job. Achievement of a higher rank than the father's was almost twice as frequent as downward mobility to a lower rank, with 31 percent achieving nonmanual employment and 9 and 10 percent reporting semiskilled and unskilled jobs respectively. With the exception of slightly less downward mobility, the pattern for sons born during the thirties was the same. This general result averages out wide variations in the balance of upward and downward mobility between crafts. At one extreme, the sons of painters show only 14 percent at nonmanual work at last job compared to 32 percent at unskilled and semiskilled work. At the other extreme, 40 percent of the sons of machinists had achieved a higher level and 7 percent had fallen to a lower level than their fathers.

Unfortunately, for most individual crafts the number of craftsmen's sons employed at two censuses is too small to support generalization. Moreover because our tracing ends with 1880 it necessarily limits career analysis to sons who entered the labor market in the fifties and early sixties. It does not show the occupational attainment of sons beginning employment during the seventies, more of whose fathers would have been hurt by the progress of skill dilution in their trades. Partial directory tracing suggests the expected result: sons of fathers in the better-paying trades did have the advantage of more frequent upward mobility and less frequent downward mobility than sons of fathers in declining trades.

Artisans' sons who remained at skilled work often did not pursue the same trades as their fathers. Of the 572 identifiable artisans' sons in 1870 who had working careers in Poughkeepsie of at least a decade, 58 percent never appeared at their father's trade and 7 percent reported it at first job but subsequently shifted to another occupation. The crafts in Poughkeepsie fell far short of being a closed, self-perpetuating world. Once again, however, wide variation exists between trades. Thus 57 percent of the sons of masons and 49 percent of the sons of coopers reported themselves at their father's trade at last reported job compared to 22 percent of the sons of shoemakers and a mere 11 percent of the sons of tailors. This variation reflects the diverging circumstances of these crafts, already sharp by the late sixties, and especially the impact of ready-made goods on the shoe and men's clothing industries. The prospects of following in their fathers' trade locally were even less favorable for the sons of cabinet makers in Poughkeepsie and only a few did.

Cabinet Makers

Cabinet making declined as a craft as soon as wood turning became automatic. Improvements in the stocking lathe made that machine capable of reproducing even the curlicues in vogue in furniture then. Factory work in other cities brought contraction of local manufacture; by 1865 Poughkeepsie's cabinet makers already had been reduced to less than three quarters of their number in 1850. But as late as 1865 two firms employed ten workers each. By 1880 only 21 cabinet makers remained in the city and their production was so insignificant that the first historian of the county failed to mention furniture and coffin making in an otherwise remarkably comprehensive discussion of small manufacturing in Poughkeepsie. Symptomatically, the *Eagle* reported in 1877 that the Baptist Church had ordered its new pews from Chicago because they cost half as much as they would if made in Poughkeepsie.[8]

A once flourishing craft had been reduced to a small remnant, nearly one half of whom were 50 years of age or older in 1880. There was no protest from the workers, simply a gradual loss of men through a rate of disappearance similar to other crafts and through failure to replace those dying, emigrating, or shifting occupations.[9] By 1880 the businesses of both of the largest employers of 1865 had passed into the hands of men untrained in the craft. One native had been a dry goods merchant, merchant tailor, and—briefly—mowing machine manufacturer previously; another, the city's most versatile and peripatetic businessman, had been in half a dozen kinds of business in the previous ten years. A third shopowner—a newcomer to furniture dealing who would have the city's biggest store in that line by the turn of the century—had been a craftsman but in a different industry. This Irish Catholic had apprenticed as a carriage trimmer, had had his own shop in that trade first in Newburgh down the river and then in Poughkeepsie, but by the mid-seventies had shifted into auctioneering and commission selling before entering the furniture business.[10] The triumph of dealers trained in retailing rather than in cabinet making was nearly complete in Poughkeepsie by 1880.

The state of cabinet making as a craft and the changing opportunities for those who remained in it can be seen in the later careers of some of the city's older and better known craftsmen. A few journeymen did succeed in opening their own businesses after 1880. They did so primarily in undertaking, long an important auxiliary business for cabinet makers who made the coffins and by the seventies coming into its own right as a separate business if not yet a professional calling. Storm Conklin had literally grown up with the firm founded by J. P. Nelson in 1849, having apprenticed in cabinet making in his teens, and continued working for Nelson and his son for 28 years. By the late seventies Conklin devoted himself to their undertaking business. Not until Conklin was 56 years old in 1891 did he open his own undertaking business.[11]

Other cabinet makers had less happy endings to their careers. David S. Mallory had started his shop in 1836 and been the second largest employer in 1865 with the "best custom in the city." Bad investments in a spring bed company and embezzlement by his bookkeeper weakened Mallory so that he sold out his business in 1878 just before making an assignment to creditors. Mallory went to work as a salesman for his successor, but subsequently resumed his craft in a small repairing shop off the main street. Long before Mallory's time of troubles, credit reporters had pegged him as a good mechanic, industrious and prudent, but not a good businessman. One commented in 1858 that he "always gets hold of the short end of the whiffletree."[12]

John Coxhead, an English cabinet maker, also received accolades as an "expert workman" but by 1871 he was reported as having "no store, simply runs a little repair shop, one house affair." Actually Coxhead continued to make desks and bookcases to order. One son began working with his father but left in 1879 when he "obtained a position in a large cabinet making establishment in New York City."[13]

Judged by occupational mobility alone both Mallory and Coxhead belong with the success stories, having achieved and maintained self-employment. Coxhead never prospered much, however, and Mallory lost the substantial property he had accumulated. Their careers remind us of the limitations of occupational change as a measure of social fluidity.

Shoemakers

The shoemakers show the process of adaptation to skill dilution even more clearly than the cabinet makers because in 1870 a largely mechanized shoe factory became the city's largest employer with from 200 to 400 operatives depending upon the state of business. Yet in 1870, 111 men still identified themselves in the census as shoemakers and boot and shoe dealers, a majority of the dealers having apprenticed in the craft. Unlike cabinet making, the decline in the total number of male workers did not begin in shoemaking until the sixties and then fell only from 124 in 1860 to the 111 of 1870. As late as the manufacturing census of 1860, 29 shops reported producing 7,116 pairs of boots and 12,890 pairs of shoes in a city of 16,000 persons.

A 20 year old journeyman in one of these shops survived into the twentieth century to reminisce about the state of his craft then. In 1860 Anthony Barth had only recently arrived from Wurttemberg; in 1908, now 68, Barth saw the middle decades as the "good old days." "Now girls are working in the factories and hundreds of good shoemakers are looking for something to eat. Over half of the shoemakers who formerly worked in the shops are working at other lines of business and making more money."[14]

This sad state contrasted with "thirty years ago when all shoes were made by hand, the shoemaker earned a fair salary from $12 to $16 a week. Every shoe shop had from five to ten shoemakers working." Like so much twentieth-century nostalgia about artisan manufacture, nostalgia which misled sociologists like W. Lloyd Warner and the Lynds about how distant the golden age of craftsmanship was, Barth's reminiscence not only makes the "good old days" better than they were but also more recent. "Thirty years ago" the Whitehouse shoe factory had already been going for nearly a decade. Barth himself had his own shop but employed only two men in 1880. Although reporters praised him as steady, attentive, and honest, he had a credit rating of COD. He was one of the many shoemakers in the seventies and eighties who shifted progressively from custom manufacture to a largely repairing business. By 1883 one credit reporter noted that Barth did "a cobbling business which keeps him pegging away all the time in order to take care of his family which consists of a wife and thirteen children."

The good times Barth described did not last much beyond the time of his own arrival on the eve of Civil War. Moreover, a variety of evidence suggests that subdivision of the craft was well-advanced in Poughkeepsie a decade before then. The chief effects of the influx of immigrant shoemakers like Barth seem to have been to set back temporarily manufacture in medium-sized shops, to reduce employment of women in these shops and to increase the number of very small shops employing one or two men, thereby strengthening temporarily practice of the whole craft by journeymen. Fragmentary evidence suggests that the newcomers cut into the trade of the older, larger shoe houses by selling at lower prices; if so, the increase in small shop manufacture came at the cost of marginal reward.

Four shoe houses had reported employing 12 or more workers in 1850; one fourth to one third of the employees in each of these firms were women who undoubtedly did the lighter sewing. The proprietor or principal partner of each firm was a man of native parentage. A decade later these firms employed fewer workers and reported a decrease in value of product. Women suffered most from the loss of employment in the larger houses, declining from 16 to 7 workers compared to the decrease from 36 to 23 male workers. As in other cities in the northeast the surplus of immigrant artisans in Poughkeepsie at mid-century tended to drive women and children out of the labor force temporarily.[15] Of the 22 firms first appearing in the 1860 census, three had four or five workers, the rest had fewer and the owners were overwhelmingly of German and Irish parentage. One English dealer employed one woman; all the other new shops employed men only.

The competition of immigrant shops and journeymen exacerbated the already difficult situation of native journeymen. The decline of village population in Dutchess County with the shift from grain to wool and then to dairy farming brought a swarm of village shoemakers to the city, usually as the first stop in a migration westward. Annual directory tracing done by Edna Macmahon shows that about half of the 437 journeymen ever listed between 1845 and 1880 also disappeared within the five year period during which they were first listed. The highest rate of disappearance, 61 percent, occurred during 1860-64 and the next highest, 60 percent, during 1845-49, the first five year period analyzed. Of all shoemakers in these thirty-five years, 34 percent were listed in Poughkeepsie only in one year.

Because census tracing misses so many of the more transient, it only hints at the extent of drifting from place to place in search of work as shoemakers found themselves faced simultaneously with the drying up of employment in the villages and countryside and with the competition of immigrant artisans in the cities. The native-born consistently disappeared more frequently than the Germans but not the Irish. The absolute number of shoemakers of native parentage declined steadily and sharply in the four censuses from 1850 to 1880: 77, 53, 38, and 19 men respectively. By contrast the Germans show 26, 40, 35, and 26 workers and the Irish — contrary to their general pattern of comprising a declining proportion of the whole male labor force after 1850 — show 16, 19, 25, and 13 shoemakers. Except for the seventies, newcomers to the work force account for more than half of the shoemakers at each census. Almost all these newcomers were journeymen coming into the city from other places rather than young residents just entering the labor market.

In the sixties further inventions in the ongoing technological revolution in shoemaking made centralized production in large factories profitable. As early as 1863 the city's *Daily Press* published a forecast from the Newburyport, Massachusetts, *Herald* of the consequences of that revolution for craftsmen. The *Herald* had noted that work previously had been scattered but that the new pegging and stitching machines then coming into use — one of them capable of doing the work of more then ten men — were being set up in factories. Shoemakers would soon have to follow the business to the places where factories located.[16] Seven years later Poughkeepsie had its own shoe factory. But J. O. Whitehouse employed more women and girls and boys in their teens than adult men and very few of the men had apprenticed as shoemakers. Largely evicted from shoemaking by immigrant small shop manufacture in the late fifties and early sixties, women returned to the industry by way of the factory.

The small shop and, increasingly, the isolated craftsman at his bench faced an ever more difficult struggle for survival. Signs of marginality in artisan shoe shops began to increase in the credit reports of the R. G. Dun & Co. in the late sixties, but the seventies first fully revealed their plight. Depression wiped out the prosperity of those self-employed artisans who still managed to do fairly well. One native had kept a small store and employed two men in the fifties. But by 1867 credit reporters described him and his son as "mostly custom work, both work at the bench, have very little stock on sale" and by 1874 said that the son, now alone, "depends principally on repairing." After more than twenty years working for himself in the city, an English shoemaker was reported in 1870 as "a very small affair, works at bench only, just lives from hand to mouth."[17]

The most pathetic victims of the revolution in shoemaking were older journeymen who lost employment when local shoe merchants largely gave up manufacturing for themselves. Once before in his mid-forties, John Hermance had been unable to find work at his trade and then had been strong enough to labor temporarily at the furnace. By 1876, now 73, this journeyman with a "good education" who still "can work at his trade" found himself unemployed and destitute. Hermance entered the poor house and died six months later.[18]

The wiser and more ambitious artisans who remained associated with their trade pushed into retailing ready-made goods as quickly as they could. An Irish Protestant in the early fifties "commenced here with little or nothing, and worked at the Bench, gradually worked up and now [1868] has a stock of goods and seems to be doing well." He advertised that year for a shoemaker "to work on repairing and assist in the store."[19]

For an artisan with little capital the shift to retailing was hazardous, however. He faced competition throughout the period from merchants who already had or could afford to invest immediately in a big stock of ready-made goods, well assorted in size, style, and price. When a native opened a "fine large Boot and Shoe store" in 1855 a local reporter nevertheless warned that "Poughkeepsie was well enough supplied with stores of this kind so doubt they'll Succeed." The firm prospered, but the observation of overcrowding in the shoe business persisted. A German tried to branch out into retailing in 1875 but had to return to the bench. A credit reporter had observed, presciently, that Maar "recently added a stock of ready-made goods in which it is thought he will do only a limited trade."

Those who pushed into retailing after the Civil War produced only one big success story. Michael Timmins, son of an English shoemaker whose parents had been born in Ireland, had come to America as a child of five and had seen his father eke out a living for his family of six children as a self-employed shoemaker. When his father left Poughkeepsie for a time in the late sixties, young Michael went into business on his own. A credit reporter described him by 1871 as "thrifty, carries stock, and works at Bench" and by the mid-seventies as having a "very good cash business in cheaper grade of goods . . . mainly among the lower classes."

Timmins expanded the volume of his business during the depression, apparently by selling at little profit ready-made goods produced elsewhere. By 1880, now reported as doing the most business in his line in Poughkeepsie, he employed three journeymen for his custom and repairing work and two clerks of German parentage. During all this time Timmins stayed in his original shop on a side street in one of the city's most polyglot working-class neighborhoods and near its largest concentration of Germans. He continued to reside above the shop although by 1880 he owned three properties assessed at $9,000. Finally, in 1882 he opened a second shop in the heart of the central business district to appeal to the quality trade. He succeeded there. The next year a credit reporter said he had the "nicest shoe store in town, full stock." When Timmins died in 1888, his sons carried on the by now "profitable" business.[20]

The attempt to escape the plight of the craft by shifting into retailing reached its peak on the eve of the depression of 1873 when the classified section of the city directory reported 26 boot and shoe dealers, one third of whom were men who had depended primarily on custom previously. After the depression the number reporting themselves as dealers never exceeded 19 and was only 15 in 1900 —

the same number as the firms primarily dependent on retailing in 1870 — despite the 20 percent increase in population in those thirty years.

Directory tracing also shows that shifts into unrelated occupations were slightly more important than the shift into retailing. Of all shoemakers listed between 1843 and 1880, a little less than 6 percent became shopowners in the trade and slightly more shifted to other kinds of jobs, nearly half of them in trade and service. Occupational shifts between censuses magnify the importance of this kind of adaptation because they omit the many journeymen who appear in the city only briefly and entirely at their craft. The census analysis shows more than one fourth of the shoemakers who persisted in the city during the sixties and also during the seventies shifting to different jobs.

By the end of the sixties, seven of the persisting shoemakers of 1860 had found nonmanual employment, five reported themselves at such disparate skilled trades as moulder, painter, butcher, and cigar maker, and four took factory and service jobs. For example, a native shoemaker who in 1866 had been "doing a safe business, with two or three men hired, himself, mostly small custom work" had opened a meat market by 1870 and sold fruits and vegetables as well.[21]

Two journeymen of 1870 had entered the shoe factory by 1880, the only exceptions to the generalization that artisans did not enter the factory. The children of shoemakers more frequently took factory employment. One old resident who had a shop on Main Street in 1869 but had failed by 1873 and worked as a journeyman thereafter saw his son employed in the shoe factory by age 18. A 30 year old daughter of another old timer, always a journeyman, worked there in 1880. A larger number of children entered other factories in the city, however.

The decline of shoemaking as a craft appears most clearly in the frequency with which sons took up other occupations. By 1870, 71 percent of the identifiable shoemakers' sons employed at two censuses in the city had never appeared at their fathers' craft, one of the highest proportions among the skilled crafts. Another 8 percent had first appeared as shoemakers but then had shifted to other jobs. Moreover, a decreasing number of sons of any city residents appear at the trade. Of those who did, about three fourths of the fathers also were shoemakers and the next most common father's occupation was ordinary labor, both facts suggesting the craft's lack of attractiveness for boys with no familial relation to it. By contrast, a steadily increasing number of local sons apprenticed in an expanding trade like that of machinist, and the proportion of fathers previously at the trade was much less.

Success in the retail shoe business increasingly belonged to men not trained in the craft although this change came more slowly than in cabinet making because of the smaller investment required. The one large new store opened during the depression, D. L. Heaton and Son, represented money earned in agriculture now being invested in city trade. Heaton, formerly a farmer in neighboring Ulster County and director of a bank there, came to the financial rescue of Smith Gildersleeve, a Dutchess County farmer-turned-shoe merchant, and his son Elmer, previously a clerk in another city shoe store. When the Gildersleeves failed in 1875, Heaton bought in but kept young Elmer to run the business. Later Elmer would start off on his own again, becoming the biggest shoe merchant in the city by the turn of the century, a member of the Board of Trade, and President of the Retail Merchants' Association.[22]

Coopers

Turning from shoemakers to a consideration of coopers in Poughkeepsie during the middle decades is like entering a different world although both trades belong to the traditional handicrafts deemed essential in rural as well as urban communities. Skill dilution did not pose any serious threat to cooperingbefore the seventies and in most local firms in 1880 the individual journeyman continued to perform much of his craft. Coopers clung to their trade despite low wages, the difficulty by the end of the period of achieving self-employment in it, and marked fluctuations in the employment of journeymen due to frequent fires as well as to shifts in demand. Coopers stayed at the manufacture of barrels and woodenware; their sons followed the same occupation more frequently than the sons of workers in most trades.

In 1850 the industry numbered six shops in Poughkeepsie, the largest employing six men. These shops together with journeymen employed in other industries like brewing and porkpacking account for the 37 coopers in that census. The industry grew faster than any other in the city during the next decade, quadrupling in work force.

One firm, Sleight and Paulding, grew from 20 men in 1851 to 80 in 1860, or nearly two thirds of the total that year. Manufacturing extensively for the southern market, especially whiskey and turpentine barrels, the firm lost heavily during the Civil War through unpaid southern notes and failed twice in the next two decades. By 1865 it reported only thirty workers.[23]

The industry as a whole continued to grow slowly although no one firm ever dominated it so thoroughly again. It depended heavily upon markets at a distance, shipping to New York City and Philadelphia houses as well as directly to the southern market, with all the financial vulnerability that such dependence implies. By the sixties the industry also went further for materials. Sleight and Paulding initially had procured all its staves in New York State but discovered it could buy them much cheaper in Michigan. The firm soon found itself acting as purchaser for the vicinity; other coopers in the city and along the river applied to it for their supplies.[24]

During the fifties coopering provided jobs for more immigrants than any other skilled trade in Poughkeepsie. The sixty Germans and Irish in the trade comprised nearly half of its work force in 1860; those nationalities had made up only one third of the much smaller force of 1850. Some of the newcomers found employment in shops owned by their countrymen. Two Irishmen already had small shops in 1850; one of them expanded from 4 to 16 workers during the next decade. But neither these men nor several other smaller Irish and German shops explain the influx into the trade. From the beginning, native manufacturers employed newcomers as well as natives.

Within each firm subdivision of the craft was minimal before the seventies and immigrant workers had as much independence and responsibility as natives. By 1866 Sleight and Paulding used machinery for dressing and heading staves, employing 10 men for these tasks and for shipping. But each of the remaining 40 coopers did all the other tasks associated with any product they made, whether butter firkins, lard kegs, or ale barrels. Thus, on the ground floor devoted to barrel making each man took a certain portion of the staves and headings and proceeded "to the construction of barrels by piece work, the article not leaving his hands until finished."[25]

The piece work system encouraged competition between journeymen. Even the local newspaper held up an example from the past of how much more the quicker, more skillful cooper could earn. The *Eagle* reported that one 91 year old still working at the trade had made a soup tub recently for $3.75, then added, "He made at times an average of $2.50 per day. Young men should take a lesson." Since the average daily wage reported in local cooperages for the previous decade was less than $2.00 per day, his prowess needed no further demonstration.[26]

The system also made the scale of prices for individual products the chief issue between bosses and journeymen and especially the variations in scale from firm to firm and from place to place. By 1863 that issue, together with long hours, prompted 60 of Poughkeepsie's coopers to respond to the appeal of three traveling delegates of the New York State Coopers' Society, recently organized in New York City and Brooklyn, to form themselves into a local branch. The new branch elected a German as president and an Irishman as secretary.[27]

A month later the coopers at Sleight and Paulding went out on strike because the firm's prices did not meet the union scale. The day before, a majority of the boss coopers in New York City had agreed to the advance demanded by the union. The Poughkeepsie bosses refused to comply, but the strikers had sufficient support so that nearly all the cooperages shut down within the week. Led by a band from the village of Saugerties up the river, the strikers paraded through the streets. The *Daily Press,* the newspaper friendly to immigrants and least hostile to labor organization, described them as a "very respectable group." The *Eagle* simply ignored them altogether.

At a meeting following the parade, P. O. Farrell of the New York society claimed that "the cooper's trade was a slave trade, compelling men to work from 13 to 15 hours to earn as much as other mechanics. The first object of the Poughkeepsie branch must be to introduce the ten hour system and secure at least an average wage of $2.00 per day." Farrell brought financial aid and the strikers also received money from Troy and other cities in the state until at least the beginning of November. Officers of the New York society also hired strikers who were willing to go to New York City to work for employers there at the union scale.

One German boss in Poughkeepsie and the Vassar brewery did put their journeymen back to work at the advanced scale but other employers held out. Both the strike and the local branch seem to have foundered during the winter although the union's officers remained at work in the city. The *Press* reported early in November that "a large number of the Poughkeepsie coopers have gone to New York where they now get 50 cents per day more than they can in Poughkeepsie." In the seventies the city's employers contributed to the defeat of the Coopers' International Union by selling to one of Standard Oil's barrel suppliers during the strike at Standard's Ohio barrel works.[28]

Whether the largest bosses in 1863, all men of native parentage except the Austrian partner of Weddle and Hill, attributed the strike primarily to the immigrants in the trade remains unknown. They did apparently prefer native journeymen in hiring during the slower expansion of the industry in the sixties. Native workers increased by half whereas Germans decreased slightly and more than half of the Irish disappeared from the trade during the sixties, mostly by leaving the city. In no other decade did so large a proportion of coopers remaining in Poughkeepsie leave their trade, and immigrants accounted for almost all of these changes in occupation.[29]

The failure of the largest Irish boss cooper during the early sixties undoubtedly influenced the sharpness of Irish decline in the trade. But the mixed ethnic composition of most firms suggests that his failure cannot fully explain their loss. Several who remained in Poughkeepsie appeared subsequently at ordinary labor suggesting that they may have been marginal workers with little or no training in the craft. Such workers might find jobs during the cooperages' great expansion in the fifties. As the last to be hired, however, they may also have been the first to be fired during the much slower growth of the sixties.

The Irish never recovered the proportion of the craft which they had comprised on the eve of Civil War. About two thirds of the Irish coopers at any census had disappeared from the city by the end of the decade, a higher rate of loss than for any other group. The Germans did consolidate their foothold in the seventies primarily through second generation sons entering the craft. By 1880 first and second generation together exceeded their proportion in 1860. But men of native parentage continued to have a comfortable majority in the craft.

The proportion of coopers recruited from other occupations in Poughkeepsie did increase slightly in the seventies suggesting a little more use of green hands. But the main tendency in recruitment —

characteristic of an injured trade even when contraction in numbers has not begun — was the steady decrease in the proportion of young workers and corresponding increase in workers 50 years or older. There was no easy escape sideways to related trades in Poughkeepsie. With the exception of the more mechanized sash and blind factories, all the woodworking trades declined in number of workers during this period. A few cabinet makers shifted into a building trade, carpentry, but coopers did not. Older workers may have been trapped by their inability to adapt readily to other kinds of skilled work.

The lack of opportunity to shift into small businesses related to cooperage, whether retail or repairing, discouraged the frequency of flight from the trade apparent in both shoemaking and cabinet making. So did the fact that extensive subdivision of the craft and use of machinery came later to coopering than it did in those trades. The largest and strongest firm in the seventies, Lown and Company, did invest in $25,000 worth of machinery. The more specialized titles given by some of Lown's employees in the 1879 county directory also suggests increasing subdivision and mechanization: they include machine cooper, finishing cooper, pail turner, and varnisher.[30]

Changes in the ownership of two other large firms suggest that the greater impersonality and preoccupation with efficiency of bigger national businesses increasingly would prevail in the industry in Poughkeepsie. By 1879 Paulding had lost the ownership of his cooperage and acted as agent for a firm in Flint, Michigan. "They hire Paulding by the month as foreman of their shop and he has no further authority." The same fate befell a German boss cooper in the eighties. By 1880 he employed more than 30 men but increasingly he relied on jobbing for New York City coopers, who advanced him money. By 1882 he, too, had become merely the agent for an absentee owner.[31]

One former journeyman, briefly a partner in Paulding in the early seventies, did succeed in starting up his own shop subsequently but his cooperage remained a small and feeble affair. The scale of the biggest firms by the eighties and increasing investment in machinery made self-employment by former journeymen unlikely for the future. But achievement of self-employment always had been too exceptional to explain the extraordinary loyalty of coopers to their craft, a loyalty which had not died by 1880. Of the coopers

who remained in Poughkeepsie during the seventies, 92 percent
remained at the trade. Sons continued to follow their fathers far
more often than in most crafts. Fifty-eight percent of the coopers'
sons of 1870 also appear at the trade at their last reported job in the
city.

The local press suggested in 1879 that journeymen identified
themselves with their shop as well as their craft. "Coopers always
consider themselves in the employ of a shop, whether business keeps
them constantly at work or not, so that it is impossible to state
exactly the increase in employment." Journeymen did change employers within the city, especially when fire or failure temporarily
shut down a cooperage and they also moved readily to other cities
when work was short locally or wages better elsewhere. Four Poughkeepsie coopers set out for a point as distant as Kansas City, Mis-
souri, in the mid-seventies, having heard of better opportunities for
coopers there. But a general sense of greater rootedness than in most
crafts persists, a rootedness which seems all the more impressive because of constant hazards to employment in the industry.[32]

In 1866, for example, 40 workmen lost their tools and their jobs
when fire swept the Sleight and Paulding and the Lown cooperages,
both of which had burned down previously in 1858. Employees who
stayed on in Poughkeepsie lost about a month's work; both firms re-
built and resumed business in that time. A month later a third cooperage, William Moore's, was destroyed entirely by fire. Moore had
been burned out before in 1861 and on that occasion the *Eagle*
noted that that was the third time John Moore had lost his coopering
tools in a fire. When Weddle and Hill burned in 1876, all 29 coopers lost their tools as well as their jobs. Losses for the ten who had
no insurance averaged $38.50, roughly a month's wages.[33]

Each time Paulding failed in business, between 30 and 50 men
lost work for up to half a year. Even when firms suffered neither fire
nor failure, changing demand brought frequent fluctuation in the
size of work forces. Commenting on the good fall trade at Paulding's
in 1879, with 40 men working, the *Eagle* said, "Last year he had not
so many men and they were not all working full time. Apple crop
orders were better last year, but New York and Philadelphia orders
are better this year."[34]

None of the usual considerations of opportunity and reward
seems adequate to explain fully the tenacity with which coopers
clung to their trade. Their national historian, Franklyn Coyne, con-

veys a sense of craft pride, camaraderie, and distinctive rhythm of life, which does seem to be an essential part of any explanation. In Poughkeepsie coopers also were set apart physically to an unusual degree. More often than members of other crafts they shared dwellings and clustered near their places of work along the waterfront. Their long working day encouraged this proximity; as late as 1880 cooperages reported averaging 14 hours from May to November and 12 the rest of the year. Journeymen "go to work sometimes as early as 3 o'clock in the morning and continue their labor until night."[35]

Except for the small minority who had saved a little money and tried to start a grocery or other small business, there is almost no evidence in the occupational behavior of coopers to suggest that members of this craft shared in even the more modest dreams of independence and success promoted by publicists in the middle decades. Rather Poughkeepsie's coopers seem like artisans set apart by the regimen and rituals as well as the economic circumstances of their craft.

Carriage Makers

The very distinctiveness of coopering as a craft and the frequency with which journeymen clung to it despite low wages and lack of opportunity for self-employment contrast with another industry which also began contracting in work force during the seventies. Carriage making employed not one but at least four very different skills, those of carriage maker or builder of the wooden body, smith, painter, and trimmer. Unlike shoemaking and coopering, two of these skills—smithing and painting—could be transferred readily to other industries such as the manufacture of agricultural implements and chairs or to the most common craft employments at horseshoeing, general blacksmithing, and house and sign painting. A 40 year old journeyman carriage smith had saved a few hundred dollars to start his business in 1850 but sold out within the year. By his midfifties he worked in the blacksmithing department at the Buckeye mower and reaper works. As the industry contracted after 1870 some craftsmen found other employment at their trades in Poughkeepsie. The *Eagle* noted that "one of the finest carriage and sleigh painters to be found in the country" had painted the cars of the city railroad company before taking up house and sign painting.[36]

But even those craftsmen who remained in the industry had more favorable prospects than coopers in the same period for several reasons. Although local manufacture declined in the face of mid-western competition, the carriage repairing business remained important and could be carried on satisfactorily by self-employed individuals or by contractual business arrangements in which the participating craftsmen retained substantial independence. Thus, a carriage painter and his son worked for themselves in the early seventies. Another painter developed a business arrangement with a carriage maker who "superintends the wood work" and a smith who "does the blacksmith or iron work." "They have no regular company or partnership; each man buys his goods for his particular branch of the work and in his own name . . . Their business is principally repairing; when they do any new work, they agree on a division of the proceeds to be derived from the sale of same before the work is commenced."[37]

Because the custom and repairing business still offered a livelihood even in small shops and little "factories" of 10 to 15 men, the opportunities for self-employment remained much better than in coopering. Local men who had apprenticed in the trade continued to own businesses in 1900; one of them had apprenticed as a trimmer during the industry's boom in Poughkeepsie in the late fifties when several firms employed 20 men each.[38]

In the forties and fifties the carriage industry had seen a succession of journeymen start up for themselves, most of them failing or selling out within a few years. As a credit reporter commented in 1850, "Our carriage makers have not been hitherto very fortunate." The owners of a few large firms became rich during the middle decades but the pattern of many short-lived ventures continued even into the years of contraction in the industry. As late as 1887 a reporter noted that Edward Delameter had been in business for more than 12 years, "a very good record for the industry." Delameter assigned to creditors the same year, apparently fulfilling the prophecy of another reporter four years earlier, "Don't believe there's much money to be made in the line in which he is engaged."[39]

But Delameter resumed and in the later days of the industry firms became longer lived. Six firms advertised in the city directories of 1880 and of 1896: five of these in the later year had the same owner or the principal partner of 1880. Delameter himself went on to make the transition to the automobile, securing the local agency for several cars. In 1911 the firm straddled the old and the new; in its new garage and small three-story factory it "builds light carriages and automobile bodies and does all classes of repair work connected with automobiles and carriages."[40]

Poughkeepsie's middle class at mid-century had boasted many men who moved up from apprentice to journeyman to employer in their crafts. That avenue to membership in the city's business community, and especially its larger establishments, had become less common by 1880, the end of our census tracing period. Impressionistic evidence from the last two decades of the century as well as evidence from other cities reinforces conjecture that skilled manual workers would never again have as much opportunity within their own careers to become not simply self-employed but also rich by the standards of the local community, say, among the top tenth of its taxpayers. The passing of the old substantial artisan middle class which had successfully combined manufacturing and retailing left a more obvious gap between the city's big and little businessmen.

Men like Edward Delameter, however, also show how late the crafts in some industries continued to spawn local success stories. They remind us how exuberant small business remained during the heyday of the trust. Traditional craft manufacture might be obsolete in most industries, but manual workers continued to act upon dreams of independence and prosperity through businesses of their own. Sometimes they tried to capitalize on a new specialization in manufacture as artisans long had done; but just as often we suspect they tried retail and service ventures unrelated to their skill as earlier artisans also had done. In these unrelated ventures they already faced increasing competition by 1880 from less skilled workers.

The narrowing differences between strata within the manual world in frequencies of achieving nonmanual work, primarily self-employment, during the middle decades showed that the old, sharp division in opportunity between artisans and laborers had been blurred just as skill dilution had diminished the differences in their work. In an age of increasing scale and specialization the usual ceiling for the occupational mobility of skilled workers lowered as that for less skilled workers lifted somewhat; increasingly both came to occupy a common working-class world. A minority of artisans, however, began to form a new aristocracy among manual workers, performing the most skilled tasks and the supervisory positions required by an increasingly industrialized economy.

8

Immigrant Success
in the Handicrafts

THE NARROWING OF differences in occupational mobility
between artisans and laborers by 1880, and especially the diminishing importance of artisan shopowners within the city's prosperous
middle class, changed the meaning of opportunity for craftsmen.
The last chapter showed that an important minority of craftsmen,
often self-employed, experienced real hardship during the years of
skill dilution and transition to larger scale manufacture in their industries and that older craftsmen, as might be expected, more often
suffered from this obsolescence.

This chapter will analyze the situation of the various ethnic
groups within particular trades. Its chief purpose is to assess the significance of the impressive occupational mobility of immigrant
artisans in Poughkeepsie at mid-century and so determine how far it
contradicts the conventional gloomy picture of opportunities for
immigrants in industrializing America. That picture shows the newcomers entering the labor force at the bottom and only slowly, after
much hardship, overcoming this initial handicap; in the case of immigrants coming with craft skills, it emphasizes their contribution to
a glut in the labor market in their trades in large cities and partici-

pation in the resulting degradation in standard of living and frequent unemployment.

Preliminary comparison of skilled workers in Poughkeepsie does not conform to this picture, revealing instead ethnic differences in mobility which favor the newcomers with one exception. (Table 8.1) The record of the Germans and the British, both first and second generation in America, and even of the native-born of Irish parentage is much better than that of white artisans of native parentage in rising above journeyman status and in avoiding descent to less

TABLE 8.1. Occupational mobility of workers starting at skilled jobs by decade and nativity

	Decade	Number of cases	Remain skilled (percent)	Rise to white collar (percent)	Fall to low manual (percent)
Native-born	1850 – 60	260	69	23	8
— native	1860 – 70	328	72	22	6
parentage	1870 – 80	420	74	15	11
British-	1850 – 60	37	73	27	—
born	1860 – 70	49	74	20	6
	1870 – 80	42	74	19	7
Native-born — British parentage	1870 – 80	43	74	19	7
German-born	1850 – 60	34	56	35	9
	1860 – 70	110	53	42	6
	1870 – 80	116	70	23	7
Native-born — German parentage	1870 – 80	62	63	27	10
Irish-born	1850 – 60	46	67	24	9
	1860 – 70	93	71	13	16
	1870 – 80	106	83	4	13
Native-born — Irish parentage	1870 – 80	60	67	18	15

skilled jobs. Only the immigrant Irish show less favorable frequencies of upward and downward movement than the natives. This apparent native disadvantage cannot be dismissed as concerning a negligible proportion of native workers. The 429 whites of native parentage reporting skilled work in 1870 and persisting in Poughkeepsie in 1880 comprised one third of all native whites persisting in that decade and were almost equal in absolute number to the persisting men of foreign birth or parentage starting skilled.

The superior upward mobility of immigrant craftsmen does reflect primarily the frequency with which they became shopowners, often within their trades. But they also succeeded ultimately in passing their advantage on to their sons (Table 8.2). Analysis of intergenerational mobility for all sons born in the forties shows a sharp difference in ethnic advantage between first and last reported jobs. Native skilled workers, like native white-collar workers, had a better chance than immigrant fathers at that level of seeing their sons begin at nonmanual employment. By last reported job, however, the sons of native skilled workers suffer by comparison with a

TABLE 8.2. Intergenerational occupational mobility of sons of skilled workers by father's nativity (sons born between 1840 and 1859)

Father's nativity	Number of cases	Occupational level of son		
		White collar (percent)	Skilled (percent)	Low manual (percent)
		Son's first job		
Native	182	21	53	26
British	39	10	64	26
German	57	19	68	17
Irish	45	18	44	38
		Son's latest job		
Native	97	23	52	26
British	25	32	48	20
German	42	26	67	7
Irish	27	44	44	11

higher percentage of unskilled and semiskilled jobs and a smaller percentage at nonmanual employment than the sons of immigrant fathers.

In less than a generation immigrant artisans at mid-century comprised a majority of journeymen in many of the city's skilled trades and a majority of shopowners in a number of them. In the traditional handicrafts this new competition often reduced the number of native proprietors within a decade or two and in both shoemaking and tailoring temporarily reduced the number of female workers in Poughkeepsie.

Whether the perpetuation of small shop craft manufacture ever resulted in more than marginal economic returns remains in question and so, therefore, does its significance in immigrant adaptation to an industrializing economy. If certain handicrafts continued to offer as good an opportunity as the industrial trades and the more attractive factory jobs—even in the short run—then the apparent native advantage in hiring in the latter appears in a different light. Although handicrafts like shoemaking suffered early from skill dilution, others like cigarmaking and baking remained relatively intact longer and some products would not face serious competition from ready-made goods before the turn of the century.

The Germans pose the question of the significance of small shop craft manufacture most acutely in Poughkeepsie as in many other northeastern cities at mid-century. By 1880 men of German birth or parentage in Poughkeepsie accounted for one sixth of the city's labor force but comprised half or more of all workers in shoemaking (excluding the shoe factory), tailoring, baking, butchering, brewing, and cigar making and well over half of the shop owners in these trades (Table 8.3). Rates of persistence within these trades for Germans exceeded the rates for other ethnic groups. In coopering, cabinet making, and watchmaking where artisans of native parentage continued to predominate, Germans accounted for between 19 and 27 percent of the work force by 1870.

By contrast, they comprised less than 12 percent of the blacksmiths and carriage makers and less than 8 percent of the moulders, machinists, carpenters, painters, and plumbers. In none of the building and new industrial trades in Poughkeepsie did the proportion of self-employed workers exceed 11 percent whereas in all but one—baking—of the six food and apparel trades 22 percent or more owned their shops. These trades with the highest self-employ-

TABLE 8.3. Nativity of workers in nine crafts, 1850 and 1880[a]

Craft	Census	White of native parentage (percent)	Irish (percent)	German (percent)	British (percent)	Number of cases
Shoemaker	1850	62	13	21	4	124
	1880	25	25	41	9	76
Tailor	1850	31	17	22	23	78
	1880	19	13	50	12	103
Baker	1850	58	13	18	8	40
	1880	15	24	48	10	71
Carpenter	1850	82	9	1	5	188
	1880	74	12	8	6	235
Mason	1850	55	27	4	14	71
	1880	32	40	14	11	111
Painter	1850	80	5	3	10	60
	1880	68	15	7	9	121
Machinist	1850	79	—	2	18	56
	1880	68	13	6	13	94
Moulder	1850	68	12	—	20	25
	1880	48	41	2	2	46
Engineer	1850	78	—	—	22	18
	1880	62	15	10	12	52

[a]The Irish, Germans, and British comprise both the foreign-born and the native-born of foreign parentage of these nationalities.

ment, however, reported lower wage rates for journeymen throughout the period than any of the building and industrial trades.

To evaluate immigrant success in the handicrafts, this chapter compares three trades — tailoring, cigar making, and baking — which the Germans dominated with those building and industrial trades that men of native parentage continued to dominate throughout the period.

Tailors

Immigrants made the greatest headway earliest in tailoring as they did in many other American cities at mid-century.[1] Already by 1850 even in this relatively small city, nine shops reported more than ten workers and four of these employed more than twenty. Tailoresses were thrice as numerous in the largest firm as tailors. Despite division of labor within the craft, organization of the business still belonged largely to men who had apprenticed in tailoring. Entry into business on a fairly substantial scale remained possible for journeymen with limited savings. When 26 year old John Dobbs entered into a partnership in merchant tailoring with two other young "practical mechanics" in 1849, the three collectively were worth no more than $2,000. They employed eight men and three women the following year. A decade later Dobbs, now in business alone, had increased his work force to 15; he prospered until the seventies on custom work being "patronized by many of the first class in the city." Even small shops still offered a good livelihood.[2]

Merchant tailoring for the better classes would still be the source of prosperity for a few men in large firms in the future, but ready-made goods had already begun their invasion of the working-class clothing market. Barnum and Co. of New York City ran eleven inches of advertisement for ready-made as well as custom-order clothes and dry goods in the Poughkeepsie *Telegraph* by 1851 and a very reputable local dry goods house also advertised ready-made. In 1852 alone two new Jewish houses began with that specialty.[3]

Ready-made manufacturing began in Poughkeepsie during the fifties but accounted for only a small portion of the garment making then. In 1850 a small grocer, Robert Taylor, began production for the southern market. He failed in 1855, resumed manufacturing for New York and Philadelphia houses, and failed again in 1858 "in consequence of the failure of his debtors in Philadelphia." Taylor continued to "get his living by tailoring and selling sewing machines," but by 1860 he employed only four men and three women and two years later he left the city. The King brothers and Benago Lockwood, strangers to the city who probably came to take advantage of its immigrant workers at a time when jobs were short, in 1858 "engaged in manufacturing clothing and . . . keep a grocery to pay the hands." Their business lasted until nearly the end of the Civil War.[4]

The largest employers in clothing in Poughkeepsie still depended upon custom work in 1860. But the proportion of German and especially of German Jewish houses had increased sharply by that date. Of the ten houses reported in the manufacturing census of 1850, only three had been owned by Germans, two of these Jewish. Of the 21 reported in 1860, 13 were German and 11 of these Jewish. The change in journeymen was equally dramatic.

Among men reporting themselves as tailors in the census, the

Germans and their native-born children comprised less than one fourth in 1850 but nearly one half by 1860, whereas whites of native parentage fell from nearly one third of the total to about one fifth in the same decade; most of those remaining were merchant tailors and clothiers rather than journeymen. Irish and British workers together comprised another fifth. Initially black tailors suffered most obviously from the influx of newcomers, four out of five disappearing during the fifties.[5] But after the Civil War the surplus of male tailors created by immigration also greatly reduced the employment of women in the manufacture of men's clothes in Poughkeepsie.

The greater stability of the German workers in the trade shows up clearly during the fifties. Nearly two thirds remained in the city and at their craft compared to half of the British and one fourth of the Irish and the whites of native parentage. In the next two decades, slightly more than half of both the German and the British tailors persisted at their trade. The persistence of the Irish and whites of native parentage was similar during the sixties, but less during the depression decade of the seventies. The native-born of foreign parentage, including German, comprised only 12 percent of the work force even by 1880, one sign that the trade did not attract young Americans. Of 44 tailors' sons employed at two censuses in Poughkeepsie only five were tailors themselves at last reported job and only one other son had begun in the trade. More than two thirds of the newcomers among the city's tailors in each decade were immigrant craftsmen who had not been employed in Poughkeepsie previously.

Prior to the seventies only four men reported as tailors shifted to other jobs in the city at the next census and none of these shifted to manual work. Ten changed occupation during the depression decade: two of these reported themselves as laborers and three at the trades of painting, cigar making, and printing. This shifting out is only one of many signs that the situation of most journeymen tailors — unfavorable even in 1850 — had grown worse in the postwar years. Wages reported compared unfavorably with other crafts except those suffering skill dilution, like shoemaking. Consumers benefited at the expense of the journeymen tailors; as the *Eagle* noted in 1877, "It is an undisputed fact that clothing is cheaper than anything else in proportion since the close of the war."[6]

The cutters, aristocrats of the trade, remained the great exception, being more highly paid than any other manual workers in the city except locomotive engineers and a few of the most highly skilled and inventive machinists. Correspondingly, opportunities for starting new clothing businesses with much chance of substantial prosperity were confined primarily to these aristocrats and to merchant adventurers with no apprenticeship in the craft. In 1866 a 31 year old English cutter reported an income of $1,543. Six years later he was "supposed to have saved several thousand dollars out of his salary" and was taken into partnership by his employer.[7]

Ordinary journeymen tailors had even less chance of successful self-employment. John Gilligan, born in Canada of Irish parentage, first appeared in Poughkeepsie as a journeyman at 24, starting his business for "making, repairing and cleaning clothing" nine years later. A reporter noted that he had "commenced by working at the bench, got in a little stock and now does a fair trade." But Gilligan never got beyond keeping "a few samples of cloth upstairs, not strong enough for credit in New York"; he failed a year before the panic of 1873 and left the city for good during the depression.[8]

The principal partners in the most successful clothing firms tended not to be tailors themselves. The largest proprietor in 1860, B. R. Tenney, employed 45 men and women and was himself a cutter. But Tenney achieved that preeminence with money advanced him by his brother-in-law, the dry goods merchant W. H. Crosby. When Tenney failed in 1862, Crosby took over the business, retaining Tenney as foreman and salesman. By 1875 when Crosby took another former dry goods merchant, George Candee, into partnership, the firm was the second largest employer among the city's merchant tailors. The largest firm by the early seventies was Hayt and Lindley and its founder, the son of a wealthy Fishkill farmer, had started in business at age 26 with a playboy reputation.[9]

Ethnic stratification within the biggest merchant tailoring firms was sharp and clear. Hayt and Lindley relied heavily on German and Irish journeymen as well as employing a former fugitive slave, but the bookkeeper, four clerks, and cutter all were whites of native parentage and, for the most part, of local respectability. Even the German Jewish houses in the central business district flattered prevailing prejudice by employing one or more native clerks.

By 1880 one Prussian-born tailor was well on his way to becoming the biggest merchant tailor and clothier not only in the city but in the mid-Hudson region. The methods of M. Shwartz's success, however, suggest that he was the exception that proves the rule, in this case the rule that skill in business rather than in the craft was the key to prosperity in tailoring in Poughkeepsie by the end of the period. In 1877 Shwartz advertised himself as a "One Price Clothing House" with the "largest stock of men's, boys' and children's ready-made in the city."[10]

By his own account in the *Poughkeepsie Illustrated* of 1887, Shwartz "saw that if goods were bought direct from the manufacturers and . . . a sufficient number of garments could be sold to give employment to a regularly organized corps of finishers, there was no reason why good clothing could not be made here even more cheaply than in the larger cities, where living is more expensive." In 1880 the firm employed 60 male tailors; by 1887 it boasted that "seven to eight cutters are employed steadily the year around, and from 100 to 150 hands making garments, while 14 or 15 men are employed as salesmen and stockkeepers."[11] M. Shwartz's stepsons began their careers in the family business as clerks, not as apprentice tailors. Generally, sons did not follow fathers in this craft, not even among the Germans. The supply of journeymen for the future as during this period would come primarily from immigrants.

Cigar Makers

The influx of German tailors during the fifties displaced workers of other nationalities, especially natives, but the trade was still polyglot in 1880. By contrast, the rapid development of the cigar industry — negligible in Poughkeepsie in 1850 but producing nearly two million cigars annually by 1866 — saw an initial competition between native and German journeymen but finally extreme domination by the Germans.[12] The 15 cigarmakers of native parentage and 20 of German parentage in 1860 had become 19 and 58 respectively by 1880. Whereas only a few native-born sons of German parentage followed the immigrants in apprenticing in tailoring, the second generation rushed into cigar making. Eight percent reported that trade in 1880, a greater concentration in one craft than existed within any other nativity group that year.

Whether this concentration by second generation German-Americans represented attraction to a superior opportunity more than failure to find entry into a wider range of opportunities than their parents had remains uncertain, but on balance the evidence available favors the latter explanation.

On the one hand, even relatively small cigar manufacturers in Poughkeepsie were able to prosper modestly as late as the eighties. A credit report on a German in 1870 commented that he had "been here a number of years . . . manufactures some little and sells over the counter"; a report twelve years later said he "began without anything, has made money." On the other hand the frequency with which men reporting themselves as cigar makers appear previously at other jobs and the frequency with which they shift subsequently to unrelated trades suggest some employment of "green hands." Hand methods did not become obsolete in cigarmaking until the turn of the century, but larger shops and subdivision of the craft were apparent by the late sixties and early seventies.[13]

At least half of Poughkeepsie's cigar makers had joined the Journeymen Cigar Makers' International Union by 1868, but wages remained only a little better than for shoemakers and tailors, among the most poorly paid craftsmen. The union could not control John Schwartz, who already had emerged as the city's most successful organizer of cigar manufacturing with "large sales to county dealers." Schwartz fired on one Saturday in 1868 all of his employees who belonged to the union. When all hands struck in response, he went to New York City for replacements.[14]

By 1889, however, organization had improved the wages of cigar makers throughout the state. All of Poughkeepsie's cigar makers now belonged to the union which reported "no difficulty with our employers, save one, who has grossly violated the apprentice law."[15] The trade may have continued to attract younger workers of German parentage partly because the opportunities for self-employment remained so high. No capital being required, one fourth of the cigar makers listed in the city directory that year had their own shops.

Bakers

Although Germans also became the largest immigrant group in baking and confectionery, the work force in those trades differed in several important respects from the tailors and cigar makers. The contrast points up the variations in opportunity for newcomers even within the traditional handicrafts. The most striking trait of the food workers was their instability, the frequency with which they left their trade or the city. Even in the decade of the seventies when half or more of the workers in most skilled trades remained in the city, nearly two thirds of the bakers and confectioners disappeared and another one sixth changed jobs. A mere one fifth persisted in their trades in Poughkeepsie and most of these were proprietors.

Youthfulness matched volatility. Two thirds or more of the workers at every census after 1850 were less than 30 years old and one fourth were in their teens. By the end of the period most of these youngest workers were native-born sons of foreign parentage. Although German immigrants and their children comprised nearly one half of the total by 1880, the increase in their proportion in the food trades had been more gradual than among tailors. The Irish and especially their native-born sons found jobs in baking and confectionery more often than they did in garment making in Poughkeepsie.

Native-born and British proprietors also loomed larger. The preeminence of two firms—the cracker bakery owned by the native Bartletts and the combined bakery, confectionery, and restaurant owned by the Scotch-Irish Smiths had no parallel in clothing. As early as 1860 these two firms employed more than two thirds of those males reporting themselves as bakers and confectioners and the proportion was not much lower in 1880. The early profitability of the cracker bakery appears in the fact that all three bakers who reported $2,000 or more annual income in 1866 were members of the Bartlett family.

By 1880 half of the bakeries and confectioneries would be owned by Germans, but none of these firms approached the scale of the cracker bakery or Smith Brothers and the next two largest firms also were owned by a native and a British immigrant. By the end of the century Jacob Schrauth and his sons would develop an extremely profitable regional ice cream business and compete locally with Smith Brothers in confectionery and baking, but in 1880 Jacob employed only two men compared to the 16 men, 25 women, and 5 children reported by Smith Brothers.[16]

That all workers who described themselves as bakers and confectioners were not craftsmen becomes apparent as soon as the cracker bakery is examined more closely. Of the 25 workers reported there in the manufacturing census of 1880, only 11 can be identified by means of census and city and county directories combined. But the traits of these 11 are so consistent as to leave no doubt about the character of this bakery's work force. Four are identified as working in the cracker bakery, four list themselves as bakers, one appears in the census as a laborer, another as a carpet weaver, and one—most accurately—as "cracker factory." With the single exception of the 30 year old foreman, all of these identifiable workers were less than 23 years of age and mostly in their teens in 1880. The foreman was born in Ireland but came to America as a child of three; all but one of the remaining ten were native-born sons of Irish parentage whose fathers overwhelmingly were employed at ordinary labor.

The foreman and one worker remained at the cracker bakery 20 years later; three more workers stayed between three and five years, but the others left the city or took up radically different jobs. By 1882 one reported himself a printer, then for at least five years at no specified occupation and finally in 1900 as a machinist. By 1885 the son of a gardener reported himself a bookkeeper, by 1890 as a grocer, and by 1900 as a letter carrier. Several other teenage sons of Irish parentage reported themselves in 1880 as "works in bakery" rather than as "cracker bakery" but the careers of the few who remained in the city in their twenties are similar. The son of a grocer reported himself as a painter by 1881 at age 18, as a clerk in his father's grocery by 1890, and at no specified occupation by 1900. Three second generation bakers of 1870, aged 17, 15, and 14, had become carpenter, brick mason, and painter respectively by 1880.

The frequency with which these second generation sons of unskilled and semiskilled Irishmen shifted occupations reflects the character of their work: ill-paid, routine, and requiring little skill or responsibility. The cracker bakery had begun in 1841 as a supplier of "pilot" or ship bread employing only four men working by hand. By the late forties the bakery shifted to butter and soda crackers, purchasing machinery to roll and cut them which doubled the product per hand. In 1863 with business booming so much that the firm could not keep up with orders, installation of one of Knapp's Patent Mechanical Reel Ovens saved the day: "ingredients for crackers are placed in the mixer and never handled until they emerged baked—all mechanical." The boys at the cracker factory who reported themselves as bakers were not learning a craft.[17]

Boys of Irish parentage also found employment at Smith Brothers. They were learning trades. James Smith had brought his family from Canada to Poughkeepsie in 1847, opening a candy store and restaurant which grew rapidly under the patronage of dockworkers and Irish laborers building the Hudson River Railroad. Credit reporters first described James in 1850 as "Keeps an Irish liquor store, tobacco" but by 1866 found his sons "making money fast, cash business entirely in their (dining) saloon, supply the country stores with confectionery and segars." The Smith Brothers had a less specialized business than the cracker bakery and do not seem to have been mechanized except in their cough drop line, which became very profitable by the seventies.[18]

Many of Smith Brothers' employees lived above the shop at 13-15 Market Street under the eye of the founder's widow and practiced their crafts there for years or began their own businesses elsewhere. One confectioner boarded with the widow from 1862 to 1868, left Poughkeepsie for Binghamton to open his own confectionery and restaurant, but returned to work and board by 1873, appearing as shop foreman by 1880.[19] A Scottish-born confectioner had been associated with the firm for more than 20 years by 1880. The native-born son of an Irish moulder would open his own confectionery a few blocks away by 1882 at age 22, having been employed by the Smiths since his teens. He remained in business for himself at the same address in 1900. And the New Hampshire-born son of an Irish carpenter was a baker at Smiths' before he was 20 and still employed there at age 50.

Looking back on the situation of journeymen bakers in America's leading cities before the mid-eighties, their national union described it as "worse than that of slaves in the South." The hours of continuous toil amounted to between 14 and 18 hours daily, many men were compelled to board with their employers, and "the temperature in which these men worked, ate and slept was almost unbearable."[20] If the manufacturing census can be believed, the situation in Poughkeepsie by 1880 was not so extreme. Some firms worked a 12 hour day all or part of the year but others reported 10 hours all year round and most workers did not board with their employers. Some firms paid the common rate for skilled labor of $2.00 a day but others reported only $1.50 and two reported a mere $1.00, the going rate that year for ordinary labor. To say the situation was not so extreme as the union's generalization is not to say that it was favorable, however. The situation and future prospects of journeymen hardly encouraged loyalty to the food trades. Baking and confectionery yielded a comfortable annual income for a few immigrant proprietors—George Geopfert reported $1,150 as early as 1866— but the rewards for most shopowners were much more modest.

Although the Irish and their children predominated at the cracker bakery and at Smiths', journeymen of German parentage formed the mainstay of the city's smaller bakeries and confectioneries, whether owned by native, English, or German proprietors. These journeymen were almost as volatile as the sons of Erin although they more often achieved self-employment. The odds of low wages, long hours, and the substantial capital usual in bakeries employing even three to four men—at least $3,000 by 1860—were against many journeymen bakers saving enough to open their own businesses.

The career of Hesse-born John Haupt illustrates the difficulties of saving enough to open a shop and also the frequent changes in employment among journeymen in a trade notorious for bad working conditions. Not until Haupt had become head baker for a Poughkeepsie firm in 1865 at age 20 did he earn as much as $12 per week including board. At that rate his maximum earnings for a year could be no more than $600, less than the salaries of the better-paid clerkships in retailing even when board is considered. Haupt had begun his career in baking at age 13 soon after arrival in Brooklyn; seven years and six employers later, he had worked himself up to second hand in a New York City bakery.[21]

Haupt worked for two native proprietors in Poughkeepsie, as foreman for one and cake baker for another. But he also took employment subsequently with a German baker, Charles Arras, and with two other firms in New York City before making his first try at business for himself in East New York. Failure there was followed by six years further employment with Arras in Poughkeepsie. Not until 1878, now age 33, did Haupt succeed in establishing himself in a modest business.

Limitations on the prosperity of most individual bakeries and confectioneries did not prevent them from multiplying in number as the city expanded. On the contrary, by the turn of the century the demand for freshly baked bread as well as for cookies, cakes, pies, and pastries supported twice as many shops in Poughkeepsie as in 1870 although the population had increased by only 20 percent. Not until the twentieth century would regional and national manufacturers' invasion of local markets sharply reduce the opportunities for local craftsmen in the food trades.

Small scale and hand methods survived longest in cigar making and most obviously in retail baking and butchering — reduced to the specialty of meat cutting by the 1890s — and immigrant artisans continued to benefit from this survival. But the early if usually modest success of so many German craftsmen at mid-century occurred in a greater variety of handicrafts, a success reflecting the special circumstances created by coincidence of the deteriorating situation of artisans in the German states and the limited progress as yet of specialization and mechanization in most handicrafts in the United States.[22]

The organization of German crafts and the competition within them prepared emigrants to capitalize upon the uneven pace of industrialization in America, especially the lag between the time ready-made goods became common and the time they took to dominate local markets. By 1880 the limitations of the initial prosperity of German artisans in Poughkeepsie and their upward mobility as shopowners had become evident, pointing up how much their successful adaptation had been a fortuitous result of the right people arriving at the right time.

The German artisans who emigrated to America during the thirties and forties and to a lesser extent during the fifties stood at the opposite pole in mentality from the proverbially inventive Yankee, ever in search of new ways of making his fortune. They were refugees from change, specifically, from the overpopulation and the extension of economic freedom within the German states, which threatened not only their individual prosperity but also the stability and cherished old ways of the small home towns from which they so frequently came. Especially before the Revolution of 1848, these artisans tended to be masters with their own shops, property, and families rather than apprentices or unmarried journeymen, masters who still had enough property to pay for their travel and to set up in business for themselves in the New World.

Such self-employed artisans comprised almost all of the 28 Germans in the 1845 directory for the village of Poughkeepsie. Newcomers in the censuses of 1850 and 1860 more often were single young men and included an important minority of unskilled workers, but the artisans among them — 50 and 60 percent of the census totals respectively — seem to differ from the first arrivals only in the greater frequency with which they worked for other employers before setting up their own shops and changed trades during their youth.

The conservatism of these emigrating artisans had a special character which shaped their occupational adaptation in America. They looked back with nostalgia to a social system which integrated the political, social, and economic life of their town so as to ensure the virtue and livelihood of its citizens and exclude alien, disrupting elements of every kind.

Morality, respectability, prosperity, and the status of family man and citizen inhered in proper initiation into and practice of one's craft. Dominant in practice during the eighteenth century, that ideal continued to motivate the losing battle artisans fought in the German states during the first half of the nineteenth century to perpetuate guild regulation against the progressive encroachments of economic liberalism. Such an ideal hardly encouraged a pragmatic, opportunistic approach to occupational adaptation in the New World.

At the same time, the facts of an evident surplus of artisans in Germany by the 1840s and increasingly ruinous competition among them taught new lessons about the tactics necessary for survival. In the larger towns and cities many masters lost their independence for all practical purposes when merchants and dealers were given the legal right to accept orders for custom work and repairing as well as to sell finished goods. Owners of small shops soon found it necessary to supplement their direct orders from individual customers with orders they filled for merchants more cheaply or else to become wage-earners working in their own homes.

The very marginality of the shops to which so many German handworkers were accustomed better prepared them as immigrants for a close struggle for survival. American artisans could not easily compete with them in habits, standard of living, and expectations. The 1860 report of the New York Association for the Improvement of the Condition of the Poor described the impact of the Germans "who settle in our large towns, where they almost always monopolize certain branches of trade and industry. They can work for less wages than Americans, and live where an Irishman would starve. As they limit their wants to their necessities, and rarely spend all they earn, they generally become prosperous money-making citizens."[23]

Within the limits of the handicraft tradition, Germans in America showed as much adaptability as men of native parentage. They do not seem to have been handicapped by any strong sense of commitment to particular crafts, whether the crafts of their fathers or the crafts in which they first apprenticed. Indeed, as the guild system broke down, impatience with the traditional apprenticeship mounted within the German states themselves. Young men shortened their training and also switched trades when opportunity beckoned.

Among the 25 relatively successful German immigrants in Poughkeepsie for whom detailed biographies exist, father's occupation in Germany is specified for 12 sons. Only five of these sons first apprenticed in their father's trade or profession and only two, a butcher and a shoemaker, pursued it for life. Only 10 of the 25 subjects followed the trade they themselves started in. One finished an apprenticeship as a combmaker in Wimpfen, Hesse, and then spent two years learning butchering before coming to America. Another apprenticed as a cooper at Kreuznach in the Rhine province but began learning the baker's trade as soon as he arrived in New York City. And change of trade was not confined to the period of apprenticeship.

The careers of the most successful Germans do mislead in one important respect. While these proprietors made money initially within their trades at a time when older methods of manufacture still prevailed, their increase in fortunes primarily reflected subsequent shrewd investment. Peter Thielman, the shoemaker-turned-shoe merchant, Jacob Bahret, the merchant tailor, and Jacob Blankenhorn, the butcher, became moneylenders and landlords to their countrymen who emigrated later. Charles Kirchner, the butcher, speculated so successfully in local real estate that he became the largest taxpayer in the city by 1900. Only Mark Shwartz, the next richest German, depended primarily upon his trade for his fortune.[24]

Most German artisans achieved more modest prosperity. While their record in achieving independence, in going into business for themselves and advertising in the city's business directory, far exceeds the performance of any other immigrant group, their careers in business tended to be easier and more successful in the fifties and sixties than in the seventies and eighties. A comparison of Germans assessed in the tax lists of 1880 and 1890 is symptomatic. Fortunes made earlier have grown larger by 1890, but there are hardly any names added to the ranks of those with property assessed at more than $10,000.

We have seen the reasons for this apparent failure of later German immigrants and of the native-born of German parentage to equal the record of the earlier immigrants in the credit reports of R. G. Dun and Company on craft-related shops, especially in the trades suffering most from skill dilution. Until the mid-sixties artisans with their own shops often are reported as doing a "snug" business and "making more than a living" in trades like tailoring and shoemaking by combining custom work with a limited stock of ready-made goods. By the early seventies a growing number of reports state that the artisan has no shop or has a very small shop with a poorly assorted stock of ready-made goods, that he works at his bench at home jobbing for local stores or that he does a "repairing business," and that he barely makes a living.

In the short run, German artisans had adapted to Poughkeepsie's economy with impressive results, becoming preeminent in the food and apparel trades. But in the longer run this very concentration seems to have been a disadvantage in the competition for occupational and property mobility. The early careers of the second generation forecast the future. The native-born of German parentage number more clerks but also more factory operatives than the immigrant generation. They appear even less often than young Irish-Americans among the early graduates of the city's high school. Furthermore, young skilled workers in the second generation did not achieve—at least prior to the eighties—a more diverse and balanced distribution among the crafts; rather they tended to cluster in relatively low paying trades like cigar making, butchering, barbering, and coopering. Although 13 percent of the 408 native-born men of German parentage in 1880 reported themselves at clerical and sales jobs compared to 6 percent at ordinary labor and 5 percent at the shoe factory, 22 percent listed themselves at the four crafts just named.[25]

Ironically but almost predictably, the second generation seems to have been victimized by the success of the first generation in these crafts. Other things being equal, employers and foremen preferred to hire relatives, friends, and fellow countrymen in about that order. The native-born of German parentage apparently took the path of least difficulty, disproportionately choosing trades which satisfy two criteria: preference in hiring and reasonable likelihood of continuing employment. They did avoid, for the most part, crafts now experiencing contraction or stagnation in work force in which the immigrant generation had done well, such as cabinet making, shoe-

making, and tailoring. But they did not make much headway in
the building trades or in well-rewarded skilled industrial callings
such as machinist, moulder, and engineer. Examination of these
trades that the Germans did not enter in any numbers provides a
useful perspective on the comparative advantages and limitations of
their occupational adaptation in Poughkeepsie.

Building Trades

Men of native parentage continued to dominate carpentry, painting, and machine work. Comparison of these crafts with three other
building and industrial trades paying high wages, in which the Irish
soon became important, heightens this initial sense of native advantage. In iron moulding, stone and brick masonry, and plumbing,
the first and second generation Irish together were more numerous
than natives by 1870. These three trades involved more heavy, dirty,
and hot tasks than the customary work of carpenters, painters,
machinists, and engineers.[26] Moreover, their skills could not be
transferred as easily to other occupations. Even in these trades with
less attractive tasks, natives remained the second largest group,
comprising a little less than one half of the moulders and the
plumbers and gas fitters and more than one third of the masons. (In
all three, natives claimed a larger proportion of employers.) Only in
masonry did first and second generation Germans together comprise
more than one tenth of the work force and this strong a foothold in
the trade did not develop until the seventies.

Domination of the skilled trades with the highest wage rates gave
men of native parentage some economic advantage over immigrant
workers in the handicrafts but less than the rates alone suggest. The
building trades show the limitations of that advantage for achieving
sustained occupational mobility within and especially between generations. Because these trades remained relatively unaffected either
by skill dilution or by extra-local competition, they also emphasize
the pervasiveness of insecurity in the careers of artisans and bosses as
well as journeymen.

While building technology and financial arrangements evolved,
the construction industry continued to be more largely local with
more room for the small, independent operator than most industries.[27] Although some work previously done by carpenters in their
own shops during the winter now passed increasingly to specialized

outsiders—notably the manufacture of sashes, blinds, stairs, doors, and mouldings—the building crafts on the whole remained less subdivided than manufacturing crafts. Experienced journeymen continued to perform the variety of tasks associated with their trades.

Journeymen faced no major obstacles in becoming self-employed, needing no more than the reputation and ability to organize a crew of workmen, to find a client willing to contract, and to arrange credit. Writers of success manuals often advised young men to choose these trades precisely because they offered an easier avenue to self-employment.[28] In masonry and plumbing and gasfitting where the Irish provided the most workers, Irishmen also figured as bosses and shop foremen, if not in equal proportion. Most of the biggest employers continued to be natives, the major exception being the boss mason and general builder and contractor, William Harloe, an Irish Episcopalian who employed many of his Catholic countrymen.

Harloe was no exception, however, to the fluctuations in fortune endemic in construction. The city's biggest builder, he maintained offices in New York City and undertook major projects throughout the Hudson valley, employing anywhere between 30 and 80 men. Reports to R. G. Dun and Company chronicle his ups and downs between 1860 and 1880.[29] On the eve of the Civil War, he already had a reputation for doing a large business on little capital. By 1861 a credit reporter predicted that he would make money on his many contracts for "Vassar Female College," but the rise in the cost of building materials during the last two years of war ruined him. Harloe had to give up the contract and took advantage of the bankruptcy act to escape creditors.

By the early seventies he had resumed and was "doing quite a business in building mostly out of the city." By 1877 reports circulated that he had a good chance of securing the contract for the new state capitol at Albany. But by 1878 the prolonged depression made his heavy involvement in real estate embarrassing financially. A year later, having just been elected mayor of the city, he called a meeting of creditors pleading for an extension of time on maturing obligations until he could complete some contracts. Soon afterward, however, he made an assignment with liabilities of $86,000 and assets of only $7,500. This second failure did not prevent him from continuing in business as an architect and builder.

Two of the largest builders with a predominantly local business, both carpenters by trade, found themselves periodically in a financial pinch although neither actually failed. Of one of them a credit reporter commented in 1871, "has been a builder here a long time, does good work and is quite popular. Takes contracts, speculates in real estate sometimes . . . he is always short of money and is slow pay."[30]

The bigger builders rarely went out of business even temporarily; but the swings of building activity and personal fortune sometimes forced bosses to resume as journeymen or take other jobs whether or not they actually failed in business. A boss painter who employed a number of men from the mid-fifties to the end of the Civil War was described in the postwar slump as keeping "a small shop but works by the day most of the time." By 1873 he had recovered, employing "sometimes as many as thirty or forty men . . . best business here and making money."[31]

In the middle of the depression of the seventies, one credit reporter generalized: "All our builders here are poor and seem to make but little money."[32] Most industries suffered in the swing from boom to depression, but few showed such universal reduction in personal circumstance among employers. The precariousness as well as the limited extent of prosperity among bosses in the construction trades may help explain why their sons so often failed to rise above manual work, not infrequently remaining journeymen in their fathers' trades. Well over two thirds of all sons of businessmen and other nonmanual workers ended their own careers in nonmanual employment, a proportion which averages marked differences between occupations. At one extreme, nine tenths of the identifiable sons of dry goods, lumber, and commission merchants sustained their fathers' occupational level at last job in Poughkeepsie. The sons of boss carpenters, masons, and painters fall near the other extreme, with only two fifths at nonmanual jobs—a slightly lower proportion than that of the sons of saloonkeepers and peddlers.[33]

If employers in the building trades seem closer to the world of manual work and to the more marginal types of business than to the more solid sectors of the business community, their journeymen in certain respects seem to be among the more fortunate craftsmen. Employers never comprised more than one tenth of men listing themselves at carpentry, masonry, and painting but in the first two trades one fourth or more of the men reported owning some real estate at every census, a higher proportion than in many trades. The proportion partly reflects the greater frequency of older workers but also the higher incomes of those who found the steadiest employment. Among carpenters, in particular, longevity in their trade in Poughkeepsie was striking, nearly a hundred men appearing at each of three or four censuses between 1850 and 1880.

The greater irregularity and uncertainty of work in the building trades, however, meant that many journeymen did not have as much economic advantage over craftsmen in the skill-diluted food and apparel trades as they seem to in a comparison of average daily wage rates. The most highly paid, the stone and brick masons, also had the shortest working year; most bosses reported that they had given their men only six months employment in 1880. Boss carpenters and painters reported between eight and ten months work. Boss plumbers reported at least part-time employment year round.

Periodic unemployment, whether seasonal or due to interruptions of work, encouraged migration in search of jobs elsewhere, especially among masons. The *Eagle* reported in September 1879 that unemployed masons "complained of being laid off a long time to await the arrival of certain material, and some of them left town and went to other places." Local newspapers frequently reported on jobs available in masonry throughout the region, urging unemployed journeymen to take advantage of them. Noting that the superintendent of Sing Sing prison down the river had advertised for bids for an immense wall, the *Eagle* commented, "Here is an opportunity for some of our Poughkeepsie masons to get employment."[34]

Only about two fifths of the masons at any census persisted in the city by the end of the decade, a low rate for the crafts. Those leaving sometimes spent much of their careers far from home. A Poughkeepsie-born mason learned his trade in the city but pursued it for years in Bedford, Ohio, and Lowell, Massachusetts, as well as nearer towns in New York like Newburgh and Kingston before returning in his fifties as agent for a plaster manufacturer.[35] The rates of persistence for stonecutters and marble workers ranged between a mere one eighth and one third persisting each decade. Marble workers employed in local monument works stayed most often. Stonecutters overwhelmingly proved transient because they depended upon the larger building jobs.

Stonecutting and masonry became the most polyglot of the construction crafts. Work crews of mixed nationality were usual, but the success of an immigrant boss normally meant better opportunities in the trade for countrymen. The Germans developed a firm foothold in only one trade by 1880, masonry, helped by the success of Eli Spross, a Bavarian Catholic, and Ernest Hochstadter, a Prussian Lutheran. Hochstadter, who spent his early years in Brooklyn in trucking and then in paving, came to Poughkeepsie in 1871 with the contract for building most of the city's sewers. Spross had come to Poughkeepsie directly, doing the mason work at the furnace with his brother and later at iron works in Cold Spring, Peekskill, and other places along the Hudson. He began contracting on his own account after seven years and in the seventies won major contracts for work on the insane asylum.[36]

Industrial Trades

The pattern of expanding immigrant employment in trades where their fellow countrymen had some responsibility in hiring characterized the new and highly paid industrial trades, too. Once again, immigrants other than the English and Scotch made headway only in the trade which had the least pleasant working conditions, iron moulding. Immigrant foremen helped. In 1880, for example, Irish-born but Brooklyn-educated James Carroll had been boss moulder and shop foreman for fifteen years at the city's largest foundry; with the single exception of one black tin and sheet iron worker, all of the seven moulders, one melter, and three helpers listed at the foundry in an 1879 county directory were first or second generation Irish. At the smaller Dutchess Iron Works where the foreman and master moulder was English, the other moulder and three machinists listed there in the same directory were all native-born.

By 1880 sons of Irish laborers and immigrant laborers themselves who had learned the trade on the job in Poughkeepsie had become a substantial minority among moulders. The capital required for a foundry precluded self-employment in that line for poor immigrants, but moulding did provide one of the quickest ways to accumulate money for small businesses in other lines. By 1881 James Carroll had saved enough from wages of $4 per day to open a meat market; in 1880 another moulder of Irish parentage started a shoe business.[37]

Men of native parentage dominated machine work throughout the period, the English and Scottish forming the largest minority. Since skilled workers formed a much larger proportion of both nationalities than they did of the Irish, there is no surprise in the greater frequency of craftsmen rather than laborers among the fathers of machinists and engineers. There is a suggestion of preference in hiring in the recruitment each decade of some natives previously employed at less skilled jobs in the city; almost none of the relatively few immigrant machinists and engineers ever report another occupation.

Most members of both trades worked in relatively large establishments with secure as well as highly paid employment. An employee by job definition, the engineer normally worked alone in all but large factories. He raised the steam in the morning, shut down at night, and had "plenty of work to do Sundays, washing out boilers, keying up engines, making joints, grinding valves and many other things which we cannot do while steam is up."[38] He also had the most transferrable of skills, needed in every kind of manufacture employing steam power.

The well-trained machinist had fewer options in employment than the engineer but more versatility than most other craftsmen. The increasing importance of precision metal working for a variety of manufactures brought a rapid expansion of the trade in Poughkeepsie as in other cities during the middle decades. Throughout the period, a small minority achieved self-employment, usually manufacturing some specialty—frequently a patent of their own invention. As often as not, the business came to grief or earned not much more than a livelihood for the owners and an assistant or two.[39]

In the late fifties several local machinists formed a partnership with financial backing from a rich family to manufacture a mill patented by one of the firm; the partnership soon dissolved, the inventor went on alone but failed two years later and then started up again in New York City. Another machinist persuaded local capitalists to incorporate an unsuccessful venture for manufacturing his patented churn. Even small machine shops doing a more general business often had a hard time. Gale and Spencer went out of business not long after a credit report describing them as "good mechanics, . . . in business six or seven years, have never made much money."[40]

For journeyman machinists, wages and working conditions as late as the early seventies remained more favorable than in almost any other trade. But the continuing expansion of industrial trades during the depression decade brought a sudden sharp rise in the proportion of the work force recruited locally from other and mostly unrelated occupations. Twenty eight percent of the machinists of 1880, 23 percent of the engineers, and 20 percent of the moulders had been employed in Poughkeepsie in 1870 at other kinds of jobs. This influx of "green hands" and the fact that the employers enumerated in the 1880 manufacturing census reported daily wage rates similar to those prevailing in many crafts that year, suggest that the deterioration of the industrial trades so widely complained of in the eighties was under way. By the latter part of that decade machinists' unions throughout the state reported "managers and owners putting at work inexperienced hands, which has degraded the skill of an old apprentice or a mechanic who has served his time . . . The tendency of wages is downward in our trade owing to improvements in machinery and boy-labor, although the improvements and inventions are our own nine times out of ten."[41]

Unlike skill dilution earlier in the traditional handicrafts, the increasing use of green hands in machine work after the seventies did not bring much increase in the proportion of first and second generation Irish and Germans. In the 1896 directory German and Irish names were a little more common among the city's machinists and engineers, about one fourth of the total. But men of native and British parentage clearly still predominated. Three fifths of the moulders of 1870 had been of Irish and German birth or parentage; names associated with those nationalities comprised only half of the 1896 total. The industrial trades grew faster than Poughkeepsie's population, but the city did not experience the rapid and sustained expansion of producer goods manufacturing which occurred in major industrial centers during the late nineteenth century. Such an expansion might have increased employment for the native-born of Irish and German parentage in the industrial trades. For men of native parentage in these trades there was no ready escape from skill dilution by the eighties. The upsurge in unionism showed how ubiquitous and serious the problem of "green hands" had become throughout the skilled crafts.

The occupational alternatives for even the former aristocrats of the skilled trades increasingly would fall within the same range as those of most manual workers. The upper ceiling for their careers usually would be petty white-collar status, whether as proprietors of small businesses or as clerks and salesmen. Machinists and engineers might have more opportunities as supervisors in large manufacturing establishments than other manual workers, but they ordinarily would not become employers themselves. Their children who began at white-collar work may have done so more often by the turn of the century, but those careers extend beyond this tracing.

The narrowing range of occupational mobility for skilled artisans and other manual workers suggests the gradual emergence of a working-class world in which most manual workers would have more in common with each other than they would with substantial businessmen and other members of the "solid" middle class. The broad separation between business and working-class worlds which the Lynds described for Middletown in the twenties seems to us the probable result of the tendencies in occupational mobility in Poughkeepsie by 1880, as the discussion of mobility among factory operatives and their children will suggest even more strongly in the next chapter.[42] As specialization progressed toward the minute subdivision of work and close supervision promoted by scientific management after the turn of the century, the work in most industries except construction would become more similar in scope and organization than in the middle decades.[43]

National data on range in wages between 1860 and 1890 does not show any narrowing. Specialization upgraded some jobs while downgrading others. To the extent that certain specialized tasks remained more valuable and difficult to learn, rewards for those tasks would be higher than for practice of the whole craft previously. Moreover, wherever skill dilution resulted from mechanization rather than from division of labor, displacing men outright rather than limiting the tasks they performed, then journeymen who kept their jobs often benefited from the increased productivity by improvement in wages. The upper and lower extremes of the hierarchy in wages for manual workers in the United States apparently widened a little between 1860 and 1890. Workers identified on company payrolls by the name of a trade rather than a task slightly increased their advantage in wages over men identified as laborers. More revealing of the impact of specialization, the differentials between foremen and journeymen and between journeymen and apprentices and helpers also increased slightly. How much this small improvement in the wages of skilled compared to other manual workers owed to unionization, especially during the eighties, has not been determined.[44] Nor can one do more than speculate whether the rise in real wages in the last two decades of the century and corresponding improvement in standard of living eased the adjustment of artisans to a world where they no longer had ready access to the prosperous middle class.

The protests of American craftsmen throughout the eighties — including the testimony of artisans gathered by the Senate Committee on Education and Labor and by the emerging state bureaus of labor statistics — suggest that they had not been impressed with a sense of improvement but rather that they were painfully conscious of the limitations on their traditional avenue of mobility, self-employment at their trade. In a growing number of crafts self-employment usually offered little more than a livelihood, if that, and almost never the substantial prosperity formerly possible.

Artisans of every nationality suffered this consequence of skill dilution. Men of native parentage, however, had the advantage in construction trades and newer industrial trades where dilution had the least impact before 1880. The consequences for immigrants and their children, especially the Germans, seem more severe not only because dilution came earlier on the whole to the handicrafts the newcomers dominated but also because self-employment in these crafts had been their major avenue of occupational mobility and the basis for the early prosperity they had won in their New World home.

9

Factories as Levelers

THE ONE CLEAR hierarchical division for manual workers traditionally had been between craftsmen and less skilled workers. Artisans had been set apart by their superior opportunities for independence and prosperity as well as by the nature of their work and training. Increase in specialization within the crafts lessened these differences as we have seen, but the expansion of factories blurred traditional distinctions most as this chapter will show. In Poughkeepsie the growing number of operatives trained to limited tasks rather than to trades received higher wages than ordinary laborers and sometimes as much as those paid journeymen in trades injured by skill dilution. Longevity in employment at one factory for many of these operatives blurred another traditional distinction between the artisan and the laborer, the usual irregularity of the laborer's jobs.

This chapter compares the opportunities of native whites and of first and second generation newcomers, especially the Irish, in factory employment. Although immigrants never came close to monopolizing factory work in Poughkeepsie as they did in some American cities, it provided an important means of improvement for the unskilled among them. No blacks obtained this type of employment between 1850 and 1880.

Unlike the chapters on other occupational groups, this one depends primarily upon directories to identify its subjects. For with the exception of the chair and the sash and blind factories, the federal censuses did not specify factory operatives with any fullness or consistency prior to 1880 in Poughkeepsie. Even in the case of the chair factory, employment there often must be inferred from the census specification of tasks—such as bottomer, caner, and varnisher—rather than of the factory itself.

Because the census enumerators asked for occupation rather than place of employment, most artisans who worked in factories in Poughkeepsie reported only their trade; unskilled and even semiskilled workers in factories usually identified themselves merely as laborers. Fortunately, several city directories in the mid-forties and the fifties identify many of these laborers in factories and a remarkable county directory in 1879 not only does that but also identifies place of employment for many skilled craftsmen in factories like the mower works. Information on their probable tasks in local sources is spotty so that our attempt to reconstruct the work process in individual factories has had to rely in part upon inference from accounts of the industry elsewhere in America at that time.

Launched three decades before the famine immigration, textiles had been Poughkeepsie's first major industry and also its first industry to dwindle. In the thirties several hundred workers manufactured woolen yarn and carpets and cotton and silk fabrics. The census of 1850 showed only one of three carpet factories surviving with 57 male and 36 female employees, one of three cotton factories still making cloth with 25 male and 45 female workers and a small yarn factory employing 12 men and 9 women. All but Pelton's carpet factory, already converted to steam by 1850, would be gone by 1860.

The skilled textile workers had formed a distinct ethnic enclave, living close to their factories along the ponds of the Fallkill. Four fifths of the 55 weavers enumerated in 1850 had been born in England and Scotland as had almost all of the spinners, carders, and dyers. The weavers alone comprised 14 percent of all male workers of those nationalities in the village that year. By 1860 the number of weavers had been cut in half; never again would the British in Poughkeepsie concentrate so heavily in one industry. The few new weavers appearing in the sixties and seventies were youths of Irish and German birth or parentage, very probably "green hands."

The diminishing remnant of English and Scottish weavers became progressively older; a high proportion disappeared from the trade by departure from the city or by shifting to other occupations there. In the fifties alone, three quarters of the 44 British-born emigrated or died; of the eleven who remained in the city, three appeared in 1860 as grocer, brewer, and farmer. For the departing British weavers, geographic mobility within the United States was not new. Of 41 weavers reporting children in the census at Poughkeepsie, 11 listed sons and daughters born in other states, suggesting frequent movement between textile centers. An English-born carder in 1850 reported five children born in New York State ranging from 21 to one years of age, but interspersed were a 12 year old born in Pennsylvania and a 3 year old born in New Jersey.

The Irish and Germans who entered the city in such numbers in the late forties and early fifties were never as heavily concentrated in one industry as the British, but German and Irish immigrants together comprised a majority of workers in three of the city's largest manufacturing enterprises in the fifties: the brewery, dye wood mill, and furnace (Table 9.1). True to stereotype these enterprises employed more unskilled than skilled labor and offered the unskilled tasks that were unusually heavy, dirty, or hot and sometimes all three. Yet economic necessity alone does not adequately explain the relation of immigrants to these industries. The sharp contrast in stability of employment between the furnace and dye wood mill suggests that loyalties could be created — as they apparently were at the furnace — by a coincidence of better pay, nepotism, and a sense that the work itself did not demean, that its very difficulty had dignity.

The blast furnace, opened in 1848 and enlarged in 1852, provided the largest number of relatively permanent jobs in manufacturing for Catholics, German as well as Irish. A pastor of the German parish recalled that some of these Catholics "were trained iron mongers from outside and therefore they were very welcome here."[1] Although whites of native parentage as late as 1856 comprised nearly one third of the 38 identifiable furnace employees, they moved away from the city or changed jobs within it far more frequently than the immigrants. The Germans and Irish, each about one third of the total, shared a common Catholicism, a higher frequency of relatives

TABLE 9.1. Ethnic composition of factory work forces[a]

Factory	Year	Native-born native parent (percent)	Irish-born (percent)	Native-born Irish parent (percent)	German-born (percent)	Native-born German parent (percent)	British-born (percent)	Native-born British parent (percent)	Number of cases
Furnace	1856	31.5	34.0	—	28.9	—	2.6	2.6	38
	1879	8.3	56.3	6.3	19.8	9.4	—	—	96
Dye wood	1879	31.0	44.8	13.8	3.4	3.4	—	—	29
Chair	1850	78.8	6.3	—	3.8	—	3.8	—	80
	1860	49.4	11.2	2.2	15.7	4.5	7.9	1.1	89
	1880	71.1	—	10.5	2.6	10.5	2.6	—	38
Buckeye	1879	60.2	11.0	5.1	8.5	5.1	3.4	2.5	118
Skilled only		65.3	10.7	2.7	8.0	4.0	5.3	4.0	75
Unskilled only		51.2	11.6	9.3	9.3	7.0	—	—	43
Shoe	1880	49.1	14.5	18.2	1.8	10.0	2.7	2.7	220
Glass	1880	35.4	7.3	31.7	2.4	4.9	18.3	—	82
Skilled only		46.2	2.6	10.3	2.6	—	38.5	—	39
Unskilled only		25.6	11.6	51.2	2.3	9.3	—	—	43

[a]Data for the years 1850, 1860, 1870, and 1880 come from the federal census; data for 1856 come from the *Poughkeepsie City Directory—1856-57* (J. I. Underhill, Publisher) and for 1879 from the *Dutchess County Directory* published that year by G. Lawrence.

also at the furnace and greater stability in employment there. These newcomers anticipate the general tendency of their countrymen to settle down in Poughkeepsie in occupations where they became pre-eminent or even a large minority.

The German Adamses, Stouts, and Millers remained furnacemen from the fifties to the eighties, some of them moving to the stacks near the upper landing in the sixties and others remaining at the older lower furnace. Germans became foremen and yard bosses at both. Burnses provided continuity for the Irish, one of them becoming foundryman at the lower furnace in the sixties. The Irish steadily increased their proportion until by 1879 they comprised nearly two thirds of the 96 identifiable furnace workers compared to more than one fourth for the Germans and less than one tenth for whites of native parentage. Three fifths of this work force had been employed in Poughkeepsie for a decade or more, a degree of stability unmatched in most manufacturing enterprises. The lower furnace closed during the eighties, but two fifths of the 1879 upper furnace workers still worked there in 1890 or nearly 70 percent of those who remained in Poughkeepsie at that date.

This stability of immigrants at the furnaces does not lend itself to easy explanation by any notion of superior opportunity. The reward for laborers there remained better than for casual labor, but improvements in the construction of blast furnaces increased productivity without increasing the skill required of workers. The work there remained hotter, dirtier, heavier and more dangerous than in most of the city's manufacturing.[2] Bad times brought extended layoffs; the *Eagle* noted in 1876 that one stack at the Upper Furnace was being blown out for the first time in three years in response to increased prosperity.[3] Children did not go on to better occupations usually. The number of sons working in the city at skilled metal trades was negligible; the vast majority appear at laboring or no designated occupation. More of the employed daughters appear as servants than as dressmakers.

The furnaces seem to have valued experience and fragmentary evidence suggests a camaraderie among furnacemen, the toughness of their work enhancing its manliness. By contrast, the dye wood mill, neighbor to the upper furnace, depended primarily upon younger and relatively transient workers. A mere one fourth of its identifiable workers in 1879 had been employed in the city a decade earlier. Machines cut and ground the woods imported primarily

from the West Indies; the woods had to be unloaded at the river
front and moved through the phases of manufacture, but the work
was less demanding and dangerous than a furnaceman's.

The Irish comprised two thirds of that factory by 1856 and only
slightly less in 1879; they provided what little continuity in work
force existed. Patrick Hannan still walked the mile or so down the
river slope from his house on Bridge Street, his oldest son now joining him at the mill. But Hannan was the exception even among his
countrymen. Native workers in the mill appear even more frequently to be drifters from job to job. Massachusetts-born Edwin
Stearns had reported himself previously as a moulder, than a saloonkeeper; 24 year old William Robinson had been a painter and
would later work on the railroad; his father had reported himself
successively as laborer, boatman, and shoemaker.

Unlike the furnaces which evidently valued experience and loyalty, the dye wood mill depended primarily upon younger and relatively transient workers. Few men spent their working lives in the
mill; sons rarely followed their fathers there. Tracing subsequent
occupational careers indicates that mill employment did not pre-
pare men for better opportunities. Overwhelmingly they remained
in less skilled manual jobs and so did their children. The three
younger sons of Patrick Hannan started at the shoe factory and two
of them later became ironers in a laundry. Other Irish millworkers'
children found employment as servants, workers in other factories,
and laborers on the railroad, the new bridge or occasional tasks.
The one great exception became president in 1907 of the city's large
overall factory, succeeding the son of the native banker who
founded it. Starting as an office boy at that factory, William J. Leahey "advanced through all grades to the top."[4]

Irish and German workers did not comprise a majority of the
work force in any other industry in Poughkeepsie which was
dominated by large shops or factories. In the manufacture of agricultural implements and — except from the mid-fifties to the early
sixties — of chairs, two thirds of the wage-earners remained men of
native parentage. The proportion of newcomers increased in factories opened during the seventies, but by then the second generation
benefited more than immigrants. In the new Whitehouse shoe
factory founded in 1870, males of native parentage accounted for
about half of the 243 male workers in 1880 or the same as they did in
the labor force as a whole. The native-born of foreign — especially

Irish—parentage made up nearly one third and the foreign-born one fifth. The same tendency to greater representation of the second generation than of immigrants appears in the garment factories founded during the depression and in the glass factory opened in 1880. Younger workers predominated in the new enterprises of the seventies. Although the foreign-born remained half again more numerous than the second generation in the male labor force as a whole, the second generation already was nearly five times more numerous among workers less than 30 years old in these factories.

The continuing predominance of men of native parentage in so many of the city's factories poses two questions. First, did these factories offer much more highly skilled or remunerative work than the furnaces, dye wood mill, and brewery? Second, within these factories did men of native parentage hold the more highly skilled jobs? Comparing the two factories where native advantage remained greatest, the answer to the first question is yes—but the native proportion does not correspond consistently to the level of skill required.

The Buckeye mower works had the highest proportion of skilled craftsmen; machinists, moulders, and blacksmiths comprised a majority of its work force, not including more specialized workers such as grinders and file cutters. These craftsmen had more freedom in pursuing their work than operatives in most factories.[5] They identified with their trades more than with their place of employment or the product they made; two thirds of the workers ever designated as skilled there reported themselves by their trades throughout their working careers in Poughkeepsie. If less skilled first jobs are eliminated then the proportion so reporting themselves rises to more than three fourths.

By contrast, the greater subdivision of labor at the chair factories required less skill of most workers. By 1860 these factories reported an array of specialized woodworking machinery, including boring, morticing, tenoning, doweling, turning, and planing machines. These machines made possible the employment of greener hands. Unlike skilled workers at Buckeye who reported themselves at their trades, almost all these workers reported themselves as chair maker or as at the chair factory. Moreover, of the 73 men so designated in the census who also remained employed in the city for at least a decade, little more than half reported themselves again at those designations or at closely related trades like those of cabinet maker, turner, carpenter, or painter. Wages correspondingly were lower than at Buckeye. Whereas the rate for skilled labor at the mower works exceeded the going rate in most firms, the pay for supposedly skilled labor in the chair factories by 1880 was no more than the average for ordinary labor in the city.

The chair factories subcontracted for some of their work to be done outside. The caning of seats consistently had been put out to women who did the work in their homes, this task employing an estimated 200 to 300 persons around 1880. Some of the work done by men, notably varnishing and painting, also could be done outside the factory. Throughout the sixties a chair finisher and painter took contracts from Arnold & Co., his prosperity and number of men employed fluctuating with the volume of their business.[6]

Even though the chair factories were less remunerative and less skilled, Buckeye in the long run proved to be more hospitable to the employment of immigrants. By 1880 men of native parentage comprised 71 percent of the chair factory workers compared to 61 percent at Buckeye. For the few years before and after 1860 when chairmaking boomed in Poughkeepsie, half of the work force became foreign-born. But as the industry declined, so did the proportion of German and Irish workers.

This decline did not result from the foreign-born persisting less often in the factories but rather from an increase in men of native parentage in new hiring in the industry. Whether this increase owes more to employer preference for native workers or the willingness of these natives to work for less cannot be determined; but certainly these new recruits had no apparent advantage over immigrant chairmakers who left the factories for other employment. All of the foreign-born who shifted out as chair making contracted took up skilled work or vending. Several Germans worked only briefly in the factories before opening shops in unrelated lines like shoemaking and groceries, suggesting that they may have chosen factory employment as a stopgap until they could find opportunities to practice as journeymen the skills they brought with them or to find capital for self-employment.

The possibility remains that the immigrants who found employment at Buckeye or other factories with more highly skilled work forces were confined to unskilled jobs and that their children also fared less well than the children of skilled native workers. At one extreme, a clear stratification of workers by ethnic origin did occur in the glass works; native-born workers of Irish parentage comprised one half of the ordinary labor there but less than one tenth of the skilled blowers, nearly half of whom were native and nearly two fifths British. The company imported the blowers, some earning as much as $125 per month, but hired local laborers — predominantly teenagers — to serve as mould, snapping-up, carrying-in, and gathering boys.[7] Even at Buckeye which did employ first and second generation immigrants at its skilled trades, men of native parentage still accounted for nearly two thirds of employees designated with skilled trades compared to one half of those designated "works Buckeye." Buckeye may have been less willing to train newcomers in skills they did not already possess. Only two of the 15 machinists of foreign birth or parentage had been enumerated previously at unskilled labor compared to eight of the 25 machinists of native parentage.

Neither possible native advantage in hiring and on-the-job training nor the underrepresentation of men of foreign birth and parentage among Buckeye's craftsmen, however, predict the opportunities for children of immigrants who found any employment at the mower works. For the children of Buckeye workers show little difference in occupational achievement regardless of whether fathers were skilled or unskilled or had native or foreign parents. A minority of the sons and daughters of both found white-collar employment, mostly petty in character; a smaller minority appeared at other factory, service, or unskilled jobs; and the remainder, a bare majority, listed themselves at skilled jobs with metal trades predominating and some sons specified as working at Buckeye. A native had one son who became a draughtsman but another labored at the glass works. The son of an Irish-born machinist worked for some years in a machine shop before becoming a letter carrier.

Unskilled workers at Buckeye do not seem to have been at any disadvantage compared to the skilled in persuading Buckeye's foremen to train their boys as machinists and moulders. A native's oldest boy started at the silk factory but then became a moulder at Buckeye, later working at that trade for the Separator factory; another son also learned moulding. The son of a Dane became a machinist. In this way Buckeye helped narrow the differences in opportunity one might expect between the children of the factory's skilled and its unskilled workers.

Skilled apprenticeships for sons of unskilled workers at Buckeye constitute only one, if a rather special, instance of an apparently general tendency of Poughkeepsie's factories in this period to level differences in occupational background among their workers, at least to level those differences which could be anticipated in occupational careers within and between generations. Admittedly, this index of leveling is rather broad; the hierarchy of economic reward and job security among factory operatives remains unknown in the absence of payrolls.[8] But the index does suggest that increase in manufacturing's scale and specialization progressively undermined the previously sharp distinction between artisan and laborer for men of every nativity who remained at manual work. Differentiation in occupational status became more subtle and complex and did so well before censuses and city directories began to reflect the state of specialization with any adequacy.

The most striking instance of this apparent leveling tendency appears in the coming together of sons of Irish laborers and sons of native skilled workers in the Whitehouse shoe factory, the largest single employer in Poughkeepsie during the seventies. The shoe industry had moved to a full-fledged factory system by the time Whitehouse opened in 1870 and that system had been perfected before the rebuilding of the plant in 1879 after a disastrous fire. The operatives in the new plant worked about 300 machines; more than half of them were sewing machines, but the remainder included machines for burnishing and trimming, heeling, leveling, tacking, and breasting.[9]

Because Irish in the immigrant generation concentrated so heavily in casual labor whereas manual workers of native parentage much more often reported trades, this conjunction was likely wherever their children found common employment. The improvement for the immigrants' children was substantial, if only because the minimum shoe factory wages were better than the going rates for ordinary labor. Any gain for the sons of native artisans seems dubious; the very youthfulness of the Whitehouse work force — nearly two fifths of the male workers being less than 20 years old and more than two thirds less than 30 — suggests that most of its tasks required little training or experience.

Lack of specification of tasks and responsibilities at Whitehouse makes it impossible to determine how much advantage the sons of native artisans had within the factory, but comparison by ethnicity of fathers' occupations with sons' occupations ten years after their listings at Whitehouse suggest that a narrowing of differences may have occurred at the factory. The occupational distribution of operatives of native parentage had not improved upon that of their fathers; but the proportion of native sons of Irish parentage at white-collar jobs was significantly higher and the proportion at unskilled labor lower than among their parents.

Immigrants and their children who entered Poughkeepsie's factories shared with native operatives common patterns of upward and downward occupational mobility. As long as factories did not differ too greatly in range and distribution of skills required in them, then strong similarities appear regardless of variations in the ethnic composition of their work forces. Operatives in the chair, mower, and shoe factories resemble each other in the skill levels of their fathers and in their own skill levels prior and subsequent to listings at those plants (Table 9.2). About one tenth of the fathers had been white-collar workers; a similar proportion of the operatives themselves had started at that level and would achieve it subsequently. The proportion of sons subsequently at unskilled work was less than the proportion of fathers. The most striking difference, however, suggests limitations in the significance of this upward and downward mobility. A higher proportion of Buckeye workers and their fathers appears at skilled trades in all listings; they also appear slightly less often in white-collar work. These most highly skilled and rewarded factory workers less often became clerks, grocers, saloonkeepers, cigar and variety store owners, and so on, perhaps for the good reason that much of such apparent upward mobility among former operatives did not bring more security or reward usually than Buckeye workers already had.

A few plant superintendents and shop foremen rose well above their skilled beginnings. The superintendent of Buckeye, an English machinist and inventor, was in a class by himself with an income of $1,935 by 1866 and a fashionable residence. Of the two superintendents of the shoe factory in 1879, one was only temporarily interrupting a career as carpenter and builder after failing during the depression of the seventies. The other superintendent also soon left the factory, opening a confectionery by 1885 and later resuming his previous trade of machinist. Foremen at the shoe factory seem to have been equally transient although the majority of operatives there were not. Of four identifiable foremen only Michigan-born George Hine remained at Whitehouse through most of the eighties; he left only to set up his own shoe factory in Poughkeepsie.

The foremen of Buckeye's assembling room, foundry, and

TABLE 9.2. Father's occupation, prior and subsequent occupations of identifiable members of three persisting factory work forces[a]

	Unskilled (percent)	Other semi-skilled (percent)	Factory (percent)	Skilled (percent)	Clerical (percent)	Proprietorial (percent)	Professional (percent)	Number of cases
Father's occupation								
Chair factory	25.0	5.0	17.5	40.0	–	10.0	2.5	40
Mower works	17.1	17.1	–	60.0	–	5.7	–	35
Shoe factory	23.9	21.7	4.3	35.9	2.2	8.7	2.2	92
Prior occupation								
Chair factory	36.8	–	10.5	42.1	10.5	–	–	19
Mower works	39.2	1.4	1.4	52.7	5.4	–	–	74
Shoe factory	38.5	7.7	7.7	30.8	15.4	–	–	13
Subsequent occupation								
Chair factory	14.3	5.7	28.6	34.3	5.7	10.0	1.4	70
Mower works	17.6	5.4	20.3	52.7	–	4.1	–	74
Shoe factory	18.5	5.6	44.4	17.7	4.8	8.1	0.8	124

[a]All workers in this table who were identified in factory employment between 1850 and 1880 were traced backward to 1850 and forward to 1900 through censuses and city directories. Only workers persisting at least a decade after their first identification in a factory have been included.

machine, knife, and wood shops show more stability, perhaps because their wages gave them better annual incomes than those of many small shopkeepers. Foremanships in large factories could tempt even a modestly successful proprietor. A grocer, once a chair painter himself, sold out his interest in a partnership in 1870 in order to take charge of the Finishing Department of a chair factory in New York City. The factory was partly owned by the Chichester family who had launched the first factory in that line in Poughkeepsie.[10]

The majority of factory supervisory workers who can be identified show the same range of employment as other skilled workers, however, many of their children remaining at manual work. Men of native and British parentage monopolized the top positions throughout the middle decades, but workers of German and Irish birth or parentage frequently appear as foremen. The exceptional success was James Carroll, an Irish boss moulder, who used his savings from the foundry to open a meat market; his five children became lawyers, professional nurses, and a clerk. More typically, one of the sons of a German yard boss at the lower furnace became a brakeman and then a conductor on the railroad; his brother became an engineer first at Buckeye and then at the glass works. The brother's sons joined him there by 1900; another found employment in the Separator factory.

With the exception of native-born George Hine, foremen in Poughkeepsie had no more success than other skilled workers in entering the city's entrepreneurial class after 1850. Recent immigrants also were rare among factory owners. The apparent exception, the Caire family from Bavaria which acquired the pottery works in 1842, rarely employed more than 20 workers. Like other factory owners and like many immigrant employers in craft shops, the Caires hired workers of different nationalities. Only the balance of nationalities varied from firm to firm.

In the greater tendency of native workers to hold the more attractive jobs and for the Irish especially to hold the less attractive employments in large manufacturing establishments, the factory world in Poughkeepsie reflected a general bias in hiring at mid-century. But in the frequency with which natives and newcomers came together in the same establishments, resulting in very similar patterns of subsequent occupational mobility, factories promoted a leveling between ethnic groups within the world of manual work. Immigrants and their children shared the skilled as well as the unskilled work with men of native parentage and seem to have benefited as much from it.

10

From the Bottom Up

NEITHER THE LEVELING tendency within Poughkeepsie's newer factories nor the relative stability of their work forces had many parallels in service jobs or unskilled jobs outside factories. Rather the traditional bottom rungs of the occupational hierarchy exhibit with great clarity both the economic vulnerability of the least skilled workers and ethnic stratification among them. The patterns of mobility for men who performed Poughkeepsie's menial and servile tasks confirms both the nineteenth-century faith in America as a land of opportunity and the common sense criticism then and now that those who began without advantages had the least favorable prospects. They might not be trapped at the bottom, but their progress upward would be slow and almost always by small steps.

This chapter describes the relative advantages of natives and newcomers in finding jobs within and ultimately—in the lives of their children if not their own—escaping from the city's least attractive jobs. It focuses upon whites of native parentage, blacks, and the Irish, who held most of those jobs. The British and Germans and their native-born sons together never comprised more than 15 percent of the city's unskilled or 20 percent of its service workers, being underrepresented compared to their proportion of the male labor force in both categories. Native whites also were underrepresented proportionately but comprised about one third of all unskilled workers from 1860 to 1880 and about two fifths of the service workers.

With a few exceptions, notably the craft of barbering which also is a personal service, the occupations discussed in this chapter show constant exchange of workers. They reveal the ease with which men could shift between different kinds of jobs at this level and correspondingly the low valuation of experience in them. This chapter will explore these shifts in some detail both because horizontal mobility exceeded vertical mobility among these least skilled workers and because occupational instability and low reward made them so vulnerable to extreme hardship in an era without any guaranteed form of social security.

Until 1880 when a fairly full listing of the numerous shoe and glass factory workers tipped the balance, service workers accounted for a majority of the semiskilled in Poughkeepsie during the middle decades. Correspondingly, with the exception of workers designated at chair and sash and blind making and a scattering at other factories, our census tracing of the semiskilled represents the opportunities of service workers. In general these workers were the most volatile in occupation within the manual labor force. Less than 60 percent of the semiskilled remained at that level in any decade; between 15 and 22 percent fell to unskilled employment, and roughly a quarter improved their occupations — rising more often to white-collar than to skilled jobs.

Ethnic and racial stratification according to desirability of jobs characterized service occupations as much as factory employment but with even greater visibility because of the addition of black workers. The contrast in frequency of employment between blacks and the whites of native parentage points up the comparative desirability of the major service occupations. In 1870 the whites comprised 59 percent of the teamsters, carmen, and carters — occupations with opportunities for self-employment — but only 36 percent of the drivers and coachmen, 16 percent of the gardeners, and none of the waiters. The black percentages in these occupations had almost the opposite tendency: 5, 23, 7, and 77 percent. Irish immigrants and their native-born sons spread themselves more evenly, becoming a majority among gardeners and the largest minority in each of the other occupations. Only the Irish provided much competition for blacks in private service, notably as coachmen.

While service workers of every ethnic and racial origin alternated frequently between semiskilled and unskilled jobs, this alternation occurred most often among the Irish and especially the blacks. Of the Irish who began any decade at semiskilled jobs, less than 40 percent of those persisting in the city ended the decade at unskilled work whereas in both the fifties and the sixties more than 40 percent of the blacks did so. By contrast, less than 20 percent of the semiskilled whites of native, British, and German parentage suffered this downward mobility in each of three decades.

Very often the shift to inferior jobs or no occupation proved temporary, pointing up the constant flux in opportunities among the less skilled as well as the marginal significance of some of these shifts. One Irishman appeared successively as cartman, driver, laborer, and coachman; another began as a hostler but later reported himself as a carman, laborer, and cartman. A black laborer in 1850 was enumerated subsequently as waiter, laborer, and white washer; another black started as a waiter but appeared next as a boatman before reporting himself again as a waiter. For blacks service jobs provided the only substantial employment outside unskilled labor.

Until the sharp increase in 1880 in the census designation of factory jobs, the predominance of service occupations in our semiskilled stratum explains its higher proportion of older workers, workers largely recruited from other strata. These occupations often served as culminations for careers spent in kinds of manual work demanding more strength or skill. Older men appear most often among custodial employments which tended to be less arduous; most of these workers already had spent several decades in skilled or unskilled work locally. But they also were overrepresented in service occupations which employed more men: gardeners, teamsters, carters, coachmen, and hackmen.

Upward mobility from semiskilled jobs occurred more often at younger ages, following the pattern for most occupations. In every decade, semiskilled workers who achieved self-employment or other nonmanual work exceeded those entering the skilled trades. Since factory operatives already in woodworking account for some of those achieving skilled work, the importance of proprietorships and clerical work in the upward mobility of service workers was even greater than the proportions indicate. Many service occupations offered chances for self-employment and some led easily to sales work in other lines.

Upward mobility within service work most often came to men who had pursued their occupations from a young age. Thus experienced gardeners could set themselves up as nurserymen and florists. M. J. Lynch, a Catholic born in County Limerick, had worked for the Earl of Clare before coming to America. Employed on a succession of estates along the Hudson river, Lynch launched himself as a florist in Poughkeepsie in the seventies. By 1897 he had a mail order seed store as well as ten greenhouses with five men employed all year round. Moreover, the incidence of self-employment among gardeners was higher than the directories or censuses reveal. Even in the midst of the depression in the seventies, the *Eagle* claimed that besides three florist shops the city had half a dozen or more dealers without stores, each of whom had his own hothouse and shipped all around the Hudson valley.[1]

The difficulty of estimating self-employment among men involved in horse transportation proves to be even greater because such men continued to designate themselves as teamsters, carmen, or carters and normally did not advertise nor report a separate place of business. The drivers employed by national and local express companies or local industries cannot be distinguished from men working for themselves. At the extreme of marginality, Jonas Place never appeared in the city directory as anything more than a scavenger and in the census as a laborer, yet the *Daily Press* announced in 1868 that "the well-known man of all work, has lately come into possession of a horse and wagon, through the assistance of friends, and is prepared to attend to all orders in the carting line that he may be favored with, promptly and with dispatch. Lend Jonas a helping hand."[2]

More successful in the long run as well as illustrative of the frequency with which service workers shifted jobs was William E. Gurney who spent more than a decade working for himself in trucking and express but appeared in the census and city directory simply as carman. Son of a farmer in the interior of the county, Gurney had worked on farms before coming to Poughkeepsie at age 30. He spent four years as a milkman in the city, one year in a meat market, and four years on the police force before shifting to the trucking and express business. After 13 years in that business and now 51 years old Gurney became a clerk in the city's post office.[3]

Since teamsters like Place and Gurney did not achieve solid prosperity, the inability to identify such self-employed men systematically seems superficially a small loss for a study of occupational mobility. Few of them did as well as the advertised native expressman who owned real estate assessed at $5,900 by 1880 or the native-born Baptist son of an Irish mason who at age 30 had won the contract for carrying the mail between the post office and the railroad depot and in 1880 already had property assessed at $3,400.[4]

On the other hand, self-employed teamsters sometimes employed other drivers and laborers to help them and often prospered as much as the proprietors of small retail, service, and craft-related shops. At the height of his career, one Irish Catholic owned three teams, did a large business, and accumulated a fair property. His old age as "Blind Tom," a nearly penniless newspaper peddler, reflected personal tragedy rather than any limitation of teamstering: his wife left him, his eyesight failed him, and he lost his property.[5]

More than shop-centered businesses, successful employment in horse transportation required aggressive tactics in searching out customers and, if need be, warding off rivals. The competition for business was fierce, the hours long when business was good and the work heavy. Success went to the hardy who could hustle and hustle fast, traits which undoubtedly helped those workers who moved on to other kinds of businesses. The newspapers praised carmen as a "hardy and laborious" breed who would tackle any assignment. They "soon get over being frightened by a piece of 7 x 9 pork." Their business often came in spurts such as spring moving time when people changed residences; during these spurts they worked extremely long hours. The *Press* noted in October 1863, for example, that the carmen had been made very busy by the "laying in of coal by citizens and heavy invoices of goods received by our merchants. One carman says that for the past five working days he has averaged seventeen hours per day and most of that time he and his horse have been engaged."[6]

Despite the long hours, heavy work, and fierce competition, teamsters, cartmen, and carters enjoyed an independence denied to drivers who worked as coachmen for private individuals. Blacks employed in horse transportation most often served as coachmen.

To be sure, the very rich sometimes paid their drivers handsomely — Matthew Vassar, Jr., gave his man more than $500 annually during the late seventies — but black coachmen do not seem to have received such rewards. Nor did they often enjoy much security in employment.

Of the 11 blacks who appeared employed at two censuses, two worked only as coachmen and a third reported himself twice at that occupation after working as a waiter and then as a driver. The other eight had no such stability. For example, one appeared twice as a coachman, than as a hostler; another shifted back and forth from ordinary labor at least twice; a third began as a laborer and ended as a whitewasher; and a fourth, a coachman in his mid-thirties, reported himself a laborer at the next two censuses and a house servant in his mid-sixties.

The total number of black coachmen in Poughkeepsie fluctuated in the four censuses: 13, 4, 15, and 8. The drop in the seventies coincided with greater recruitment and persistence of Irish coachmen. Directories for the eighties suggest that the Irish maintained the preeminence they had achieved during the depression decade; first and second generation Irish accounted for 11 of the 22 coachmen listed in the 1885 directory compared to only three blacks.

The displacement of blacks among the city's coachmen suggests the difficulty which members of the race encountered in trying to hold on to more skilled, responsible, and dignified employments during the middle decades and especially after the Civil War. More than any ethnic group in Poughkeepsie they specialized in a few occupations but had difficulty maintaining their position even in the more attractive of these. The skilled service calling in which blacks had prospered most frequently, barbering, expanded rapidly during the period but whites and especially first and second generation Germans account for the increase. Of 12 shops advertising in 1862, three had been owned by blacks; of 23 shops in 1885, three also, and the proportion of black journeymen in the trade had fallen comparably. Blacks remained more important in the most menial male occupations such as those of porter, hostler, and house servant (Table 10.1).

Blacks dominated one service occupation. Thirty-one listed themselves as waiters in the 1880 census in Poughkeepsie; together with 17 hostlers they accounted for one third of all black male workers in the city that year. Concentration encouraged some orga-

TABLE 10.1. Nativity of workers in five service occupations at four censuses[a]

Occupation	Census	White of native parentage (percent)	Black (percent)	Irish (percent)	German (percent)	British (percent)	Number of Cases
Barber	1850	36	27	9	18	9	11
	1860	35	15	5	30	15	20
	1870	41	19	5	24	8	37
	1880	29	13	5	50	2	56
Gardener	1850	24	—	34	10	29	41
	1860	22	4	38	15	20	76
	1870	16	7	44	14	18	105
	1880	22	3	41	20	13	111
Teamster, carter, or carman	1850	74	2	15	2	7	46
	1860	52	5	26	8	7	87
	1870	59	5	25	8	2	126
	1880	53	1	27	13	6	109
Coachman or driver	1850	34	43	14	3	6	35
	1860	56	15	24	5	—	41
	1870	36	23	37	1	2	87
	1880	30	18	31	19	1	77
Waiter	1850	20	55	25	—	—	20
	1860	18	82	—	—	—	11
	1870	—	77	8	—	8	13
	1880	3	97	—	—	—	36

[a]The Irish, Germans, and British comprise both the foreign-born and the native-born of foreign parentage of those nationalities.

nization of social life around the job. Thus, in 1877 the "colored waiters" at the Nelson House hotel threw a Calico Ball at a local dance hall. Members of the most prominent black families participated in this occupational specialization. In 1879, the year Gaius Bolin became the first black student to matriculate at Williams College, his older brothers waited on table at the Poughkeepsie Hotel and at the Morgan House. Another brother worked as private groomsman for a gentleman.[7]

Occupational specialization meant no more security of employment among waiters and hostlers than it did among coachmen. Typically, the older Bolin brothers had worked as gardeners in their teens and the one who remained in the city worked at ordinary labor during the eighties and nineties. A John F. Davis was the exception rather than the rule in service jobs. Born in New Orleans and brought to Poughkeepsie by Colonel George Parker whose body servant he had been during the war, Davis served the Parker family for years. Through them he also obtained employment for three terms as janitor at the post office.

Whites assumed that certain unskilled jobs belonged to blacks. Thus, no white man ever listed himself as a whitewasher, but a few blacks did at every census. By the time one farmer, George Frisch, died in 1868 at the age of 106, his experience in business for himself was a rarity among Poughkeepsie's blacks, but otherwise his life typifies the usual range and variety in the occupational careers of blacks. Born in Vermont in 1762 Frisch had moved to Virginia with his parents, been a servant on William Henry Harrison's staff at the Battle of Tippecanoe, and later a waiter in a private house in Culpepper Court House. He fled Virginia at age 50, stayed in Pennsylvania a few years, and then went to Newburgh, New York, where he opened a shoe shop. He came to Poughkeepsie in 1840 and opened a shoe blacking shop but, according to the *Eagle,* "was compelled by colored rowdies to give it up" and turned to whitewashing which he continued until he was too old.[8] He then became a janitor.

No other group in the city remained so consistently depressed and limited in the kinds of occupation open to them. The Irish in the immigrant generation showed slightly less mobility upward from semiskilled to nonmanual employments than blacks did, but their native-born sons fared better. Blacks did not improve their occupational position between generations; rather they remained largely trapped in unskilled work and in the specialized niches in service work which whites expected them to occupy. Even their occasional achievement of nonmanual status usually occurred within these bounds. Whereas the semiskilled immigrant Irish who became proprietors usually opened groceries or saloons catering to their countrymen, the more successful blacks continued to serve whites.

Although a gardener reported himself subsequently as a missionary agent, a cook more typically became a steward on a river steamboat and that only in his late forties. Blacks who did not know their place in society soon discovered the costs of being "uppity." That a few blacks like Joseph Rhodes, the dyer and bleacher, did run their own shops, and that Rhodes went so far as to challenge segregation in Poughkeepsie's schools tells us more about their resourcefulness, tact, and courage than about the receptivity of the white community generally to their ambitions. Despite the sympathy of an important minority of abolitionists, Poughkeepsians at mid-century had an even less flattering view of blacks than of the Irish.[9]

A majority of blacks and immigrant Irish at each census reported themselves at ordinary labor and other unskilled occupations. Whether or not either group could look to eventual acceptance as a respectable, stable element in the community depended upon the opportunities for upward mobility from the very bottom, from the irregular work at subsistence wages which gave the unskilled every-where the highest rate of transiency, disorderliness, and crime. Mobility from any stratum poses the twin questions of how much movement is a little or a lot and how significant it is, regardless of frequency. The questions seem most acute for the unskilled, the workers who had the least to offer employers and the most to gain themselves. Given the limitations in the evidence and differences in perspective on what constitutes significant improvement in occupa-tion, the answers suggested here are at best an arguable attempt to balance the claims of the various possible readings.

On the one hand, the bottom stratum of the occupational hierar-chy cannot be described as fixed or static. Even without compara-tive evidence on the chances to rise for European urban proletar-ians, the absolute frequency with which Poughkeepsie's unskilled shift to better jobs is simply too large to dismiss as unimportant. Two out of every five men employed at unskilled work at the begin-ning of the fifties and of the seventies had improved in occupation by the end of those decades and the ratio was nearly one out of every three in the sixties. If careers rather than decades are measured, then the mobility is even greater. Among young men who began in unskilled jobs and continued working in Poughkeepsie into their thirties, only 54 percent remained at the same level at last reported job.

Opportunities to rise were best for younger workers as in every stratum, especially for the achievement of a skilled trade. Relatively few older men shifted from unskilled work into the crafts, presum-ably as "green hands." In every decade between 23 and 31 percent of the unskilled reported initially in their teens appeared subse-quently at a trade compared to between 15 and 21 percent of those in their twenties and 6 to 10 percent of those in their forties.

Youths did not have as much of an advantage over their elders in movement from unskilled into nonmanual employment. Between 8 and 14 percent of the teenage unskilled at the start of any decade made that shift compared to between 6 and 11 percent of those in their twenties and 3 and 9 percent of those in their forties and fifties. The launching of small businesses by unskilled workers became more rather than less common as the period progressed, a form of mobility more common among older workers who had accumulated some savings. In the fifties only 5 percent of the persisting unskilled had become proprietors by the end of the decade compared to 11 percent of the semiskilled; by the seventies the difference had narrowed to 7.8 and 8.3 percent respectively.

This upward mobility from unskilled work includes some genuine success stories—not rags to riches, but substantial improvement even for the most handicapped of the immigrants, the Irish. The Protestant Dunwoody brothers began as laborers working in the soap factory of Jacob DeGroff, a native. When these immigrant brothers bought the factory from DeGroff, a credit reporter commented that they "had been brought up by him and he has been helping them out, has great confidence in them."[10]

Few unskilled workers among the Irish did as well as the Dunwoodys, however. John Kearney was more typical of those who started their own businesses. After laboring for two decades, Kearney reported himself as a junk dealer. He did own a modest house but the results of his efforts seem clearer in the careers of his children, all of whom started off with better jobs than he did. The oldest boy began as a grocery clerk at 15, reporting himself in subsequent censuses as a baker, policeman, and by age 40 as an inspector at the water works; the second son became an iron moulder and the third moved from being a post office clerk to superintendent of city streets. Many laborers in the immigrant generation, however, did not fare even as well as Kearney in their business attempts. The ubiquitous saloon begun at home often lasted no more than a year or so.

Among the unskilled the Irish reported achievement of proprietorship as often as any other immigrant group. Whites of native parentage had a slightly better record, about one tenth reporting that improvement in occupational status each decade compared to an average of 7 percent for the other groups (Table 10.2). Native whites had no advantage over the Germans and British, however, in moving from unskilled to skilled employments either in the immigrant or in the second generation. Here the Irish lagged far behind,

TABLE 10.2. Occupational mobility of unskilled workers by decade and by nativity

Nativity	Decade	White collar (percent)	Skilled (percent)	Semi-skilled (percent)	Unskilled (percent)	Number of cases
White of native parent- age	1850 – 60	9	27	21	42	99
	1860 – 70	14	17	13	56	90
	1870 – 80	14	16	21	49	125
Black	1850 – 60	5	5	25	65	20
	1860 – 70	–	–	20	80	15
	1870 – 80	3	6	30	61	33
Irish- born	1850 – 60	2	9	11	78	114
	1860 – 70	6	4	13	77	201
	1870 – 80	7	4	13	76	257
Native of Irish parent- age	1870 – 80	11	26	13	51	55
German- born	1850 – 60	5	30	15	50	20
	1860 – 70	9	17	9	65	46
	1870 – 80	11	13	30	48	61

reporting that improvement about one fourth as often as the other ethnic groups in any decade and no more often than unskilled blacks.

The always sharply limited opportunities for blacks to become craftsmen would not improve whereas the native-born of Irish parentage beginning at unskilled work would surpass whites of native parentage in the frequency with which they acquired trades. During the depression decade of the seventies, one fourth of the second generation Irish among the unskilled acquired a trade compared to one third of the second generation Germans and a mere 16 percent of the whites of native parentage. To be sure, the disproportionate number of young men among these second generation Irish and Germans in Poughkeepsie largely explains the apparent disadvantage of whites of native parentage; most shifts between unskilled and skilled work occurred early in a man's career.

For all except the immigrant Irish and blacks, the proportion reporting changes from unskilled to semiskilled employments in any
decade was less than the proportion finding skilled employment except during the seventies. In every decade three fifths or more of all
unskilled workers reported no improvement in job status, but the
differences between ethnic groups once again mirror their relative
advantage in the labor force: at the extremes, a little less than half
of the native whites in two decades remained unskilled compared to
more than three quarters of the Irish. The Germans, the British
—some of whom had Irish parents—and the blacks fell in between.
The slight superiority of the blacks to the immigrant Irish in proportion remaining unskilled reflects the blacks' greater concentration
in service jobs.

Although whites of native parentage comprised no more than one
third of all unskilled workers between 1860 and 1880—a substantial
underrepresentation for a group who still accounted for half of the
male labor force even in 1880—this minority retained the advantage
in occupational mobility. Their record makes questionable any presumption that the mid-century influx of unskilled immigrants, especially the Irish, meant that thereafter only the dregs of native
society—the least competent, lazy or shiftless—accepted unskilled
jobs.

Even for native whites, however, progress upward normally occurred only in small steps just as it did for members of all groups in
movements from any stratum. One man reported himself as a laborer until his fifties, then as a mill foreman. Another, born of
"humble parents" in nearby Hyde Park, began the duties of a
farmer's boy at age 12 and appeared in Poughkeepsie by 18. After
attaining a first lieutenancy during the Civil War he returned to
Poughkeepsie, married an Irish girl, and divided his time between
farming and teamstering. A third reported himself as a laborer at
18, at farm work a decade later and at shoemaking in his thirties,
probably as a "green hand" or repairman.

Men of native parentage remained preeminent in certain unskilled occupations notably those of boatman and farm laborer.
They also climbed to better jobs from these beginnings more frequently than they did from unspecified labor. Some boatmen
became pilots or captains and a few farm laborers became farm
proprietors themselves; more often, both groups rose in unrelated
kinds of work. The son of a local cooper went from farm labor at 20

to house painting at 30 and to stone masonry in his forties. The 16 year old son of a farmer reported farm work in 1850 but appeared at the next three censuses as a carpenter, achieving modest success building houses first in partnership and then on his own. The son of another farmer who had retired to Poughkeepsie went to sea when he was 13. By the time he came of age, he was working as a boatman on the Hudson. At 30 he reported himself as a gardener and at 40 as a stonemason. Soon afterward he purchased his family's homestead farm in nearby LaGrange and spent the rest of his life there.[11]

The Irish, by contrast, dominated casual labor throughout the middle decades and reported themselves more often than natives at a specific place of employment such as the gas works or a cemetery. They also frequently appeared temporarily at positions of some responsibility on the railroad, notably as flagmen, switchmen, and brakemen. The Irish became a decreasing portion of unskilled service workers like hostlers and porters and an increasing proportion of the city's gardeners, teamsters, drivers, and policemen, occupations with greater responsibility. Those who shifted from casual labor to specified employments in manufacturing and construction most often became bricklayers, moulders, and workers in less attractive factories like the dye wood mill, rope works, tanneries, furnaces, and brewery.

Employment on the railroad provides a revealing illustration of the slowness with which the unskilled Irish found better occupations in Poughkeepsie. Well before 1880 the Irish had achieved a monopoly on unskilled construction and maintenance work on the Hudson River Railroad, the first jobs for a majority of the famine refugees in Poughkeepsie during the late forties and early fifties and an important source of unskilled employment throughout the middle decades. "Don't the paddies have to work," observed a student at the Poughkeepsie Collegiate School in 1849 after watching the blasting and clearing of rock along the railroad route.[12]

Since occupations on the railroad ran the gamut from unskilled labor to more highly paid skilled and clerical jobs, numerous opportunities for the Irish to rise to such jobs could have existed within the railroad organizations. Locomotive engineers, for example, were the city's most highly paid manual workers; railroad conductors earned as much as many clerks though less than the engineers. The 124 employees of Vanderbilt's railroad in Poughkeepsie whose jobs can be identified in the 1879 county directory show some occupa-

tional mobility for immigrants and their children, but the majority
of the Irish still clustered in the less skilled occupations.

No immigrant appeared as a conductor, but three out of nine
conductors did have foreign parents. One father was Irish, a laborer.
The ten locomotive engineers included one born in Ireland and two
born in America of Irish parentage. By contrast, six of the 23 brakemen had been born in Ireland and four more had Irish parents. All
but one of the nine switchmen and flagmen were Irish and all but
two of these were immigrants. The Irish accounted for all of the 24
men listed as trackhands and railroad laborers.

The previous and subsequent careers of these workers in
Poughkeepsie reinforce the impression of slow gains. At least one
half of the railroad laborers of 1879 had been in Poughkeepsie for a
decade and seven had been employed there for 20 years. Some of
these workers had been listed at railroad employment previously; all
but three had never reported themselves as anything more than laborers, one having worked initially as a gardener, another at the
brick foundry, and the third apparently as an engineer. Newness in
the city does not help explain the lowly position of these Irish. Nor
did these laborers improve their lot subsequently. Of the 12 still employed in Poughkeepsie in 1890 and the six still listed in 1900, none
reported any occupation other than laboring.

A larger number of the Irish employed by the railroad in 1879 had
achieved limited occupational mobility in the form of more responsible and better paid work as brakemen, switchmen, and flagmen.
All but one of the nine switchmen and flagmen listed in the county
directory were of Irish birth or parentage compared to half of the
brakemen. Just before the 10 percent wage reduction of 1877, railroad laborers had received $1.00 a day or a usual average of $26 for
a full month compared to $40 per month for switchmen. Brakemen
did a little better than the switch tenders at $1.75 a day. The switch-
men who had been employed previously in Poughkeepsie all had
been ordinary laborers and several would so report themselves after
1879. Some listed themselves alternately as switchmen and laborers
or appeared at one designation in the census and at the other in the
city directory. This wavering in reportage together with the wage
rate for switchmen—less than that for most artisans and almost
identical to the going rate for a carman with one horse—strengthen
the impression of a limited and precarious mobility similar to that of
many service workers.[13]

The slightly better paid brakemen had no greater occupational stability. Between 1850 and 1900, for example, one Irishman appeared successively as laborer, brakeman, laborer, brakeman, and switchman. Furthermore, brakemen had the more dangerous job with a higher frequency of death and crippling accidents, especially injuries sustained while coupling cars. In general, railroad employees needed hospital attention so often that they collected more money among themselves for a contribution to the city's St. Barnabas hospital than had been given by their employer, Mr. Vanderbilt. [14]

Firemen received the same pay as brakemen but clearly comprised a different class of workers. This occupation served as the most common apprenticeship for locomotive engineers so that sons of engineers and conductors appear at this designation in their early twenties. Of the seven engineers previously employed in Poughkeepsie at other occupations, four had reported themselves as firemen and one each as machinist, brakeman, and engine wiper. Four of the seven men listed as firemen in 1879 became engineers subsequently; two of the three who did not were the only Irishmen among the firemen that year.

The locomotive engineers formed the apex of the hierarchy of manual work on the railroad, several earning more than $1,000 a year in the mid-sixties. The lowest among the seven engineers reporting annual income in 1866 — all men of native and British parentage — claimed $871. The relationship of the engineers to other railroad workers appears in simpler form in the bonuses Vanderbilt gave in 1877 in partial compensation for wage reductions that year; engineers got $30 each, passenger conductors $20, baggagemen $10, and brakemen $9. [15]

The Irish had appeared as locomotive engineers before 1870. In that year the newspaper described one as a veteran engineer and young Richard Whalen had just joined him in the occupation. Whalen and two young native-born firemen of Irish parentáge about to become engineers would still be running locomotives and residing in Poughkeepsie in 1900. But as of 1880, more than a generation after the famine influx, the Irish progress into better jobs on the railroad they had so largely built remained limited. Symbolically, only one man of Irish parentage in his twenties reported himself as a conductor in 1879 and before 1900 he had shifted to an occupation in which his countrymen had become prominent by 1880, that of policeman.

The police force in Poughkeepsie provides one of the clearest

signs of the growing assimilation and recognition of the Catholic
Irish in the life of the city just as it was the avenue of success for one
of the more dramatic careers among the famine refugees. Peter
Shields first appeared in Poughkeepsie in the 1850 census as a
pauper at the Alms House, then as a laborer, next as the city's Chief
of Police—already conceded to be one of the most influential
officers in the municipal government—and by 1880 as Deputy
Sheriff of Dutchess County.

As late as 1866 Poughkeepsie had had only two day police, paid a
mere $350 a year, and four night police, paid $547.50. The newspapers complained frequently about the force's insufficiency and in-
efficiency. By 1870, 12 men appear as policemen, ten of them men
of native parentage and mostly at less skilled work previously. The
seventies, however, saw a rapid expansion in the size of the force and
in the proportion of Irish members. Whites of native parentage
comprised six of the 16 policemen at the 1880 census compared to
three men of Irish birth and four of Irish parentage. Whereas five of
the six natives had been skilled and sales workers in Poughkeepsie in
1870 and the sixth already a policeman, five of the seven Irish had
been ordinary laborers previously. Judged by wages alone these
laborers had improved their situation, earning more than they had
at unskilled jobs or could get at many service jobs. In addition, they
had achieved the dignity of being an officer of the community with
limited authority over other citizens.[16]

The progress of the native-born sons of Irish laborers in achieving
skilled trades after beginning at casual labor like their fathers
offered more hope for the future than domination of the police
force. As we have seen, one fourth of the second generation workers
who persisted in Poughkeepsie during the seventies made that improvement, mostly scattering through the better paid industrial and
building trades. How much this progress owed to exposure to these
trades in their first reported jobs as laborers cannot be determined.
But the early importance of immigrant laborers in foundries and
furnaces and as hod carriers on construction sites as well as the early
prominence of Irish masons and iron moulders in the city
undoubtedly made it easier for members of the more assimilated
second generation to work in these industries and so find opportunities on the job for learning the trades they later report.

Many in the second generation who began at unskilled work
continued there—half made no improvement during the

seventies — but the advance into the trades encouraged optimism for the future. Even if the unskilled among the immigrant Irish remained overwhelmingly trapped at the bottom of the labor force, they could hope to see their children improve upon their position. Within the second generation a few sons of laborers rose all the way to respectability and public prominence. Richard Connell, for example, began at ordinary labor like his father, but moved progressively from carriage painting to newspaper reporting and editing to Congress and saw his son attend Harvard.[17]

If even the Irish — so often distressed and distrusted, even despised by natives during the fifties — could make this much headway in Poughkeepsie by 1880, then few grounds existed for believing that the growing division of labor created a permanent and depressed underclass, certainly not a substantial one. Judged by occupational mobility, opportunities for the unskilled regardless of national origin had improved during the thirty years after 1850.

While recognizing the importance of this mobility, the optimistic view it suggests needs to be balanced by the mass of evidence on the painful uncertainties in the lives of so many unskilled workers, primarily the precariousness of their livelihoods. Even among native-born farm workers who generally improved their occupational position more often than any other group of the unskilled, a minority show a pattern of changing jobs at or near the bottom, a changing which sometimes included absences from the city presumably to work on nearby farms or in rural villages.

Only one third of those reporting themselves as farm hands at any census remained in the city a decade later and of those who did almost all reported another occupation. The accidents of the season of the year when the census enumerated unskilled workers often determined whether those who sometimes worked on farms during the summer months ever appeared at agricultural labor.

Among the young natives who listed themselves in the census as farmers in their teens or twenties, one reported himself later as a hostler and then at ordinary labor. Another was gone at the next census but reappeared as a laborer and a third also left, returning as a railroad peddler. Like farm workers, boatmen remained predominantly whites of native parentage and totally unstable in occupation. Even in the seventies when half remained in the city, less than one tenth continued to report themselves as boatmen.

The impression of vulnerability would be much greater if the cen-

sus specified more often the place or kind of employment for the unskilled. The simple designation laborer accounts for more than two
thirds of the unskilled at any census and those who persist at that
designation comprise two thirds of all laborers remaining in the city
each decade. Conceding that as many as one third of these laborers
may have been employed regularly by the railroad and manufacturing establishments, most of the remainder depended upon casual
and fluctuating employment. Moreover, unskilled workers in river
transportation as well as farm hands had only seasonal employment
at those occupations. As the *Daily Press* noted in late February of
1868, "What a longing among boatmen, merchants and dock laborers for reopening of navigation." It had been a hard winter "especially for poor laborers whose funds are nearly run out." The year
before, the *Eagle* had noted however that the "boss boatmen don't
like to see the river open till some time in March, for the reason that
there is scarcely any work for boats to do before the latter part of
that month, and even then it doesn't pay."[18]

During periods of extensive local construction, whether booms in
house building or in construction of public works such as the new
water works, sewage system, and state insane asylum erected during
the early seventies, ordinary laborers might find work readily available for all but the winter months. In the absence of local booms,
opportunities in other towns in the county or along the Hudson River
sometimes drew enough laborers away from Poughkeepsie to improve the situation of those who remained. The *Daily Press* noted in
1863 that "laboring men and mechanics are very scarce in this city at
present. Some have gone to Cold Spring, where the owners of the
furnaces are creating dwellings for their employees. The laboring
men are receiving $1.62 per day." Casual laborers like skilled work-
ers responded to shifts in demand and wages within a regional market.[19]

Apart from construction, however, the least skilled and specialized workers rarely found steady employment for extended periods
of time. They depended instead upon a wide variety of temporary
employments for their livelihood, many of these employments lasting only a day or so. In the springtime, for example, householders
who could afford to often employed a laborer to dig up a kitchen
garden. In one of its perennial complaints about idlers lounging
around Main Street, the *Press* found their presence intolerable "in
the season of industry when even an ordinary laborer, to spade up

the ground, can't be had for less than $1.50 a day." May Day, the customary time for moving, brought demand for men to help teamsters and carters with the transfer to the new residence of furniture and other family possessions. The *Eagle* commented in 1877, a depression year, that "it was a good day for the unemployed, for men were in demand although the wages were not as high as a year ago. One horse load brought from 75¢ to $1.00 with an extra man to help thrown in, and two horse loads brought $2.00 to $3.00 with a man to help the driver."[20]

In favorable times casual laborers could earn at least a subsistence and some did better. But the precariousness of their lot appears in a variety of circumstances. A rapid rise in prices hurt them badly and immediately. The *Press* claimed in 1864 that a laborer couldn't support his family on the then prevailing rate of $1.25 per day because of wartime inflation.[21]

More obvious and poignant reminders of the economic vulnerability of casual laborers occurred every winter and especially during times of severe cold when the numbers turning to the Alms House for temporary relief increased sharply. The *Press* accordingly offered this sermon in 1868: "By November 30th it will be too cold to labor much out of doors. Also necessaries of life cost more in winter. So get fuel and all the provisions your surplus earnings permit in now. Last winter was long and cold and many poor families needed comforts they couldn't obtain, but if they will economize in season, they may guard against contingency."[22] In 1870 the Alms House admitted 254 males during January and December alone, including 151 Irish and 73 whites of native parentage. Furthermore, that winter the city gave outdoor relief to 300 families with unemployed heads of household.[23]

Business depression showed most clearly the ordinary laborer's vulnerability in unemployment in comparison to more skilled workers. Of the 350 families receiving outdoor relief in the form of groceries and coal during early 1877, almost all the male heads of household appeared in the city directory that year simply as laborers or with no occupation. When the city gave work to 51 of the unemployed quarrying and breaking stone for street repair, laborers and men reporting no occupation were the primary beneficiaries—comprising 36 of the 43 who can be identified in city directories. Four fifths of those receiving work relief were Irish, suggesting these immigrants' increasing political muscle in the city. The Republican

Eagle complained that "it is next to impossible for anyone not a
Democrat . . . to get employment in the work."[24]

Moreover, regardless of nationality, the poorer, the less skilled,
the more transient, and, among the stable, the least upwardly
mobile appeared disproportionately among those idenified in newspaper accounts or court records as being in trouble with the law,
mostly for petty violations such as intoxication, disorderly conduct,
and assault and battery. The incidence of trouble with the law
tempts speculation about the existence of a class of people "under"
the social system, pariahs when they are not literally strangers, and
even of a "culture of poverty". A study of occupational mobility
cannot settle questions of social psychology, but it does offer some
cautions about what should not be presumed about the least successful.

Although those who most frequently suffered unemployment
often moved from place to place hunting for jobs, it cannot be
assumed that the least successful invariably were transients, part of a
"floating" proletariat. Among the most stable of Poughkeepsie's
laborers are men who moved in and out of the Alms House a
number of times, men whom the officer admitting usually described
as intemperate, lazy, or otherwise likely to be a frequent charge
upon the public. Calvin Drury, the Vermont-born laborer who
appeared in Poughkeepsie at every census from 1850 to 1880, was
one of these stable n'er-do-wells and his adult son followed him into
the Alms House at one point. Poughkeepsie had its town drunks, its
regular frequenters of "low" amusements of all kinds, and its re-
peating criminals, well-known to newspaper readers. These persis-
tent residents do fit the contemporary definition of the degraded or
"pauperized" poor.

By no means do all those who remained in menial occupations fit
contemporaries' notions of the undeserving poor. Throughout the
city a substantial number of families resident for all or most of the
period show all male members in successive generations employed at
unskilled and semiskilled work but the men do not appear at the
Alms House, on outdoor relief or in the courts. No attempt has been
made to systematically determine the kinship of unskilled and semiskilled male heads of household with the same surnames, but the
frequency of some distinctive Dutch and English surnames present
in Poughkeepsie from colonial times such as Freer, Ferdon, Pal-
matier, Travis, and Westervelt does suggest an important stable ele-

ment at the bottom of Poughkeepsie's working class. They played no role in the city's politics or associational life, but neither did they constitute a burden upon the taxpayer nor a problem for the police.

The dependent and deviant and the independent but occupationally immobile comprised a substantial minority of the families of unskilled workers in Poughkeepsie but never a majority. In only a minority of the familes of the unskilled did all the sons remain at unskilled and semiskilled work. In a majority, at least one son achieved skilled or nonmanual employment. Among all sons of unskilled fathers, whites of native parentage escaped less skilled work least frequently. Yet 40 percent of those born between 1840 and 1859 had done so by last reported job compared to 51 percent of the sons of Irish unskilled workers.

To be the child of a laborer was a handicap, not an advantage, in the competition for occupational mobility. Contrary to contemporary sermonizing about poverty being the best school for success, the higher up you began, the better your opportunities. But the handicap of the sons of the unskilled did not prevent a near majority of those who remained employed in Poughkeepsie for at least two decades from achieving better jobs than their fathers. Only the blacks remained confined almost entirely to servile and menial employment. Even at the bottom of the occupational hierarchy, white men of every nationality could hope reasonably to see their sons, if not themselves, achieve an occupation with greater reward, responsibility, and respectability.

11

The Employment of Women

DESPITE ITS CONCERN with the lives of ordinary people, the new urban history so far has largely ignored an already neglected group: women. Some of this neglect may reflect a lingering notion that woman's place was largely in the home and that the home did not make history, but the primary reason has been the focus on occupational and residential mobility, on tracing the careers of individual workers. Most women in the nineteenth century did not work and those who did typically took employment only for the few years before marriage. Few women had occupations or careers which could be traced through successive censuses. Furthermore, the lack of inclusive marriage records for many communities makes it difficult to estimate persistence of women in the community for even a ten year span because of the changes of women's names after marriage. Perhaps most important, the social and economic position of most families depended upon the occupation of the husband or father.

Ignoring the employment of women creates an implicit bias in mobility studies, however, heightening our sense of opportunity in nineteenth-century society by limiting our awareness of the extent to which occupational gains for some groups may have occurred at the expense of other groups. The chances of upward mobility for men are given a different perspective by showing the degree to which Poughkeepsie's economy depended upon cheap, usually temporary, labor from women. Few women persisted in the labor force and of those who did, almost none improved their occupational position; the availability of this relatively immobile group of workers increased the opportunities for men to rise just as the swelling of the manual labor force by so many immigrant men improved the opportunities for native white men to achieve white-collar positions.

Admittedly, Poughkeepsie may represent an extreme in the employment available to women. Unlike a mill town such as Cohoes it did not provide large numbers of factory jobs for women; nor did Poughkeepsie offer the metropolitan variety of jobs, let alone the glamor, which might attract a Sister Carrie. But we see no reason to doubt its typicality of opportunities for women in the much larger class of small and medium-sized cities with diversified economies. In 1860, 1870, and 1880 women represented 25, 20, and 24 percent respectively of Poughkeepsie's total labor force, proportions within the typical range for women's employment in cities with a mixed industrial base.[1]

While a career analysis comparable to that for men is neither feasible nor appropriate for women, the manuscript census population schedules and other sources permit a close description of the situation of ordinary women in the nineteenth century, especially the means by which they secured a livelihood for themselves and for their families. This chapter will describe the employment patterns of women in Poughkeepsie in 1860, 1870, and 1880 only because the 1850 census did not specify female employments. It complements our mobility analysis for men by pointing up the differences between the sexes in opportunities for economic independence and security.

The study of women from the census presents some peculiar problems. Without civil marriage records, not available in Poughkeepsie until after 1880, persistence of all women within the community cannot be calculated. However, working women's persistence in their occupations can be determined quite accurately from the census alone. Few women were lost through a change of name after marriage because few married women, especially in 1870 and 1880, reported any employment.

A greater problem is posed by the reliability of census information

on female employment. In 1860, for example, the three chair factories in the manufacturing schedules reported employing 168 women
but the population schedules listed only 32 women as chair seaters
and caners. No records of the chair factories survive to tell whether
these discrepancies arise from the census takers' failing to record
part-time work performed at home or from the factories' contracting for this work in surrounding rural towns rather than in the
city.

On the other hand, dressmakers, tailoresses, and seamstresses also
often worked at home but still were recorded by trade in the census.
In 1860 the population schedules show more tailoresses than the
total number of female employees reported by tailoring and
clothing firms in the manufacturing schedules. Finally, the census
reportage includes more occupations for women than the directory
listing which completely excluded, for example, domestic servants.
So, although it may underestimate some home work and part-time
employment and thus underestimate the employment of married
women especially, the census remains the most comprehensive
source for studying women's employment in a community.

To make the discussion of women's employment patterns broadly
comparable to that for men, a scheme of occupational classification
has been adopted. The use of similar skill categories for women,
however, suggests a greater range of opportunity and reward than
actually existed. Wages for all working women remained low. Female teachers and female janitors in the city schools, for example,
earned approximately the same salaries. Both domestic service and
factory work often paid better than some of the piece work done by
skilled women in the garment industry. Still, judged by educational
requirements and by the occupations of the fathers of working girls,
women's occupations can be classified roughly in a hierarchy moving downward from professionals to proprietors, skilled, factory,
and domestic service jobs.

Because their work required at least a high school education,
teachers and doctors have been assigned to the highest level of skill.
Most businesses run by women were modest so no attempt has been
made to distinguish between large and small proprietors. Directories
have been used to distinguish shopowners from employees or solitary
workers among dressmakers and milliners. Only those whose listings
show a shop separate from living quarters have been counted as
proprietors. Women who described themselves in the census as

boarding-house keepers are deemed proprietors. Many women who took in boarders and thereby contributed to family income did not so report themselves in the census. In 1880, if all household heads and wives who took in boarders are counted as employed, then the proportion of women employed would be 29 rather than 24 percent.

Women without shops who reported the occupations of tailoress, milliner, dressmaker, and other sewing jobs have been considered skilled manual workers. Since over 95 percent of the skilled women worked at some kind of sewing, this classification is little more than a surrogate for women in nonfactory manufacture of apparel. The level of skill required undoubtedly varied widely but it cannot be distinguished with any accuracy.

At the bottom of this occupational hierarchy, female occupations have been divided only into factory, classified as semiskilled, and domestic service, classified as unskilled. Before 1880 most female factory workers in the census were employed by the chair factory and caned seats at home. By 1880 most worked inside at the shoe, shirt, and skirt factories. Unlike domestics, who came more often from households headed by semiskilled and unskilled workers, the majority of female factory operatives, like many of the skilled sewing women, came from households headed by skilled workers.

While domestic servants in the larger households performed specialized jobs and were so listed in the census, the majority of servants performed a wide variety of tasks. To single out those who listed themselves as cooks, laundresses, or nurses as having more skill than the general servant would be misleading, therefore.[2]

Some characteristics of the employment of all white women remained constant between 1860 and 1880. At each census almost one quarter of those over 14 years old were employed.[3] Women under 30 comprised between two thirds and three quarters of the white female labor force. One major shift occurred. Among all nationalities, the proportion of female household heads and wives who were employed declined sharply between 1860 and 1870, followed by a very slight increase in the next decade. Among native white women, for example, the percentage of household heads working declined from 34 percent in 1860 to 19 percent in 1880; among the Irish, from 40 to 11 percent; and among the Germans, from 35 to 15 percent. Working wives were never very common but the proportions working showed a similar decline. In 1860, 10 percent of native wives worked but by 1880 only 3 percent. Immigrant wives in 1860 never worked so frequently as their native sisters but the percentage of Irish working wives fell from 6 to 2 percent and Germans from 2 to 1 percent. Among black women, a far greater proportion of household heads and wives always worked but the same pattern prevailed. In 1860, 72 percent of black household heads worked but only 48 percent did in 1880; 32 percent of black wives worked in 1860 and 26 percent in 1880.

But as mothers retired from the labor force, their daughters joined it. The percentage of girls between 15 and 20 who worked increased for all nationality groups except the Irish, whose rate of teenage employment remained over 60 percent between 1860 and 1880. At every census the proportion of Irish women of all ages working was higher than for other white women (Table 11.1).

The nature of white women's employment changed dramatically

TABLE 11.1. Percentage of women employed, by age group

Ethnic group	All women 15 or over	15 − 19	20 − 29	30 − 39	40 − 49	50 − 59	60 or over	Number 15 or over
Whites of native parentage								
1860	4	29	33	23	20	14	10	2,847
1880	18	35	26	14	16	12	4	3,986
Blacks								
1860	55	55	45	62	62	65	53	189
1880	57	66	61	67	43	59	50	302
Irish								
1860	38	61	49	29	25	19	8	1,129
1880	34	62	54	19	17	16	9	1,884
German								
1860	13	34	17	6	5	3	0	466
1880	21	45	33	6	8	10	6	846
British								
1860	20	27	33	11	21	6	7	294
1880	23	48	27	19	22	11	37	446

[a]The native born of foreign parentage are included in the percentages for each ethnic group.

during these years. The proportion of women engaged in the traditional sewing trades declined sharply. Much of the loss of job opportunities for these skilled women occurred in the manufacture of
men's clothing. The census listed 207 tailoresses in 1860 but only 55
in 1880. Seamstresses, vestmakers, and milliners also declined; the
number of dressmakers alone increased.

Women displaced from traditional apparel manufacture did not
find comparable jobs. To the contrary, the initial decline in skilled
employment for white women between 1860 and 1870 — from 42 to
29 percent of the female labor force — was accompanied by a rise in
the proportion of white women in domestic service — from 43 percent in 1860 to 56 percent in 1870. In 1880 the proportion in the
sewing trades had declined further to less than one quarter, but the
proportion working as domestics also began to decline as the new
shoe, shirt, and skirt factories increasingly provided employment. In
1860 and 1870 only 4 percent but by 1880 15 percent, of white
female workers appear in factory-related employment (Table 11.2).

Increased participation in the labor force by immigrants partially
explains the growing percentage of white women who worked as
domestic servants. In 1860 native women represented 56 percent of
the white workers but by 1880 only 43 percent. In 1860, 84 percent
of the Irish working women and 58 percent of the German working
women reported themselves as domestics, but those proportions had
declined to 70 and 46 percent respectively in 1880.

Whereas immigrant women began as domestics and gradually
moved into other occupations, native women more and more left
the labor force or turned to domestic service as their opportunities
in domestic garment manufacture declined. In 1860, 24 percent of
native white women over 14 were employed, in 1870 only 16 percent, and in 1880, 18 percent. Moreover, between 1860 and 1880,
the percentage of native wives who worked fell from 10 to 3 percent. Of those native white women who remained employed, the
proportion entering domestic service jumped from 18 to 33 percent
between 1860 and 1870 while the proportion engaged in skilled
sewing occupations fell from 62 to 43 percent. By 1880 domestics
accounted for a similar third of native female workers but traditional garment workers comprised only 30 percent of the labor
force. By that year factories had become an important source of
employment for natives as they had for all white women.

These shifts in employment patterns closely parallel those that
occurred in England during the nineteenth century. Patricia Branca

TABLE 11.2. Skill level of employed women, by ethnic group (percent)[a]

Ethnic group	Profes-sional	Proprie-torial	Clerical	Skilled	Factory	Unskilled	Number of employed
Whites of native parentage							
1860	11	5	1	62	4	18	695
1870	13	5	2	43	3	34	623
1880	12	4	3	30	18	33	754
Blacks							
1860	—	—	—	7	—	93	104
1870	1	—	—	1	—	98	139
1880	1	—	1	2	—	97	173
Irish							
1860	1	1	1	13	2	84	426
1870	1	1	1	14	2	82	553
1880	2	1	1	15	9	70	670
German							
1860	2	2	2	23	13	58	60
1870	5	1	5	22	11	57	65
1880	3	5	2	18	23	46	210
British							
1860	10	9	—	40	14	28	60
1870	11	5	—	41	4	39	56
1880	5	5	4	24	19	43	100

The native born of foreign parentage are included in the percentages for each ethnic group. For the total number of all ethnic groups in each skill level, see Table 1.1.

has formulated two models for women's employment during that century in Europe. In England and Germany, on the one hand, rapid industrialization, mechanization, and urbanization made domestic manufacture obsolete; women responded by leaving the labor force, entering domestic service, or less commonly by seeking employment in factories. As opportunities for working at home disappeared, the female labor force became young and single and few married women held jobs. In France and Italy, on the other hand, domestic manufacture persisted much longer, a higher proportion of women worked, and married women were more likely to remain in the labor force.[4]

To a large extent, then, the changing employment patterns found among white women in Poughkeepsie were the structural accompaniment of industrialization and urbanization on the English model. Yet in Poughkeepsie the process of displacement of women from traditional jobs in the garment industry, however inevitable, was hastened by competition from immigrant men and the rise of ready-made clothing manufactured in other localities. According to the manufacturing census some 25 firms in 1860 engaged in making men's clothing; they reported a total of 257 employees in that year, 153 of whom were women. By 1880, in an incomplete enumeration, the manufacturing census showed only five local firms making men's clothing with 85 employees, only ten of whom were women. The largest firm, M. Shwartz, employed 60 men and no women. This replacement of women by immigrant men in the clothing industry, noticed long ago by Edith Abbott in her *Women in Industry,* helps explain why the Civil War did not cause any great expansion in women's employment. Although the production of clothing increased nationwide and large numbers of men left to serve in the army, women did not replace them in the labor force. On the contrary, in Poughkeepsie as elsewhere, the decade of the sixties saw a decrease in female employment.[5]

Many women who reported no occupation did contribute to family income. There is no way unfortunately of measuring the number of wives who may have assisted their husbands in trades such as tailoring and cigarmaking or who served behind the counter in the family grocery or saloon. But women who reported boarders in their households can be counted in the 1880 census, the only one which distinguished between boarders and relatives in the household.

If wives who listed lodgers in their households are considered employed, the proportion of employed wives increases sharply for all nationality groups. By this calculation 14 percent of Irish, English, and native wives worked and 10 percent of German wives contrasted with the less than 4 percent of any of these groups of wives reporting employment in the census. Similarly, the proportion of female heads of household who could be considered working rises from about one fifth to about one third for native and for English women, from 15 to 24 percent for German women, and from 11 to 19 percent for Irish women.[6]

The majority of households that took in boarders probably did so out of economic necessity. Almost two thirds of the native white male-headed households reporting boarders were headed by blue-collar workers compared to three quarters of the Irish households and over half of the German. Over half of the wives in households with boarders were in their thirties and forties. Moreover, half of all households that accepted boarders had nonworking children at home with another quarter having at least one working child in the household. Providing housekeeping services for lodgers enabled wives to earn extra money while remaining within the home.

Not all women accepted boarders because of financial straits. Almost a quarter of the native male-headed households that accepted boarders, for example, were headed by professionals or proprietors. A prosperous dry goods dealer had his two bachelor partners boarding in his household. Few craftsmen had apprentices living in their households by 1880, but proprietors often had store clerks living with them. The large student population in Pough-keepsie tempted some of the most prosperous to take an occasional boarder. When dry goods merchant Edmund Platt first set up housekeeping with his wife, they took in a student boarder at seven dollars a week. Since Mrs. Platt also had a servant, the burden became psychological rather than physical. When their boarder went to New York City for a week Platt remarked in his diary that "we enjoy his absence very much," and they quickly discontinued the arrangement.[7]

Few women appeared in the labor force for as many as two consecutive censuses. Of the women who reported occupations in 1860, 12 percent were still employed in 1870; of those working in 1870, 14 percent still held jobs in 1880. Domestics and skilled garment workers comprised the bulk of those who persisted. Between 1860 and 1880 only 41 women who can be linked by name reported an occupation at every census, and almost half of them were Irish servants. Persistence did not mean job improvement. Of the white women employed in both 1860 and 1870, 92 percent held the same kind of job at both listings; of the women who worked in both 1870 and 1880, 88 percent did not change their occupational status.

The preceding discussion omitted black women because they differed from white women in type of employment and in persistence. Although they were far more likely to work, they had fewer occupational choices. In both 1860 and 1880 over half of all black women held jobs; in 1870 only 48 percent reported employment but that lower figure is partially explained by the census takers' apparent failure to record employment as laundresses, an occupation in which black wives predominated.

At every census well over 90 percent of employed black women worked as domestics. One fourth of the working black women in the sixties and in the seventies persisted in the labor force, a much higher rate than for white women of any nationality. In 1880 a mere 3 percent of white wives reported jobs, but in 1860 a third of the black wives worked and in 1880 one fourth worked, mostly as laundresses in both years.

These general patterns of employment emphasize the limitations in the means of livelihood available to women, but they do not convey the variation in training, reward, and attractiveness of particular occupations. For women, much more than for men, hierarchical classification of occupations is problematic, making all the more important studies of the present kind, which go behind such classifications as skilled and professional to describe the work situation, apparent status, and reward of specific occupations.

At every census about 7 percent of white working women pursued professional careers. As in the male labor force the native-born predominated, comprising 89 percent of female professionals in 1860 and 1870 and 77 percent in 1880. The majority, of course, were teachers; the feminization of that profession occurred as rapidly in Poughkeepsie as it did in other cities during the latter half of the century. Given the comparative newness of medical schools for women, the city had a surprising number of women doctors. In both 1860 and 1870 three native-born physicians were listed in the census and several other women practiced for a short time in the years between censuses. While men dominated the profession, a young girl growing up in Poughkeepsie at least had before her an alternative model to teaching.

Only Anna C. Howland appeared in both the 1860 and 1870 censuses. Born into a prominent Quaker family in Maine, she did not begin her medical career until after her marriage and the birth of four children. After coming to Poughkeepsie in 1865 with her husband, a teacher-turned-shoe merchant, she enrolled in the New York Medical College in 1866. At that time, her eldest child was 9 and her youngest 2 years old. Widowed by 1869, Dr. Howland supported and educated her children through her active practice which continued until after the turn of the century.[8]

Other women also combined marriage and medicine. Maria E. Luckey, wife of a hardware merchant, maintained an active practice from 1862 until the family left the city in 1875. Phoebe Thorne Williamson, a granddaughter of one of Dutchess County's largest landholders and leading jurists, developed an early interest in medicine by assisting her father in his practice. She was graduated from Women's Medical College and Infirmary in New York City in 1878. Although she had married in 1877, she not only practiced in Poughkeepsie for many years but also opened another office in New York City where she spent several days a week. Another graduate of Women's Medical College practiced briefly in Poughkeepsie but subsequently became a medical missionary to India, married there, and sent her children back to the United States to be educated.[9]

Two of the single doctors in Poughkeepsie illustrate chain migration among professional women and also perhaps the need for mutual support when embracing male-dominated careers. Elizabeth Gerow was a native of Dutchess County. After studying at Women's Hospital in Boston she was graduated from the Medical Department of the University of Michigan in 1875 and returned to Poughkeepsie that year to begin a practice which lasted until the twentieth century. Joining her in Poughkeepsie in the late seventies was Dr. Elizabeth Moshier, a native of western New York who also was graduated from Michigan in 1875. Although Dr. Moshier soon left the city, eventually becoming the first woman dean and professor of hygiene at Michigan, another Michigan graduate, a pharmacist, appeared in the 1880 census. She worked for a local druggist and boarded with Dr. Gerow.[10]

By mid-century medical careers for women had won the approval of many who believed that doctors should only treat members of their own sex. Poughkeepsie's female doctors usually observed the accepted sexual division of labor within medicine. Dr. Luckey's advertisements stated her belief that "there are many who are suffering from . . . maladies peculiar to women that would gladly avail themselves of the opportunity to have the advice and attention of a physician of their own sex." Only Dr. Howland's practice seems to have regularly included both men and women perhaps because homeopathic medicine was so popular but had relatively few practitioners in Poughkeepsie.[11]

Patronage from their own sex did not wholly erase the prejudice against female doctors. When Dr. Moshier left Poughkeepsie in 1877, the *News* commented that her success during her two years in the city had been remarkable "when we consider that she had to meet not only the difficulties encountered by all young practitioners, but also the objection of sex, the power of which objection can only be appreciated by those who are trying or who are watching the efforts of brave women to dignifiedly and delicately establish themselves in this noble profession." Local male doctors, however grudgingly, did extend professional recognition to their female counterparts; two women became members of the County Medical Society. Vassar Brothers hospital named Dr. Gerow to its first medical board and she and a male doctor also ran a clinic which dispensed free medical care to the poor.[12]

Other women in Poughkeepsie associated with medicine have not been classified as professionals. A few of the nurses may have taken advantage of the new professional training for that career, but they cannot be distinguished in the census. Most were teenage girls, some as young as 12 years old, and thus classified as domestics. Only one woman, a married German in her fifties, ever listed herself as midwife although the practice probably was more widespread. Abortionists never reported their occupation but newspaper accounts show that women frequently performed abortions locally and elsewhere.

Although medicine at mid-century was new and controversial as a field for women, teaching had become an accepted and approved career. Younger women predominated, especially in 1860 when only one quarter of the teachers were over 30 as compared to 40 percent of all native-born working women. In both 1870 and 1880 the proportion of teachers over 30 had risen to one third, perhaps signaling a greater commitment to teaching as a career rather than something to do briefly before marriage.

Before 1880, however, few teachers in the census continued ten years later in that work; the proportion doing so rose from 14 percent during the sixties to 18 percent during the seventies. Only a few of those who did not continue teaching could be found living under the same name in the community ten years later. Continuity was more pronounced in the public schools than in private seminaries.

City directories and the annual reports of the Board of Education regularly contained lists of teachers, their positions and salaries between 1862 and 1896, making it possible to chart increasing persistence in the public schools. Of the 25 teachers employed there in 1862, only 28 percent remained a decade later whereas of the 41 teachers listed in 1873, 34 percent remained a decade later. By contrast, of the 60 teachers employed in 1880, almost one half could still be found in 1890 and almost one quarter were still teaching in 1897. By 1890, 7 percent of all public school teachers had been teaching in the system for twenty years or more and 31 percent for more than ten years. Kate Lee, for example, joined the city system in 1865, served variously as a principal, a primary and a grammar teacher and in 1897 still taught first grade.

Increasing commitment to teaching brought no financial improvement. Poughkeepsie's Board of Education prided itself on its low costs, boasting that no other city in the state except Cohoes spent so little per pupil. Teachers' salaries reflected this penury. In 1867 the *Eagle* reported that 34 teachers received the "niggardly" salary of $229 each and five received less than $200 a year. Commenting on "Poughkeepsie's liberality," the paper estimated that it cost a teacher $273 to live without any provision for sickness.[13]

The teachers made a successful plea to the Common Council; in 1868 the lowest salary paid to a teacher was $300. By 1897, the starting salaries of primary school teachers had risen to $350. Those who had been in the system the longest did not receive much above the minimum. Kate Lee earned $350 in 1880 and in 1897 had advanced to $425; her principal had an annual salary of $425 in 1874; by 1897 it had risen to $480. Janitors in the school system frequently made as much for banking the fires and sweeping the floors. In 1884 one woman who served as janitor for two schools earned $380 when beginning first grade teachers earned $325. Those who had argued earlier for the feminization of teaching because it would save money had been proved correct.

Salaries largely reflected the level of pupils taught. High school teachers received between $600 and $750 during the eighties and nineties, but even these better-paid teachers, invariably single women, found their salaries inadequate for security in old age. When the vice-principal of the high school's second department entered the Old Ladies' Home in 1902, after 40 years as a public school teacher, the *Eagle* chastised the city: "She is comfortably situated there. Nevertheless it is but little to the credit of a civilized community that a woman who has given her whole life to the instruction of the young should find herself in her old age want for means of support."[14]

Working conditions matched salaries. The typical grammar school class had an average attendance of between 40 and 50 pupils during the eighties and primary classes had even more. First grade enrollment so far exceeded capacity that double sessions had to be instituted. In 1883 only 10 of the 53 rooms maintained or rented by the system had the proper amount of space per pupil required by the Board of Health. Some pupils had no desks and perched instead on the teachers' platforms. Conditions remained the same as late as 1898 when the state superintendent delivered a blistering report on the physical condition of the city schools. "Out of the 13 buildings in which schools are maintained . . . with the exception of Number Five—not a single building has any system of ventilation, and no means of heating except by coal stoves, in some cases within 20 inches of the desks occupied by the pupils, consuming the oxygen of the overcrowded school room. No provision is made for children's wraps, which hang about the school room four and five deep upon an insufficient number of hooks, a most unsanitary condition. Some of these buildings have water closets in the basements, the odors from which permeate the whole building."[15]

Low salaries and overcrowded classrooms filled with working-class children made public school teaching anything but a genteel and attractive profession. The proportion of teachers recruited from white-collar homes declined between 1860 and 1880 reflecting also the decline of private academies. In any census year over half of the teachers living at home with employed fathers came from working-class households and the proportion increased steadily until by 1880 two thirds of the daughters with employed fathers came from such households.

Low accreditation standards made entry into the profession possible for working-class girls. Poughkeepsie's Board not only promoted local residents but also required no training beyond high school graduation and occasional teacher institutes. By 1890 graduates of the local high school comprised more than two thirds of the public school teachers appointed after 1875, and by that time the school represented a very different mix in social origins from the private seminaries. From 1850 to 1873 one fifth of the graduates whose fathers could be identified in one seminary for girls came from blue-collar households. Once the high school became a going concern, that proportion dropped to below one tenth. By contrast, between 1873 and 1884 almost half of the girls graduating from the high school came from blue-collar families. Just as a public high school education plus the ability to read law locally enabled more working-class boys to enter a profession formerly restricted to the more elite graduates of private academies, so, too, the high school enabled working-class women to enter a profession by the last quarter of the century.

Despite their dominance of teaching, few women became proprietors of their own schools, the only lucrative positions in the profession. Women occasionally started up small seminaries but they rarely lasted more than a few years. Only one attempted to offer a comprehensive course of study. The leading seminaries had male proprietors; their wives often participated actively as teachers or matrons, but only one actually ran the school as principal while her husband, the proprietor, pursued his dry goods business.

The dearth of women among school proprietors reflects a more general reluctance of women to engage in commercial enterprises. Of the businesses reported on by the R. G. Dun credit agency between 1845 and 1880, 9 percent were owned by women. Moreover, at any census only 3 percent of the female labor force could be classified as proprietors. Although the credit reports are more inclusive because they list businesses which operated between census years, they underestimate the number of women who attempted to establish enterprises. Between 1845 and 1880 nineteen female grocers appear in the city directory who are not listed either in the credit reports or the census. Credit reporters similarly underestimated male proprietors, especially in the earlier years. In both cases, they failed to report on firms which stayed in business only a year or two, especially those who relied solely on local wholesalers and did not seek credit elsewhere.

Founding a business required capital. Although many rich widows and well-endowed daughters had substantial holdings in real estate and bank stocks, we do not know how actively they participated in the management of their estates. We do know that women of means did not regard remunerative work as appropriate to their status and that few chose to invest in their own businesses. Some wives did invest in their husbands' enterprises. The credit reports for Poughkeepsie list a few wives as a source of capital for their husbands. An occasional wife would keep a sharp eye on her husband's use of her funds; one had his business closed up by the sheriff when it did not prosper.[16]

The varied careers of the tiny minority of women who ran their own businesses do call into question the commonly held view that eighteenth-century women had a far wider involvement in commerce than women in the nineteenth century. Poughkeepsie women engaged in about the same range of enterprises often cited as proof that eighteenth-century women had vastly superior opportunities to their successors, supposedly confined to their homes by the Victorian cult of domesticity. In both centuries women's participation in business was sporadic and unusual.

While the majority of Poughkeepsie's female proprietors evaluated by R. G. Dun and Company ran businesses associated with feminine clothing, the city also had female saloon and hotel keepers, grocers, a newspaper proprietor, and stove dealers. Some of these women had succeeded to their deceased husbands' businesses and continued to run them competently. One native widow headed her husband's bottling establishment after his death in 1863. Credit reporters characterized her in 1873 as a "sharp, shrewd woman — understands how to manage her affairs." By 1882 she employed her sons in the business but she remained as proprietor in 1890. Another widow ran her husband's print works and edited a weekly newspaper for a short time after his death, while a German and a native widow continued their husbands' stove businesses for a longer period.[17]

Mary Kelly inherited $10,000 and a grocery business from her husband in 1870. When she died in 1880, she left an estate of well over $20,000. In addition to running the grocery, she invested shrewdly in real estate and became a moneylender, prospering sufficiently to back her son in the dry goods business with two native-born partners. Such widows were exceptions, however. When a male proprietor died, his business usually was liquidated or, less commonly, passed on to a male heir. Moreover, although businesses inherited from spouses include some of the most prosperous female-headed firms, they account for only one tenth of all businesswomen listed in credit reports.[18]

On the whole, firms headed by women were more marginal than those headed by men; 61 percent of the female-headed businesses whose worth was estimated by R. G. Dun and Company were valued at $1,000 or less and only 4 percent at more than $10,000. By contrast, only 36 percent of the male-headed firms were valued at $1,000 or less and 17 percent at more than $10,000. The venturesomeness and success of a Mary Brazier was unusual. After suffering a fire at her mill in New York City, she established the Fallkill Knitting Machine Company in Poughkeepsie in 1882 with an investment estimated at $30,000. Partly because the insurance settlement on the fire loss proved to be slow and inadequate, she failed in 1884. Her sister-in-law, wife of a machinist, bought the stock and machinery remaining after the settlement of debts and by 1886 the mill had started up again, selling all of its production of shirts to a New York firm. In 1890 credit reporters found it to be "a pushing and enterprising concern" and during the nineties the directory listed Mary Brazier as proprietor.[19]

At the other extreme, most businesswomen not associated with clothing ran small groceries, saloons, and confectioneries. A credit reporter's characterization of one saloon indicates the marginality of many of these ventures: "Nothing but a third-class billiard table, a few chairs and counter and poor at that." Invariably these enterprises appear at the owner's place of residence and virtually all were operated by wives or widows. For a wife with children at home or for a widow with a house and children, such home-based businesses were attractive. Single women did not engage in them.[20]

The majority of business women, both successful and unsuccessful, clustered in the more traditional lines of feminine clothing. Such firms accounted for two thirds of all firms run by women with milliners alone representing almost half of all firms ever listed in the R. G. Dun reports. At any census listing milliners and owners of fancy goods stores constituted the majority of female proprietors.

Distinctions between millineries, fancy goods stores and dressmaking establishments were blurred. Few women confined themselves to only one line. Mrs. De Groff, for example, advertised in 1858 that she had "made arrangements to carry on dressmaking in all its branches" and in 1859 that she would do "stitching, quilting, tucking and family sewing generally" as well as sell patterns, sewing machines, and materials for dressmaking. By 1862 she had added hoop skirts, corsets, notions, and ready-made garments. Credit reporters found one woman "doing a large trade not only in millinery but also in dresses, cloaks and mantillas" and another keeping "a nice stock of trimmings but her principal business is dressmaking."[21]

Whatever their specialties most of these shops remained small and vanished quickly. Of those evaluated for credit, only 28 percent were ever estimated as worth more than $1,000 and only a few lasted ten years or more. Since most women manufacturing in these lines did custom work only, space and capital requirements were minimal. Milliners often ran shops in their houses; those who located in the central business district usually rented rooms above well-established stores. One of the longest successes for years rented space above a men's clothing store and was described by a credit reporter as "doing a fair business but capital moderate like most of the milliners here." The largest firm in 1875 reported an annual product of $12,000 and five female employees.[22]

Because of its respectability and its exclusively female clientele, millinery and dressmaking attracted single women as well as wives and widows. Of the 40 women listed in the R. G. Dun and Company reports who could be identified as single, 33 were milliners and four were dressmakers. For the spinster daughters of a Methodist minister—"prudent girls working on a small capital"—millinery afforded a safe and respectable way to earn a necessary livelihood.[23]

Some wives married to incompetent husbands supported their families by very skillful management of their shops. A credit reporter characterized a female shopowner as "the man of the two" and after her husband died commented that "her great clog and incumbrance she has had to struggle with is removed . . . She is an active, prudent, energetic woman and if she succeeded with a drunken husband, she certainly will without him." Another woman's husband was found to be "sort of a dead duck" but she was "a real businesswoman and doing well." Not all wives overcame such liabilities. A corset maker's husband was a "worthless fellow and absorbs most of her profits." When a dressmaker failed in 1866, the credit reporter observed that "she was doing a large business but managed it badly by entrusting her husband with her money and he squandered it."[24]

Other wives ran their businesses as adjuncts to their husbands' firms or as means of supplementing family income. One received the backing of her husband and occupied a corner of his merchant tailor shop. Another ran a millinery business in her husband's fancy goods store. Among others, a carriage maker, a laborer, and a livery stable owner had wives who opened small shops.

Wives had once been important among workers in the clothing trades as well as among shopowners, but decrease in domestic manufacturing resulted in the virtual disappearance of married women who sewed for income. While the total number of women in the skilled trades declined between 1860 and 1880, the proportion of wives among them dropped from 25 to 8 percent whereas daughters increased from 35 to 56 percent. Competition from male workers, especially German immigrants, and the advent of ready-made clothing sharply diminished opportunities for women in work that could be performed at home rather than in a shop.

Women who worked as tailoresses suffered the sharpest loss in employment. While it has been impossible to discover what proportion of tailoresses in 1860 worked at home, the available evidence suggests the prevalence of work outside shops. Piece work was well established in tailoring by the late fifties. Newspaper advertisements, for example, called for women "to work on pants" or "to sew buttonholes." Since even the largest tailoring establishments reported no more than two sewing machines in 1860, it is likely that much of the piece work was done at home. The surviving records of one large clothier indicate that that firm did have its work done outside. Its records list variable amounts paid at irregular intervals to a number of women, some of whom appear in the census as tailoresses. Finally, the high proportion of wives among tailoresses reinforces the assumption that most women did their work at home. Over one third of the native-born tailoresses in 1860 were married women.[25]

Although never so numerous as tailoresses, seamstresses, vest makers, and shirtmakers also became fewer. Vest makers disappeared entirely by 1880, and the number of seamstresses was halved from its 1860 total. Symptomatically, both a shirt and a skirt factory opened in Poughkeepsie in the late seventies. Young girls performed most of the work on sewing machines inside the factories.

While the census undoubtedly failed to record as employed some women who performed piece work at home, the sharp decline in tailoresses and seamstresses does not seem to be a matter of census reportage. The number of dressmakers, most of whom had no regular place of work but the home, increased from 156 in 1860 to 261 in 1880. Unlike other sewing women, dressmakers continued to prosper because they faced no competition from men in that line and because ready-made garments had not yet become common in ladies' apparel.

Unlike larger cities, Poughkeepsie had few large dressmaking establishments so that the majority of dressmakers must have been self-employed. Only a few merited evaluation for credit. The largest firm, with the "trade of most of the wealthy people in the city," employed "quite a number of hands" but seems an exception. More typical was the woman who "keeps no store, just has a shingle stuck up at the corner of the house, signifying that she is a knightress of the needle, don't think she pretends to keep any goods for sale, just makes up what is brought to her." Although dressmakers far outnumbered milliners at every census, the newspapers show only an occasional advertisement for apprentices or employees in the dressmaking trade whereas advertisements for milliners appeared regularly in the spring and the fall.[26]

While dressmaking by 1880 was virtually the only line of sewing in which wives participated, it was not so compatible with family responsibilities and so it never attracted the same proportion of married women that tailoring had in 1860. While some of the actual sewing could be done at home, dressmakers often traveled to their customers' residences for fittings and sometimes for the making of the entire garment. For example, Edmund Platt noted in his diary that "Miss Tulle a dressmaker was here all day."[27]

The decline in domestic manufacture affected native-born women most severely. In 1860 over 60 percent of all employed native women had found work doing some kind of sewing but by 1880 only a quarter did so. Nor did they maintain their relative importance compared to immigrant women in the fewer sewing jobs remaining, the proportion of native women falling from 82 percent in 1860 to 58 percent in 1880. Among dressmakers, the only expanding trade, the native proportion similarly dropped from 81 percent in 1860 to 59 percent in 1880.

The question of whether native women voluntarily withdrew from sewing or were pushed out by competition from foreign-born women and men cannot be answered definitively. For wives the decline of domestic manufacture did result in retirement from the labor force but native household heads, many of whom were widows with dependent children, did not withdraw to the same degree. Many native daughters probably relinquished their needles by choice. Although the proportion of employed native daughters remained constant between 1860 and 1880, daughters employed at sewing fell absolutely from 150 in 1860 and 1870 to 97 in 1880. In 1880, a native daughter was as likely to enter the shoe, skirt, or shirt factory as to take up her needle at home.

Natives comprised more than half of the female factory labor force in 1880 and adolescents predominated. Only 12 percent of the native operatives were over 30 and over half were under 20 whereas half of the traditional native female garment workers in 1880 were over 30. The majority of the operatives lived at home, over a quarter with widowed mothers. Of those who lived at home with employed fathers, 61 percent came from households headed by a skilled worker and 33 percent from households headed by semiskilled and unskilled workers, a substantial overrepresentation of skilled workers. About a quarter of the native factory workers lived as boarders and relatives, suggesting that they probably came to Poughkeepsie to work in the factory.[28]

Foreign-born factory workers were even more youthful than their native sisters, almost two thirds being under 20. Virtually all the Irish and German girls who worked in the factory lived at home. But whereas half of the German girls with employed fathers came from households headed by a skilled male worker or a petty proprietor, two thirds of the Irish operatives came from semiskilled and unskilled households. As was true for men, the factory brought together the daughters of native and foreign-born workers and the children of skilled and unskilled workers.

While the factory regimen excluded wives and household heads, for young girls it meant new opportunity—steady work at a regular wage often higher than the remuneration for piece work in the garment industry. Although the more traditional garment makers still outnumbered factory operatives among women workers, the gap had narrowed substantially by 1880. Roughly a third of all native, German, and English employed women under 20 worked in factories while less than a fifth made garments outside them. Only among the Irish did the sewing trades remain the more important source of employment for young women.

Throughout the middle decades, domestic service provided the most constant source of large numbers of jobs for young women. Of the whole domestic labor force, white and black, the Irish in 1860 and 1870 accounted for over half of all domestics; by 1880 that proportion had fallen to 46 percent. Black women comprised a constant 16 percent in all census years while the native-born proportion increased from 19 percent in 1860 to 24 percent in 1880. Over two thirds of the female servants in Poughkeepsie were under age 30. Among the native-born and Germans, teenage girls made up approximately 40 percent of the domestic labor force. Among Irish servants, however, between 43 and 48 percent were women in their twenties and only about 20 percent were in their teens.

The Irish less readily allowed their teenage daughters to live out in strange households. In 1880, two fifths of Irish teenage domestics lived at home compared to one quarter of native-born teenage domestics. During their twenties though, four fifths of Irish women working as servants lived in the households of their employers, a proportion comparable to that of the native-born. Among German servants in their teens and twenties, about two thirds lived out.

The reluctance of Irish parents to allow their young daughters to live in other households is understandable. Unlike German servants, half of whom were employed in German households, Irish servants invariably worked in native Protestant households. The large number of advertisements specifying "a Protestant girl," "American or German girl" only underlined the religious and cultural gap between young Irish girls and their prospective employers. And the ads did not mention the usual sharp and expected difference in social class; unlike female factory operatives and skilled workers, many of whom came from households headed by skilled males, women in domestic service usually came from homes headed by unskilled or semiskilled workers. Furthermore, young women in service could not count on either the companionship of peers or expert guidance and quasi-parental solicitude from older staff members since three quarters of all households which employed servants in 1880 employed only one at a given time.

Work specialization among domestics in Poughkeepsie remained comparatively rare as it did in the nation as a whole. Even in households with several employees, the census seldom attempted to differentiate the types of services rendered. As Francis Walker commented in the 1870 census, "the organization of domestic services in the United States is so crude that no distinction whatsoever can be successfully maintained." Ralph Bartholomew's remembrance of servants in Greenwich Village epitomizes the versatility expected. "In the Golden Age each family employed one domestic, generally an Irish girl. She washed on Monday, ironed on Tuesday, swept on

Wednesday, went courting on Thursday, cleaned on Friday, and baked on Saturday. She was cook, waitress, chambermaid and butler."[29]

Typical help-wanted advertisements in Poughkeepsie specified a wide range of tasks, often ill-defined: "a girl or middle-aged woman who understands cooking, washing and ironing and general housework in a small family," "a woman as cook and laundress," "a tidy industrious girl to do general housework." While many of those looking for domestic work reciprocated by an expressed willingness to perform any or all household tasks, others sought to define the kind of work, usually the lightest, which they would like to do: "situation wanted by a colored girl as chambermaid," "situation wanted by a middle-aged German lady, to keep house or nurse sick or tend children," "situation wanted as chambermaid and plain sewing," "a respectable German girl wants a situation as a ladies' maid and seamstress or to take care of grown children," "wanted a place by a Scotch girl as waiter or any work except cooking."

Whether market conditions enabled servants to find the kinds of work they wanted cannot be known. But the newspapers from time to time ritually sympathized with employers in their quest for docile, competent help. "One of the afflictions which poor people escape is servants. Blessed are those who can do without them . . . The demand for domestic help fully keeps pace with the supply, and the ladies who condescend to the business, finding their services in demand and the pay good, become very independent and exacting in their terms."[30]

At the very least, employers could expect a constant turnover in their household help. Few women remained in domestic service for as long as ten years. Of the white servants listed in the 1860 census, only 15 percent remained as servants ten years later, and of the servants in the 1870 census only 11 percent were still servants in 1880. Ironically, despite the advertised preference for Protestant women, Irish women accounted for most of the white women who continued as domestics, 19 percent of them remaining so between 1860 and 1870 and 15 percent between 1870 and 1880. Since black women invariably worked in domestic occupations at every census, they most frequently remained as servants, 30 percent doing so between 1860 and 1870 and 19 percent between 1870 and 1880. Moreover, because a high proportion of black women continued to work after marriage, the actual percentage of those remaining as servants probably is higher. Few servants, black or white, stayed in the same households, however. Of all the white servants in Poughkeepsie, only three appeared in the same family in three censuses and only twenty-eight in two censuses. Only three black women reported themselves with the same family for two censuses and none for three.

Desirous as employers might have been of finding a faithful retainer, few rewarded service by providing security in old age. An occasional exception occurred. When a black woman died in her seventy-fifth year, her employers sent a letter to the local newspaper extolling her virtues. Noting that she had been employed by them for 37 years and had been given the best of care during her illness, they wrote that "in addition to goodness, faithfullness and industry, she was intelligent and possessed an unusual fund of common sense." The newspaper commented editorially that "the rarity of such tributes to faithful servants accounts for much of the lack of respect for the employers by the employed in this world."[31]

More typical of employers' sense of responsibility was the treatment of an Irish servant by a well-off native family. She appeared in the 1860 and 1870 census as a servant of one brother but by 1880 had become a member of another brother's household. In 1913, now age 75, she entered the poor house where she died seven years later; the admitting officer listed a member of the employing family as the "friend" who brought her. While few domestics had given the long service this Irishwoman had to one family, the outdoor relief rolls and lists of inmates of the poor house testify to the economic vulnerability of servants.[32]

Their vulnerability is the extreme case pointing up the general question of economic insecurity for women. That question can best be explored with the evidence available for this period by looking at the frequency with which women owned property, lived with their own families, took employment, and resorted to public charity and by asking how these traits differ according to ethnic origin and age. The most striking suggestion of the ultimate insecurity of women, should family support be lacking, is the infrequency of assets of their own. Real property in Poughkeepsie during the middle decades overwhelmingly remained in male hands, women accounting for only 16 percent of those assessed in 1870 and 21 percent in 1880. In neither year did as many as one quarter of the female household heads of any ethnic group own property and the proportion of wives owning property never reached 5 percent for any group.

For women over 30, the decision to work varied sharply with their marital status. Married women rarely worked. Single women reported employment far more often than widows. Among native women in their thirties and forties in 1880, for example, over two fifths of the spinsters held jobs compared to about one quarter of the widows. The differences were not so marked among native women in their fifties or their sixties, but single women still continued to report employment more often.

The expectation that women should remain embedded within their families, depending economically first upon their parents, then upon their husbands, and finally, if they survived as widows, upon their grown-up children or other relatives appears in the household situation of the majority of women in the different phases of the family life cycle. The periods as well as the circumstances in which women maintained their own households or boarded away from their families suggest economic necessity more than preference. Until they reached their sixties only a small proportion of single native women headed their own households. Two thirds of those in their thirties still lived in their parents' households but by the time they were 40 that proportion had dropped to a third. As single women aged, an increasing proportion became household heads or were taken in by relatives. Of the single women 60 or over in 1880, 43 percent headed their own households and 46 percent lived with relatives. Only a little over 10 percent of single women in any age group ever lived as boarders and the proportion who worked as live-in servants never exceeded 11 percent.

By contrast, native widows headed their households more often. About half of the young widows in their thirties presided over their own households while one quarter still lived at home. In their forties and fifties, about two thirds of native widows were household heads, most of them with working children at home. As their children grew up and left home, elderly widows began to break up their own households: only half of those sixty and over remained as household heads and one quarter went to live with their children. The proportion of native widows who were boarders and relatives hovered around 10 percent respectively for all age groups and the proportion who lived as servants never exceeded 5 percent.

The very different household and employment patterns of Irish single women and widows reflects both their greater poverty and the absence in the New World of an elaborate familial network. Single Irish women invariably worked, well over three quarters of those between 30 and 60 doing so and half of those over 60 doing so. Very few single Irish women of any age headed their own households; at every age except over 60 the majority lived as servants.

A much greater proportion of Irish than of native widows worked. Among widows in their thirties 41 percent of the Irish widows reported employment compared to 28 percent of the natives. Young Irish widows less often had family in Poughkeepsie to turn to for aid when their husbands died or deserted. Although older Irish widows continued to work more frequently than their native sisters, the differences between the two lessened as they aged, reflecting the increase of working-age children as support for both groups.

Irish widows also headed their own households more frequently than native widows. In old age, fewer went to live with their children and very few ever resided in relatives' households. The majority of those who headed their own households, however, still had children living with them. For Irish widows, as well as native, family provided, especially in old age, a vital support.

Because of women's economic dependence, the loss of the breadwinners often necessitated turning to public charity. About 10 percent of the native white household heads in 1880 appeared at some time between 1871 and 1885 on the list of recipients of outdoor relief.[33] Fifteen percent of Irish household heads likewise sought public aid but, poor as the Irish were, they were more fortunate than black women, half of whom applied for relief during the same years. About two thirds of the female relief recipients were widows and another 22 percent were married with only 3 percent being reported as single; the remainder reported no marital status. In the case of married women, the recording officer mentioned desertion by the husband as the cause of destitution in almost half of the cases; since such comments were random rather than regular, it is probable that most married women on relief had been abandoned.

The need for relief coincided with crucial stages in the life cycle of women. Of the relief recipients, women in their thirties, forties, and sixties each comprised one quarter while only 14 percent were in their fifties and 12 percent under thirty. Younger women were less likely to suffer the loss of their husbands, and those in their fifties more often had working-age children at home.

For women in late nineteenth-century Poughkeepsie, the family continued to offer the surest means of support. With the exception of physicians and a few owners of businesses, women could not earn a decent livelihood by themselves. Industrialization did not improve their opportunities before 1880. Rather, kinds of work that had been compatible with family responsibilities declined sharply in Poughkeepsie; the contraction in local demand for women in the sewing trades left those who remained at home few means of earning money beyond taking in boarders. The rising proportions of domestics and factory operatives among female workers ensured that only the young and the single would continue to find much employment in the immediate future.

The expansion of clerical and sales jobs in the city before 1880 largely benefited men. The increasing specialization and reduction in the responsibility and skill required in so many of these jobs would make them less attractive in the future to ambitious men and more available to women. But in our period the only dramatic expansion of respectable work for women occurred in teaching. The daughters of the working class benefited most from the femininization of that profession, but the gain in respectability was offset by niggardly salaries. In general, the range of occupations and of economic reward for women remained slight compared to that for men.

Conclusion

THE EVIDENCE FOR Poughkeepsie has contributed to a picture of broad similarity in occupational structure and mobility, and in ethnic advantage within both, between cities that differ in many characteristics. Recent comparisons which emphasize this similarity do rely primarily on studies of relatively diversified economies so that they may not prove to be representative of mill towns and other more specialized urban economies. Whether newer cities outside the Northeast offered more opportunities for immigrants also has yet to be determined, but it seems unlikely that the relative advantages of natives and newcomers will differ greatly.

Within a structure of marked economic inequality, a high level of geographic, occupational, and to a lesser extent property mobility will be found together with clear evidence of advantage according to social origin, both class and ethnic. Taken as a whole, blacks and immigrants will show the poorest opportunities and whites of native parentage, the best, with the second generation in America closer to natives in occupational behavior but more precarious in gains. Even a hierarchy in advantage among ethnic groups seems probable whether or not it is as distinct in other periods as the difference in opportunities at mid-century of British, Germans, Irish, and blacks.

These broad patterns derived from classification at a high level of generalization obscure as much as they reveal, not least differences in the avenues of opportunity produced by changes in the scale of economic organization and in the division of labor. Because the meaning of mobility for particular groups in particular times and places depends upon these differences, we have believed that the necessary next step in historical studies of mobility is to identify the paths of mobility more precisely through microscopic examination of the opportunities of workers in specific occupations. This refinement in analysis immediately calls attention to fundamental, if expected, differences between the era of Civil War and the twentieth century in the most frequent forms of mobility even where the social distance traversed may be regarded as broadly comparable.

In mid-nineteenth-century Poughkeepsie the achievement of self-employment remained much more common as a form of upward mobility than improvement in position within any organization. Proprietors trained to a craft still loomed large among the city's substantial middle class. The old hope that the sequence of apprenticeship and employment as journeyman would end in a comfortable livelihood earned in one's own shop had not yet become wholly unrealistic nor had the occupational worlds of wage-earners and businessmen separated as much as they have in the twentieth century.

Because Poughkeepsie lagged behind larger cities in its region in scale of enterprise, this sequence of advancement in artisans' careers and the expected movement from clerkships to proprietorships or partnerships in commerce may well have predominated longer in upward mobility in this small city. But it is this very possibility of limitation in typicality related to differences in economic development which mobility studies now need to identify, not least to understand how differences in kinds of opportunities may be related to differences between localities in social and political behavior.

What does seem to be just as true for other cities, regardless of size, as for Poughkeepsie are the marked differences we find between natives and newcomers in their dependence on particular avenues of opportunity. Given the immigrants' lack of familarity and personal connections, their disadvantage compared to natives in owning large manufacturing or commercial enterprises was expected. Less predictable was the impressive frequency with which immigrants achieved self-employment in the skilled crafts, especially in the food and apparel trades, as contrasted with native predominance in the construction and industrial trades where self-employment was less common.

Close examination of these differences yields evidence for a picture of ethnic stratification according to relative desirability of work that appears at every level of the city's labor force. Immigrants tended to predominate in crafts and factories with lower wages or less attractive working conditions. In retailing and services they appear disproportionately in marginal neighborhood ventures catering to their countrymen rather than in shops in the central business district serving a wider clientele. The most glaring ethnic stratification appears between jobs requiring least skill, but it has been obscured in mobility studies by aggregating these jobs as unskilled and semiskilled or in one rank of low manual. As it turns out, whites of native parentage predominate in jobs with the most independence and the Irish and especially the blacks in jobs most clearly servile and menial in character.

But more refined analyses of mobility patterns also make clear that, regardless of ethnic origin, the type of occupation one started with profoundly influenced the likelihood that one would continue to pursue it. The frequency with which men shifted among very different kinds of service and unskilled work argues that employers put little premium on previous experience in them. By contrast, workers in professions and the skilled crafts show remarkable stability in occupation with the only major exceptions occurring in trades declining locally and in trades whose skills were readily transferrable to other occupations. These exceptions point up the importance for assessments of changing opportunities of a closer look at kinds of occupational change which mobility studies have ignored because they have classified them as horizontal rather than vertical. Our analysis suggests that any substantial shifting from one skilled trade to others reveals differences in opportunity.

Our study covers too short a span of time to identify trends definitively. Yet the most interesting inferences from this microscopic examination concern the future. Our evidence suggests that industrialization already was producing locally a scale of enterprise and degree of specialization which made dramatic success stories by recent immigrants less likely. Moreover, by largely eliminating the traditional artisan middle class the same process helped narrow differences in opportunities between various kinds of manual workers and so created a working class.

The one clear trend we found in avenues of mobility in Pough-

keepsie is the increasing importance of clerical work rather than a
skilled trade as preparation for proprietorship. But that shift seems
to us only the most extended symptom among a variety of signs,
especially in the last decade of our study, that specialization and
division of labor was transforming local opportunities. Although
proprietorships in the food trades remained just as frequent with
new neighborhood shops opening up as the city expanded, self-
employment in most manufacturing crafts declined. What we do
not know yet — what only studies comparing frequencies of achievement of self-employment in manufacturing with other kinds of upward mobility in the twentieth century can show — is the extent to
which decline in opportunities for proprietorship in older industries
was offset by opportunities in new industries. The frequency with
which new small enterprises have continued to emerge in America
even in the manufacturing sector has been impressive.

During the seventies upward mobility from skilled manual work
to proprietorships dropped sharply as did achievement of proprietorships by clerical and sales workers. The depression undoubtedly
exaggerated the decline in both types of mobility, but the evidence
we have on scale of enterprise and ratio of firms to labor force in the
city after 1880 suggests that self-employment would be a less realistic
ambition in many lines for the future. An increasing proportion of
journeymen and clerks must have kept that status throughout their
careers. In both cases progressive division of labor meant a loss of
the versatility entailed in traditional apprenticeships in both manufacturing and commerce.

A diminished chance for self-employment was only one of the
ways industrialization limited opportunities for skilled manual
workers in Poughkeepsie. In trades whose custom manufacture suffered from competition of ready-made or factory goods from other
localities, attrition in work force occurred through a failure of
younger men to enter the trades. Older workers, including the self-
employed in some of these trades, found themselves struggling to
survive on a repairing business if they did not make a successful
transition to retailing. Skilled employments for women, heavily concentrated in the sewing trades, shrank most under the combined
impact of ready-made goods and the competition of immigrant
male workers. Opportunities for women to work in their homes
largely disappeared in Poughkeepsie by 1880 and employment became overwhelmingly that of young and single women.

The most important general consequence of the erosion of the older artisan middle class appears in the narrowing of differences between the various levels of manual work in both intra- and inter-generational mobility. The previous distinctiveness in the situation of artisans and ordinary laborers became progressively blurred as fewer artisans became shopowners and a gradually increasing proportion of less skilled workers founded small retail and service businesses or, especially in the seventies, found employment as "green hands" at previously skilled work.

Division of labor did mean an increasing differentiation of reward within skilled work itself and may well have created something like an aristocracy within the trades who performed the most difficult tasks. But whatever the situation of the most favored craftsmen, the general advantage in occupational mobility of skilled over less skilled workers decreased in our period. The newer factories contributed to this leveling process.

Artisans rarely entered the newer factories, largely in manufacturing apparel, in Poughkeepsie, but their children often did. The children's subsequent careers resemble those of the children in the same factories of less skilled workers. In enterprises like the mower and reaper works, which did employ numerous craftsmen as well as less skilled workers, the opportunities of the sons do not vary according to the skill of the father. Only in the large manufacturing establishments with the heaviest, dirtiest, and most dangerous work such as the furnaces did the children of laborers remain disproportionately concentrated in unskilled employments.

These changes in the world of manual work had profound consequences for the opportunities of immigrants and their children in Poughkeepsie. For the Irish in the second generation, overwhelmingly sons of unskilled workers, the factory leveled upward and so did opportunities in certain building and metal trades. This conforms to the conventional model which sees the more assimilated second generation improving upon the opportunities of the immigrant generation. For the Germans and, to a much lesser extent, the British, the achievement of self-employment in the crafts in the immigrant generation exceeded that of whites of native parentage and the record of the second generation did not improve upon it. Indeed in the case of the Germans, the native-born sons concentrated disproportionately in a narrowing range of crafts which can be interpreted as cul-de-sacs.

This reversal of the conventional model underscores the importance for understanding the immigrants' adaptation of the state of economic development at the time of their arrival as well as of the skills and capital they brought with them. The great influx of German artisans before the Civil War entered a local economy in which custom manufacture still predominated in most lines and in the short run the immigrants capitalized successfully upon that predominance. By the seventies, however, increasing scale and specialization in many lines of manufacture and commerce gave whites of native parentage a larger advantage in the quest for prosperity. Our evidence does not support the view that that advantage meant security for individuals or families who succeeded in a small city. The instability among Poughkeepsie's rich and the frequency of nouveaux riches is impressive.

Beyond 1880 our analyses are too limited except for the recruitment of the richest taxpayers to be able to do more than speculate about changing patterns of stratification and mobility. But it is worth emphasizing, in conclusion, the importance of increasing separation in experience between manual and other workers. With the shrinking of opportunities for artisans to become owners of large shops in their trades and so join the city's substantial middle class, and even its principal taxpayers, a previously important form of long distance mobility within a career largely disappeared. Correspondingly, the prospects lessened for men to rise to or near the top positions in their communities when they did not begin their careers at white-collar employments. As a higher level of formal education became the usual prerequisite for such employments, long distance mobility almost by definition became less common within individual careers and presumably increased instead between generations during the twentieth century.

The outlook of manual workers in the Lynds' Middletown in the 1920s suggests the shift just described. Pessimistic about the likelihood of any major improvement in positions for themselves, these workers still dreamed occasionally that their children might escape upward through education. What we need now are studies of the intervening years that specify the avenues as well as the frequencies of mobility for different groups to evaluate that sense of a sharpened difference between the business and working classes which appears in studies of Middletown and so many other communities.

We do assume that these studies will show continuing differences in patterns of opportunity between industrial cities whose economies depended overwhelmingly on manufacturing and those with more diversification. They also may show that differences in predominant types of manufacturing even in diversified economies result in significant differences in frequencies of self-employment. Perhaps they will even show more variation in mobility due to differences in region, in age, sex, and ethnic composition of the labor force, and in rapidity of change in occupational structure than the studies so far lead us to anticipate.

Whatever the structural correlates of variation in occupational mobility, we do expect microcosmic examinations to point up the differences between cities and between firms and industries within cities in negotiating the turbulent waters of economic change. Detailed studies remind us that the processes which we describe consist of individual choices, however much the choices seem to be shaped by circumstances or prevailing attitudes. They remind us that social history always must be moving back and forth between interpretation of such universal phenomena as the decline of artisan manufacture and such parochial phenomena as the lingering of that manufacture among particular groups of workers in particular localities. The necessary tension in interests was suggested by Edmund Platt in summing up his history of one city: "Poughkeepsie is not so very different from many other Eastern cities, but nevertheless has its characteristics."

Notes
Index

Notes

1. From Village to Small City

1. S. L. Walker to Benson J. Lossing, June 30, 1869, Manuscript Collection, Adriance Memorial Library; *Poughkeepsie Weekly Eagle,* 9/2/1871. Hereafter cited as *Weekly Eagle.*

2. Edmund Platt, *The Eagle's History of Poughkeepsie* (Poughkeepsie, 1905), p. 267. Hereafter cited as *Eagle's History.* The description of Poughkeepsie in this chapter draws heavily on this useful history. Stuart Blumin skillfully analyzes these twin themes of enterprise and order in *The Urban Threshold: Growth and Change in a Nineteenth-Century American Community* (Chicago: University of Chicago Press, 1976), Chapter 10.

3. At the extremes were Jersey City, N.J., the only city to more than double in population and Newburyport, Mass., the only one to lose population. Jeffrey G. Williamson and Joseph A. Swanson, "The Growth of Cities in the American Northeast, 1820-1870," *Explorations in Entrepreneurial History,* Second Series, vol. 4, no. 1 (Supplement, 1966), pp. 78-79.

4. Computed from statistics in the published volumes of the federal censuses of 1860 through 1900. Tabulations in the published volumes of the New York State censuses of 1855, 1865, and 1875 were employed for comparison of the age and sex distributions of urban populations in that state.

5. Theodore Hershberg, Michael Katz, Stuart Blumin, Laurence Glasco, and Clyde Griffen, "Occupation and Ethnicity in Five Nineteenth-Century Cities: A Collaborative Inquiry," *Historical Methods Newsletter,* 7 (June 1974), 193-194, graphs 1 and 2.

6. We are grateful to Ms. Conk for sharing with us her tables for 1870 and 1880 on composition of the work force in ten cities, which were prepared for a forth-

coming study, "The U.S. Census and Urban America: An Analysis of the Growth and Composition of the Urban American Workforce, 1870-1940."

7. In 1880, for example, a conservative estimate of the unskilled workers at the brewery, furnaces, dye wood mill, and mower works unaccounted for by specific occupational designation in the census is 260, or 28 percent of the total of 940 unspecified laborers that year. The county directory of 1879 identifies 132 of the 1880 "laborers" as employed by the above firms.

8. For changes in agriculture in Dutchess County, see David M. Ellis, *Landlords and Farmers in the Hudson-Mohawk Region, 1790-1850* (Ithaca, N.Y., 1964); *Daily Eagle,* 9/1/1866; 2/10/1865; *Weekly Eagle,* 7/9/1870.

9. Platt, *Eagle's History,* p. 239.

10. In Paterson which grew by 71 percent during the sixties, the number of grocers increased from 0.54 to 0.68 percent of the population and saloonkeepers from 0.23 to 0.80 percent between 1859 and 1870. In Poughkeepsie, which grew by 37 percent, the proportions changed less; the number of grocers decreased slightly from 0.38 to 0.34 percent and the number of saloonkeepers increased from 0.15 to 0.21 percent between 1859 and 1871. Data for both cities were taken from the directories for the years named. Herbert G. Gutman, *Work, Culture, and Society in Industrializing America: Essays in American Working-Class and Social History* (New York, 1976), p. 240.

11. R. G. and A. R. Hutchinson and Mabel Newcomer, "Study in Business Mortality: Length of Life of Business Enterprises in Poughkeepsie, New York, 1843-1936," *American Economic Review,* 27 (September 1938), 511, table 15.

12. The manufacturing schedules of the federal census for Poughkeepsie for the years 1850, 1860, 1880 and Platt's *Eagle's History* chart this uneven progress. See also the credit report for JP, p. 230, in the credit ledgers of the R. G. Dun and Company deposited in the Baker Library, Harvard University. The Mercantile Agency, organized in 1841 by Lewis Tappen, bore that name until 1859 when it became R. G. Dun and Company. The reports for Poughkeepsie begin in 1844 and, like the volumes for other cities, end in 1890. Hereafter, the credit reports will be referred to as R. G. Dun & Co., followed by the initials of the proprietor; at the request of Dun and Bradstreet, we have used only initials in citation to protect the anonymity of individuals where it seemed desirable. The credit reports for Poughkeepsie are contained in volumes 73 and 74 of the Baker Library collection, and the reports on any one individual are widely scattered. In citing page references to these volumes, we have not used any volume number if the reports are contained in volume 73; any reports for volume 74 are always preceded by the volume number.

13. R. G. Dun & Co., FC, 74, pp. 556, 700; RT, pp. 34, 41; JBT, p. 39; BL, p. 12; *Poughkeepsie Daily Press,* 1/10/1852; *Poughkeepsie Telegraph and Democrat,* 6/15/1857. Hereafter referred to as the *Daily Press* and the *Telegraph* respectively.

14. See Part III, "The Industrial City" in Gutman, *Work, Culture, and Society,* esp. pp. 254-258.

15. Theodore Hershberg, Bruce Laurie, and George Alter, "Immigrants and Industry: The Philadelphia Experience, 1850-1880," *Journal of Social History,* 9 (Winter 1975), 222-228 and Tables 3-5. For an invaluable analysis of scale of enterprise in New York State cities, see Richard H. Ehrlich, "The Development of Manufacturing in Selected Counties in the Erie Canal Corridor, 1815-1860" (Ph.D. dissertation, State University of New York, Buffalo, 1972). We have used the manuscript schedules of the federal censuses of manufactures in 1850, 1860, and 1880 for our analysis of scale in Poughkeepsie; the 1870 schedules could not be located. In computing average work force for manufacturing firms and percentage of the total

manufacturing work force accounted for by the two leading industries in cities in
New York, New Jersey, and Connecticut with populations of 20,000 or more in
1880, we have used the tables prepared from the manufacturing census which are
included in the description of each city in the "Social Statistics of Cities" volume of
the published federal census for that year.

16. A. S. Pease, *Selections of His Poems with an Autobiography and Genealogy
of His Descendants* (privately printed, 1915), p. 76.

17. Poughkeepsie's directories, unlike Boston's, did not specify the number of
old listings dropped and of new listings added, so that estimates of annual turnover
are impracticable. We have done systematic traces of a few groups of craftsmen
through directories for periods of a decade or more.

18. See Thernstrom, *The Other Bostonians*, pp. 234-235; Thomas Kessner, *The
Golden Door: Italian and Jewish Immigrant Mobility in New York City, 1880-1915*
(New York, 1977), esp. pp. 115-119.

19. Newcomer, "Study in Business Mortality," p. 512, table 16.

20. R. G. Dun & Co., GC, p. 265.

21. For analysis of how persistence in Poughkeepsie varied according to age and
property, see Stephan Thernstrom and Richard Sennett, eds., *Nineteenth-Century
Cities: Essays in the New Urban History* (New Haven, Conn., 1969), pp. 59-61.

22. See also the career of John Sutcliffe in Platt, *Eagle's History*, p. 297.

23. *Commemorative Biographical Record of Dutchess County, New York*
(Chicago: J. H. Beers & Co., 1897), p. 299; hereafter cited as *Biographical Record*.

24. *Ibid.*, p. 258.

25. *Ibid.*, p. 253; R. G. Dun & Co., SS, vol. 74, p. 411.

26. *Biographical Record*, p. 556.

27. *Ibid.*, pp. 11, 134. *Daily Eagle*, 9/3/1879.

28. *Biographical Record*, pp. 595, 846.

29. *Weekly Eagle*, 11/18/1871; *Daily Eagle*, 2/19/1864; R. G. Dun & Co., DH,
p. 395; vol. 74, pp. 518, 687; JHM, p. 36; vol. 74, p. 418.

30. *Daily Eagle*, 12/12/1879.

31. *Register of Marriages at St. Peter's Church from its foundation to 1857*,
Adriance Memorial Library.

32. The actual index of ethnic concentration by occupation for four censuses
has not been included because of length but may be obtained by writing the authors. It eliminates the effect of differences in the size of nativity groups by dividing
the percentage a group comprises of the occupational level by the percentage it
comprises of the city's labor force, creating an index number by multiplying the
result by 100. Scores of less than 100 indicate the group comprises a lesser proportion of the occupational stratum than of the labor force and, in that sense, is
underrepresented at that level. Scores higher than 100 show overrepresentation.

33. *Daily Eagle*, 7/10 and 9/25/1873.

34. *Ibid.*, 6/16, 7/4, 7/16, and 9/27/1873; Platt, *Eagle's History*, pp. 253-254.

35. *Daily Eagle*, 9/15 and 9/29, 1873.

36. *Ibid.*, 9/11, 9/24, 9/29, and 10/9/1873.

37. Edward C. Bolton, M.D., to Benson J. Lossing, October 11, 1873, Adriance
Memorial Library.

38. *Daily Eagle*, 1/1 and 4/13/1876.

39. *Ibid.*, 9/2, 3, 5, and 6/1873. For discussions by blacks of their hopes for
better education, see *Weekly Eagle*, 9/24/1870, and *Daily Eagle*, 9/23, 9/24, and
10/19/1870. A "colored men's educational convention" resolved to erect and
furnish a college to be located near the city; three prominent local blacks

incorporated Touissant L'Overture College early in 1871 but the project never materialized. *Ibid.*, 2/10/1871.

2. Perspectives on Success

1. *Eastman Business College Catalogue,* 1886, pp. 4, 6, 10-11.

2. Howard P. Chudacoff, "Mobility Studies at a Crossroads," in *Reviews in American History,* 2 (June 1974), 185; David Montgomery, "The New Urban History," in *ibid.*, 2 (December 1974), 502; Herbert Gans, *The Urban Villagers: Group and Class in the Life of Italian Americans* (New York, 1962); Ely Chinoy, *Automobile Workers and the American Dream* (Garden City, N.Y., 1955).

3. *Daily Press,* 10/18/1867.

4. Diary of Edmund Platt, December 31, 1875; *Daily Eagle,* 2/17/1877.

5. R. G. Dun & Co., LH, p. 59.

6. R. G. Dun & Co., AD, pp. 80, 106, 268; JB, pp. 76, 148, 161.

7. R. G. Dun & Co., JC, pp. 37, 343; BA, pp. 94, 244; vol. 74, p. 622.

8. For analyses of nineteenth-century success literature, see Richard Weiss, *The American Myth of Success* (New York, 1969), esp. pp. 100-101; John Cawelti, *Apostles of the Self-Made Man* (Chicago, 1965), esp. chapter 2. For local expression of this older perspective, see *Daily Eagle,* 6/13/1868, and *Daily News,* 12/12/1877.

9. *Daily Telegraph,* 3/24/1852.

10. R. G. Dun & Co., WD, pp. 228, 231, 438.

11. *Daily Press,* 5/22/1868.

12. Diary of Edmund H. Hart in the possession of Mr. and Mrs. E. Stuart Hubbard, Jr., Poughkeepsie; *Daily Eagle,* 6/19/1866; Minutes of the WCTU; Adriance Memorial Library, May 20, 1874.

13. *Daily Press,* 3/6, 4/13, 4/14, and 4/16/1868.

14. *Daily Eagle,* 7/2 and 8/28/1877; *Daily News,* 7/26/1877.

15. *Daily Eagle,* 10/24/1870.

16. *Daily Press,* 9/9, 9/10, and 9/11/1863.

17. Gareth Stedman Jones, "Working-Class Culture and Working-Class Politics in London, 1870-1900: Notes on the Remaking of the Working Class," *Journal of Social History,* 7 (Summer, 1974), 460-508; see the essay by Lee Rainwater in Sam Bass Warner, Jr., ed., *Planning for a Nation of Cities* (Cambridge, Mass., 1967).

18. *Daily Press,* 9/29 and 10/16/ 1868; *Daily Eagle,* 8/23 and 8/24/1868. The analysis of the composition of the fire companies draws on newpaper reports and especially on an 1867 listing of 372 members of fire companies and their occupations contained in the Chief Engineer's Report for 1867.

19. *Daily Press,* 1/31, 2/5, and 7/23/1868.

20. *Daily Eagle,* 7/7/1870.

21. Milton Gordon, *Assimilation in American Life* (New York, 1964); Timothy Smith, "Immigration in Twentieth-Century America," *American Historical Review,* 71 (July 1966), 1274.

22. *Jubilee Year Book, Church of the Nativity* (Poughkeepsie, 1897), pp. 5,7. We are grateful to Agnes Langdon, professor of German, Bard College, for translation of this book.

23. R. G. Dun & Co., FH, pp. 138-139, 376-377; vol. 74, pp. 506, 552.

24. *Jubilee Year Book, Church of the Nativity,* p.7.

25. *Daily Eagle,* 6/25/1866; 1/17/1874; 1/19 and 2/17/1876; 8/7/1877; 6/3, and 11/4/1879; for Americus Club officers 8/14, *Daily Eagle* 5/2/1876; 5/9/1877;

11/27/1879; for Friendship coterie, *Daily Eagle,* 1/26/1877; 7/10/1877; 5/15/1879.

26. *Jubilee Year Book, Church of the Nativity,* p. 87.

27. R. G. Dun & Co., MK, p. 33; *Biographical Record,* pp. 797-798; *Chronograph of St. Peter's Church,* p. 20; Conrad Arensberg, *The Irish Countryman* (Garden City, N.Y., 1968).

28. R. G. Dun & Co., LH & K, vol. 74, pp. 471, 520.

29. *Biographical Record,* p. 579; *Daily Eagle,* 3/10, 6/4, 6/5, 6/7, and 6/12/1866; 4/27 and 10/21/1868.

30. *Daily Press,* 10/10/1868; the marriage register of St. Peter's Church specifically recorded 27 marriages involving a Protestant between 1858 and 1880. About 10 others involve conspicuously Protestant names but were not identified within the church records as being Protestant.

31. We cannot determine, for example, the regions — let alone the counties — in Ireland from which Poughkeepsie's immigrants came. Yet the literature makes clear the existence of two distinct economies in nineteenth-century and especially pre-famine Ireland, a rural subsistence economy comprehending four fifths of the population and a maritime cash economy along the eastern coastal fringe and the towns of Limerick and Galway. Dissimilarities in social composition as well as economy resulted in minimal exchange between them. While the maritime economy included many Catholics on the lower occupational levels, they lived in an exclusively English-speaking world; by contrast, the number of Irish speakers remained high in many parts of the overwhelmingly Catholic subsistence economy. Although emigration from the latter predominated during the famine, a continuing stream came from the maritime economy. Origin in the more sophisticated or the primitive economy may have influenced mobility in the New World, but we have no way of determining such an influence. We are indebted for this analysis to Patrick J. Blessing, "West among Strangers: Irish Migration to California, 1850-1880" (Ms., n.d.) chapter 2.

32. Derived from Minutes of St. Peter's Church RCTAB Society, 1880-1885 (William Leahey, recorder), Adriance Memorial Library.

33. *Daily Press,* 5/5/1868; *Daily Eagle,* 11/10/1868; 11/16/1870; 11/7/1872; 1/5/1876; 4/21/1879.

3. Chances to Rise

1. Michael B. Katz, *The People of Hamilton, Canada West: Family and Class in a Mid-Nineteenth-Century City* (Cambridge, Mass., 1975), pp. 139-140; see also Katz, "Occupational Classification in History," *Journal of Interdisciplinary History,* 3 (1972), 63-88; Stuart Blumin, "The Historical Study of Vertical Mobility," *Historical Methods Newsletter,* 1 (September 1968), 1-13; Donald J. Treiman, "The Validity of the 'Standard International Occupational Prestige Scale' for Historical Data" (Paper delivered at the MSSB Conference on International Comparisons of Social Mobility in Past Societies, June 1972); and Clyde Griffen, "The Study of Occupational Mobility in Nineteenth-Century America: Problems and Possibilities," *Journal of Social History,* 5 (1972), 310-330.

2. Thernstrom, *The Other Bostonians,* chapter 9.

3. For examples of how the classification of occupations as white-collar and blue-collar also distorts contemporary analysis of status, see Andrew Levinson, *The Working-Class Majority* (New York, 1974), chapter 1.

4. Eric Hobsbawm, *Labouring Men* (New York, 1964), pp. 273-274.

5. See Thernstrom, *The Other Bostonians,* appendix B.

6. In the essay cited above, Donald Treiman's case for the usefulness of a precise interval scale for historical data depends partly upon confusion of stability in occupational designation with continuity in the level of skill required and partly upon overrepresentation in his historical lists of occupations at the upper and lower ends of the hierarchy where skill and status, we think, are both less ambiguous and more stable over time.

7. Before the regular introduction of a classified section in 1859, specification of shop ownership was less systematic. We used other sources to supplement the directories in identifying the self-employed in the 1850 census.

8. R. G. Dun & Co., JJ, p. 294.

9. Since this chapter focuses on individual mobility, both real estate and personal property whether or not they were part of the business itself are relevant to the differentiation. (Differentiation of petty from large businesses, however, requires a more restricted standard of capital in the business, such as the estimates of the worth of store, fixtures, and inventory sometimes detailed in credit reports.)

10. The failure of the 1880 census to report property is the primary reason for using a functional division of white-collar workers in our comparison of mobility for three decades. At the time we coded our data for the computer, we had not been able to locate the tax rolls for the city. Our vertical ranking of high and low white-collar for proprietors depends upon self-reportage of property in the censuses from 1850 through 1870, which permits comparison of mobility in and out of these ranks in the fifties and the sixties but not during the seventies. Subsequently we did discover the tax rolls and at the end of this chapter we will use our manual linking of the 1870 and 1880 rolls to analyze property mobility and its relation to occupational mobility.

Our analysis of mobility over full working careers has been blunted somewhat by the lack of self-reportage of property in 1880. In coding occupational status for men who remained in the city in 1880 we assigned to high white-collar rank those proprietors who already had reached that rank by 1870 by our property test. The 1880 tax roll subsequently showed us that the large majority of these men did in fact retain sufficient property in 1880 to qualify for that rank again so that the underestimation of downward mobility is not great. For example, of the 180 proprietors of native parentage at the high white-collar rank in 1870 who also appear as proprietors in the 1880 census, only 19, or 11 percent, did not sustain that rank judging by assessed property on the 1880 tax roll.

The effects on our career mobility tables would be even less visible than these downward decadal shifts between 1870 and 1880 suggest because the effects would be diffused. For example, a proprietor originally classified as climbing from skilled to high white-collar rank between first and last reported jobs in 1850 and 1880 would — if he lost his property between 1870 and 1880 — be reclassified as having risen only to low white-collar work and not appear as downwardly mobile in a recomputed career mobility table.

Since we did classify as low white-collar all proprietors in 1880 who had not attained high white-collar rank by 1870, we necessarily failed to capture the upward mobility of those who accumulated sufficient property for the first time during the seventies. The 1880 tax roll again indicates that correction of that underestimation would not change substantially our general analysis of career mobility over our thirty year period. What should be emphasized here is that this limitation in our career analysis underestimates rather than overestimates the magnitude of vertical mobility at the top of our five-strata ranking. There was more movement — though not much more — in and out of our high white-collar rank than our general tables on career mobility indicate.

11. The terminal years for a career analysis based on the census influence frequencies of mobility. However, with one major exception we find no suggestion of a substantial shift during this period which might mean quite different results if other terminal years had been chosen, say, 1890 rather than 1880 as our concluding year had the later census been available. As Table 3.1 on mobility by decades will show, there was little change in downward mobility between 1850 and 1880 but there was a marked drop in upward mobility during the seventies, especially in the achievement of proprietorships by skilled manual and clerical workers. That loss in opportunity was borne primarily by younger workers who entered the labor force not long before the depression of 1873; they would have had little chance to recover by our terminal year, 1880. But there is also reason to wonder whether for artisans, at least, a more fundamental change in opportunity for self-employment had occurred. Since most of these younger workers were less than 31 in 1880, however, they do not meet the age convention for career mobility analysis and so do not influence Table 3.3.

12. On an important aid for tracing the occupational careers of men after they leave a community, see Charles Stephenson, "Tracing Those Who Left: Mobility Studies and the Soundex Indexes to the U.S. Census," *Journal of Urban History,* 1 (November 1974), 75-84. The full indexing for 1900 and partial indexing for 1880 will prove invaluable for community mobility studies focusing on the closing decades of the century but will have only limited usefulness — primarily for tracing the destinations of out-migrants during the seventies — for the several studies of the years 1850-80 now under way.

13. For the comparison of cities, see Thernstrom, *The Other Bostonians,* p. 240, and table 9.4 on p. 234.

14. Most skilled workers reported an occupation so long as they appeared in the census. Our decision to classify unemployed manual workers — including old men previously listed at skilled trades — as unskilled does explain some of the downward mobility of the skilled late in life but in a majority of cases these workers actually reported a shift to ordinary labor or other unskilled jobs. We believe that even this limited bias toward mobility through our classification is justified by evidence on the frequency of economic dependency and hardship among artisans without employment in old age.

15. That suggestion finds reinforcement in comparison of the careers of skilled workers born in successive decades. Generally there are slight differences with no consistent direction in vertical mobility between these birth cohorts and the fact that only three cohorts — 1820-29, 1830-39, and 1840-49 — have careers which satisfy our requirements for analysis discourages putting any emphasis on these differences. But there is one exception, a consistent reduction in the frequency with which the skilled found nonmanual employment, from 40 percent of the oldest cohort to 36 and 25 percent. Had that reduction occurred only in the 1840-49 cohort the shift might plausibly be attributed to the depression for members of this youngest of the three cohorts were in their twenties and thirties during the seventies, the time of life when most artisans first went into business for themselves. That cohort did sustain the sharpest loss, but some decline in opportunity already appears in the next older cohort whose peak years for achievement of proprietorships coincide better with the city's second boom of the century at the end of the sixties. Cohort analysis can be no more than suggestive, but it reinforces the

importance of exploring in greater detail the changing situation of the artisan during the middle decades in Poughkeepsie.

16. The percentages are for men born between 1820 and 1849. Sons born between 1840 and 1849 faced hard times at the very period in their careers when accession to proprietorships occurred most often; 30 percent of those whose fathers pursued nonmanual callings held manual jobs in 1880. But earlier cohorts without this handicap showed rates of downward mobility between generations of 20 and 22 percent, twice the rate of downward mobility within career for men beginning at nonmanual work.

The slippage in occupational status between generations does not reflect any underrepresentation of the city's more successful families. Only sons at home at their first employment can be identified with certainty and among those who worked at least two censuses in Poughkeepsie, sons with fathers in nonmanual occupations comprise 44 percent of the total. By contrast, at the 1870 census they comprised only 38 percent of all identifiable sons, including those employed in Poughkeepsie at only one census.

17. Harold J. Abramson, *Ethnic Diversity in Catholic America* (New York, 1973), *passim.*

18. Thernstrom, *The Other Bostonians,* chapter 8.

19. Quoted in Lynn Larsen, "Educational and Occupational Opportunity in a Nineteenth-Century American Industrial City: Poughkeepsie, N. Y., 1860-1880" (Senior thesis, Vassar College, 1967), p. 20.

20. Stephan Thernstrom, *Poverty and Progress: Social Mobility in a Nineteenth-Century City* (Cambridge, Mass., 1964), pp. 22-25, 155-157. Howard Gitelman also finds earlier entry into the labor force and correspondingly less formal education among Catholics than among Protestants but argues that this difference had little influence upon their occupational experience, since formal educational requirements for most jobs remained low. Gitelman, *Waltham,* pp. 59-60.

21. Colin Greer emphasizes the "small role schools played in giving immigrants access to economic mobility" and the frequency of immigrant failure in the public schools in *The Great School Legend* (New York, 1972), esp. chapter 6. For the problems of the Lawrence, Massachusetts, school system — designed for a model town — in relating to a working class and especially an immigrant Catholic population on the eve of civil war, see Michael B. Katz, *The Irony of Early School Reform* (Cambridge, Mass., 1968), pp. 93-112.

4. Men at the Top

1. *Biographical Record,* pp. 12-13; Smith, *History of Dutchess Country,* pp. 410-412; Platt, *Eagle's History,* pp. 166, 191-192, 206, 212-223.

2. Edward Pessen, *Riches, Class, and Power before the Civil War* (Lexington, Mass., 1973), chapter 1. Unlike Pessen we have been able to assign most of the business property to individual owners, since we knew the partners and approximate divisions of property from the R. G. Dun and Company credit reports. Most of the incorporated firms in Poughkeepsie operated under simple partnership agreements, and if we lacked specific information we assumed an equal division. The problem did not arise very frequently, and the tax rolls usually specified when the property was owned by more than one individual. We excluded a few corporations whose ownership was uncertain. If a man and his wife and children reported separate pieces of property, we assigned them to the individual not the family unit. In a few cases this practice meant the exclusion of a prominent family.

With the help of an alphabetized file of all marriages reported in the *Eagle* at Adriance Library, genealogical and church records, we have been able to determine the origins of the wives of most of the richest men. Our information has been assembled from newspaper articles and obituaries, genealogies, local histories, the *Biographical Record* and the *Encyclopedia of Biography of New York* (New York, 1925). We know of no way to resolve the problem of outside investments. Probate records, for example, reveal some of this information but have the defect of not recording property a man gave away during his lifetime. Certainly some men did have substantial outside investments. Edna C. Macmahon once made a rough estimate that only about one sixth of the investments of Matthew Vassar, Jr. were local, and Platt, in his history, made the point that during the seventies many men in Poughkeepsie had invested their money outside the city.

3. Frederic C. Jaher, "Nineteenth-Century Elites in Boston and New York," *Journal of Social History*, 6 (Fall 1972), 34-73. To have chosen the top 1 or 2 percent of Poughkeepsie's taxpayers would have resulted in too few men to form an adequate basis of comparison. Unfortunately the number of men included is still small, and we are aware of Jaher's caveat that small groups allow a small shift in numbers to create large differences in percentages although only the 53 of 1857 are small enough to suffer unduly from this defect. A comparison of the top 10 percent would have included too many lesser property holders. In a small city accurate biographical information is difficult to find for even the most prominent men.

4. Platt, *Eagle's History*, pp. 123, 135, 217-218; Smith, *History of Dutchess County*, p. 384; *Biographical Record*, p. 676.

5. A comparison of the 1866 income list with the 1865 real estate rolls reveals some significant differences. The 11 richest men in the city ranked by income were also among the top 50 real estate owners, but only half of the 50 richest men ranked by income numbered among the 50 largest real estate owners. These discrepancies remind us that real estate ownership is not a totally accurate measure of a man's economic standing, but the discrepancies are less serious than it may appear at first glance. Of the 25 men in 1865 who were rich by the criterion of real estate but not by income in 1866, almost one half had been on the 1857 list of real estate owners but would not be on the 1880 list — in other words, they were members of that older elite who did not maintain their position. As for the other 14 men who were on the real estate list but not the income tax list, 4 were on their way up and would appear on the 1880 real estate list, 5 appeared as rich real property owners only on the 1865 real property list, and only 5 were among the richest on all the real property lists but their economic standing was seriously reduced when tested by income. Similarly, of the 25 men who had large incomes in 1866 but had not acquired large amounts of local real estate, 6 would appear among the richest real property holders in 1880. Of the remaining 18 who had large incomes in 1866 but never appeared as the largest property holders on any list, 6 reported no occupation (presumably gentlemen who had retired to Poughkeepsie and lived off investments made elsewhere), and 7 were manufacturers whose physical plants were assessed at a low valuation although they produced a good current income.

6. The picture does not change substantially even if we compare the same absolute number of taxpayers in each year rather than a similar percentage of the whole tax roll, as we have done so far. If we consider only the richest 53 men in both 1857 and 1880, then the proportion of the 1857 group remaining at the top falls to 40 percent and the proportion of newcomers among the 1880 group rises slightly. Since Jaher dealt with the post-Civil War period, his findings are the most easily compared although unfortunately our time spans for the measurement of the

elite differ somewhat. Jaher tabulated the persistence of the New York elite between 1857 and 1892 and found that 43 percent of the 1857 elite reappeared on the 1892 tax list 35 years later. Our longer time span of 43 years between 1857 and 1900 yielded a persistence rate of 17 percent for the 1857 elite and our much shorter timespan of 23 years between 1857 and 1880 yielded a rate of 47 percent. Jaher found that 26 percent of the New York elite of 1892 had ties with or survived from those of 1857, while only 12 percent of Poughkeepsie's 1900 elite had a relationship to the 1857 elite. Jaher's rates for Boston were consistently higher than those for New York. See Jaher, "Nineteenth-Century Elites," pp. 44-47, and Pessen, *Riches, Class, and Power,* chapter 7.

7. Some of Matthew Vassar's nephews continued to run his brewery but increasingly could not compete in the national market. By the eighties the business declined visibly and closed finally in the mid-nineties. Platt, *Eagle's History,* p. 233; R. G. Dun & Co., MV & Co., pp. 76, 89, 317; vol. 74, p. 530; GS & I, pp. 11, 344; WD, pp. 228, 231, 438; *Biographical Record,* pp. 95, 931.

8. R. G. Dun & Co., A & B, pp. 205, 265.

9. R. G. Dun & Co., ET, pp. 52-53; Record of Inmates, Poughkeepsie Alms House, May 1877-March 1878; Minutes of the WCTU, 4/11/1874, Adriance Memorial Library.

10. R. G. Dun & Co., WJ, pp. 34-35; vol. 74, pp. 416, 433. Clipping in the Poughkeepsie *Eagle* scrapbook, 1899, Adriance Memorial Library; Henry Noble MacCracken, *Blithe Dutchess,* p. 185.

11. *Biographical Record,* p. 488; Platt, *Eagle's History,* pp. 192, 205; Smith, *History of Dutchess County,* pp. 454-455.

12. *Biographical Record,* p. 317.

13. R. G. Dun & Co., JC, pp. B, 11, 176, 373; *Biographical Record,* p. 138.

14. *Biographical Record,* p. 599.

15. R. G. Dun & Co., JGP, pp. 12, 131; P & Co., pp. 276, 393; vol. 74, pp. 488, 534, 687; JPN, pp. 128, 142, 303; vol. 74, p. 493; EH, vol. 74, pp. 558, 567; CB, pp. 117, 257, 349; *Daily Eagle,* 8/19/1879.

16. William Davies' son Augustus listed himself as an artist in several directories but with no occupation in others. A son of another rich man seems to have devoted himself largely to traveling. The tendency of the sons of the rich in Boston to take up cultural pursuits has been well documented in Frederic C. Jaher, "Businessmen and Gentlemen," *Explorations in Entrepreneurial History,* IV (1966-67), 17-35.

17. *Biographical Record,* p. 116; Platt, *Eagle's History,* pp. 240-244.

18. *Biographical Record,* pp. 252-253, 899-900; Platt, *Eagle's History,* pp. 235, 287, 295-296; *Empire State,* pp. 229, 234, 238; *Poughkeepsie Illustrated* (1887), p. 29; R. G. Dun & Co., JS, p. 168; vol. 74, p. 431; JS, pp. 12, 14; S. Bros., vol. 74, p. 484; F. H. Champion, "The Ice Cream Industry, 1866-1936," typescript prepared for the WPA, pp. 1-3; Poughkeepsie *New Yorker,* 8/16/1944.

19. R. G. Dun & Co., WRM, pp. 191, 392, 403; Platt, *Eagle's History,* p. 247.

20. Platt, *Eagle's History,* pp. 216-220; *Daily Eagle,* 7/4/1871, 10/30/1877, 6/18/1879.

21. Platt, *Eagle's History,* pp. 216-229, 227-234.

22. Smith, *History of Dutchess County,* pp. 396-399. The names of bank directors for various years have been drawn from the newspaper listings which appeared every January.

23. R. G. Dun & Co., PT, p. 84; GS & I, pp. 11, 344.

24. We chose income rather than real property to compare professionals because real property can reflect inheritance rather than the comparative rewards

of the professions. Information on lawyers has been drawn from newspapers, the *Biographical Record* and local histories, esp. Smith, *History of Dutchess County,* pp. 463-465, and Frank B. Lown, "The Bench and Bar of Dutchess County," pp. 498-528, in Frank Hasbrouck, ed., *History of Dutchess County, New York* (Poughkeepsie, 1909).

25. Platt, *Eagle's History,* pp. 287-288; biographical sketch of George V. Spratt prepared by the Citizen's Historical Association, Indianapolis, genealogical file, Adriance Memorial Library; Poughkeepsie *Star,* 5/18/1932.

26. Platt, *Eagle's History,* pp. 153, 158, 168, 208-209, 220; *Biographical Record,* p. 463; *Daily News,* 11/20/1877.

27. Platt, *Eagle's History,* pp. 158, 280-281; *Annual Statement of the American Railroad Chair Co.,* 1856, and *Act of Incorporation of the Fallkill Iron Works,* Corporation File nos. 11 and 66, Dutchess County Clerk's Office.

28. *Biographical Record,* pp. 1-4; Appleton's *Cyclopaedia of American Biography,* III, 60.

29. The information on doctors was drawn from the *Biographical Record,* local histories, Guy Carleton Bayley, "The Medical Profession," pp. 528-597 in Frank Hasbrouck, ed., *History of Dutchess County, New York* (Poughkeepsie, 1909), and "An Historical Address Delivered Before the Dutchess County Medical Society at its Centennial Meeting, Jan. 10, 1906. With a Record of the Medical Profession of Dutchess County" (Poughkeepsie, 1906), and John F. Rogers, M.D., *History of the Dutchess County Medical Society, 1806-1956.* Since medical schools in the first half of the nineteenth century offered a notoriously poor education, graduation from a medical school did not necessarily signify competence. Medical schools did entail, however, an expense greater than that of reading law locally or of training with a local doctor. For a survey of the medical profession see William G. Rothstein, *American Physicians in the Nineteenth Century* (Baltimore, 1972).

30. Frank B. Lown, "Bench and Bar," pp. 523-524.

31. R. G. Dun & Co., DI, p. 314.

32. *Daily Eagle,* 9/20/1866, 10/22/1866.

33. R. G. Dun & Co., AC, pp. 153, 308, 312; *Biographical Record,* p. 913.

34. R. G. Dun & Co., JP, pp. 87, 128; vol. 74, p. 731; JF, p. 187; *Biographical Record,* p. 791; *Daily Eagle,* 3/12/1877.

5. The Precariousness of Enterprise

1. Michael Katz's study of the entrepreneurs in Hamilton, Ontario, and Peter Decker's study of the merchant community in San Francisco are major exceptions although the latter focuses upon large merchants in a major city. Both studies profited from selective use of the R. G. Dun and Company credit reports. Katz, *The People of Hamilton,* chapter 4; Decker, "Social Mobility on the Urban Frontier: The San Francisco Merchants, 1850-1880," Ph.D. dissertation, Columbia University, 1974.

2. Tabulation of firms from the alphabetical section of the directory over a longer span shows that the firms in 1873 represented a 96 percent increase over those of 1843, while the population of Poughkeepsie and four surrounding towns increased by 81 percent. In 1903 the number of firms decreased by 1 percent over those in 1873 although the population had grown by 19 percent. R. G. and A. R. Hutchinson and Mabel Newcomer, "Study in Business Mortality," *American Economic Review,* 28 (September 1938), p. 509. Hereafter cited as Newcomer.

3. Counting new partners as the beginning of a new business only affected their

results on length of life by roughly 2 percent. Newcomer, "Study in Business Mortality," pp. 501-503. Edna C. Macmahon generously shared with us the original data on which the Hutchinson and Newcomer study was based; unfortunately we do not have the actual classification and tabulations from the raw data. Our examination of this data convinced us that for the earlier years they classified some artisans as self-employed who actually worked as journeymen. In listing artisans between 1843 and 1855 the directories sometimes gave two addresses. Since directories normally put the address of a businessman's shop before his place of residence, the Hutchinsons and Newcomer assumed that the first address for a man listed at a craft meant that he owned a shop. We have found that the first address in such cases often refers to a large shop in which the craftsman worked as a wage-earner.

4. The estimated worth figures refer to the highest amount ever reported for a firm. "Estimated worth" in the credit ledgers refers to all assets that could be reached by creditors. Since it could include real estate, bank stock, and other assets outside the business, this figure may be larger than the capital invested in the business. We have used this figure because local correspondents practically always gave this estimate in their reports whereas specification of capital employed or value of merchandise was sporadic. Judged by evidence from the federal manufacturing census, newspaper reports, and other sources, estimated worth is a fairly reliable indicator of the scale and prosperity of firms in Poughkeepsie.

5. The Hutchinsons and Newcomer found a decline of 25 percent in craft-related firms between 1843 and 1873. They used a longer span of time, however, and included some artisans who were not self-employed in the earlier period. We have found a burgeoning of craft-related firms, as well as other kinds of businesses, from 1865 to 1873, followed by a decline in most lines thereafter. Newcomer, "Study in Business Mortality," p. 509.

6. R. G. Dun & Co., JC, p. 197; JC, p. 115; JB, p. 157.

7. Newcomer, "Study in Business Mortality," p. 506.

8. R. G. Dun & Co., WFC, pp. 127, 132, 188; SBA, p. 212; vol. 74, p. 436.

9. *Daily Eagle,* 2/25/1864, 2/8/1866. *Weekly Eagle,* 2/3/1872. R. G. Dun & Co., GH, pp. 176, 348; vol. 74, pp. 581, 615. *Biographical Record,* pp. 577-579.

10. Clipping from the *Eagle* scrapbook, Adriance Memorial Library, July 1907. *Biographical Record,* p. 826.

11. R. G. Dun & Co., WF, pp. 58, 61, 73, 177, 343; vol. 74, p. 498; F & W., pp. 151, 238; JGF, vol. 74, p. 456; NH, p. 280; vol. 74, p. 545; CM, pp. 103, 180. *Biographical Record,* pp. 357-358.

12. *Weekly Eagle,* 4/10/1875.

13. R. G. Dun & Co., JB, pp. 54, 66, 93, 110, 112; BT, pp. 33, 44, 124; vol. 74, p. 438.

14. R. G. Dun & Co., IC, pp. 48, 171; vol. 74, pp. 407, 457.

15. R. G. Dun & Co., HE, pp. 120, 292; vol. 74, p. 656.

16. R. G. Dun & Co., RD, p. 309; vol. 74, p. 533; FH, pp. 322, 344; PMH, p. 123; vol. 74, pp. 431, 470.

17. R. G. Dun & Co., CR & Co., pp. 97, 156; vol. 74, p. 451; JWM, pp. 36, 39, 62, 287; vol. 74, p. 451; WB, p. 200; vol 74, p. 440.

18. R. G. Dun & Co., JHB, pp. 120, 304; RD, p. 139.

19. *Daily News,* 10/2/1877. R. G. Dun & Co., JO & PR, pp. 168, 217.

20. R. G. Dun & Co., WCD, p. 290; vol. 74, pp. 478, 570; RH, p. 134.

21. Eleanor Hays, *Morning Star: A Biography of Lucy Stone* (New York, 1961), pp. 78-79, 168-172; Yuri Suhl, *Ernestine L. Rose and the Battle for Human Rights*

(New York, 1959), pp. 200-214; George Bayles, *Women and New York Law* (New York, 1911), pp. 51-55; John Proffat, *Women Before the Law* (New York, 1874), pp. 73-78; Mary Beard, *Women as a Force in History* (New York, 1946), pp. 138-144. Mary Beard and Proffat both point out that the common law restrictions on a married woman's property could be overturned in equity proceedings. Since only the very rich were likely to take advantage of the relief afforded by equity, the legislative acts, by removing the common law restraints on the married woman's possession of property, enabled all women to retain their property despite their husbands' debts.

22. R. G. Dun & Co., FG, pp. 210, 226; vol. 74, p. 402; EP, pp. 255, 298, 344; HG, p. 162.

23. P. R. Earling, *Whom To Trust* (Chicago, 1890), p. 132.

24. R. G. Dun & Co., FH, pp. 376-377, 506, 552.

25. R. G. Dun & Co., JB, pp. 3, 415; JJB & Co., p. 110; vol. 74, pp. 429, 625.

26. R. G. Dun & Co., H & A, pp. 158, 227, 474; R & A, pp. 237, 302-303; RG & B, pp. 270, 413; JJB, Jr., p. 160; JP, pp. 225, 316; vol. 74, p. 544; MB, pp. 196, 347; JW, pp. 248, 266, 340; W & C, vol. 74, pp. 476, 485.

6. Stratification in Business

1. R. G. Dun & Co., WH, pp. 328, 500; *Empire State,* p. 241.

2. R. G. Dun & Co., DC & M, p. 395; vol. 74, pp. 476, 709.

3. *Daily Eagle,* 2/27/1866, 2/28/1866, 3/1/1866, 4/16/1868.

4. R. G. Dun & Co., IM, pp. 17, 331; vol. 74, p. 589; BH, p. 51; HH, pp. 138, 183.

5. R. G. Dun & Co., MS, pp. 331, 363; vol. 74, pp. 517, 579; BJ, pp. 204, 327; vol. 74, p. 635.

6. R. G. Dun & Co., HR, p. 46; RS, pp. 29, 51, 85; HSG & Co., p. 357.

7. R. G. Dun & Co., AW, pp. 209, 364; vol. 74, p. 596; SJ, pp. 164, 364, 336. Credit reporters said of one Jewish merchant, for example, that he owns "some RE which is not often the case with 'children of Israel'." RS, pp. 29, 51, 85.

8. R. G. Dun & Co., IH, pp. 87, 178, 396; SG, p. 124.

9. R. G. Dun & Co., HW, pp. 199, 207; AH, p. 134.

10. R. G. Dun & Co., AW, pp. 209, 364; vol. 74, p. 596; IH, pp. 87, 178, 396; F Bros., pp. 190, 266, 397.

11. R. G. Dun & Co., JG, p. 57.

12. R. G. Dun & Co., JR, p. 328; UB, p. 109; AB, p. 337; *Weekly Eagle,* March 1904, clipping from a scrapbook in Adriance Memorial Library; *Daily Press,* 9/28/1858.

13. *Weekly Eagle,* 2/7/1874. The other persisting steamboat steward in Pough-keepsie was also among the few blacks who owned any property, being assessed for $400 in 1880.

14. R. G. Dun & Co., C & E, p. 175.

15. Diary of Edmund Platt, May 1, 1869, and April 30, 1870. He had paid back one year's interest and $500 of the principal. R. G. Dun & Co., LH & K, pp. 260, 396; JM, p. 36; CA, pp. 48, 68; JWM, pp. 36, 39, 62, 287; vol. 74, p. 451; T & Co., pp. 32, 130; vol. 74, p. 443.

16. *Sunday Courier,* 2/2/1896. *A Tale of Fifty Years: Luckey, Platt & Co., 1869-1919,* p. 5; Ann Silverman, "The Story of Luckey, Platt & Co., 1835-1912," paper, Vassar College, pp. 2-3; Irene Garrison, "History of Luckey, Platt & Co.," typescript prepared for the WPA.

17. R. G. Dun & Co., C & E, p. 175; GVK & Co., vol. 74, pp. 472, 514.

18. R. G. Dun & Co., HW & Co., p. 162; OH, p. 63; EW, p. 160; HT & Co., p. 88.

19. In a newspaper advertisement in the fall of 1875, for example, Samuel Samelson advertised "hats, silks, ribbons, gloves, parasols, and umbrellas," and E. C. Adriance carried "hats, gloves, ties, striped hosiery, corsets." While dry goods merchants also carried fancy goods, they advertised cashmeres, alpacas, muslins, felt skirts, mohair, silks, and dress goods. *Weekly Eagle,* 9/11/1875.

20. R. G. Dun & Co., WRM, pp. 191. 392, 403. This analysis of fancy goods dealers does not include the 20 women who owned fancy goods stores, about half of whom were foreign-born. Their stores were small, 60 percent being worth $1,000 or less and none worth over $10,000.

21. R. G. Dun & Co., MF, p. 215; vol. 74, p. 443; SS, pp. 195, 299, 344; LW, p. 194; HDB, p. 219; JD, pp. 354, 443. Since the customers of fancy goods stores were women, the numbers of wives working in the stores is not surprising.

22. Silverman, "Luckey Platt & Co.," pp. 2-3. Platt noted on April 16, 1875, that "we sometimes fear we have made a mistake in going into the cash business," but by June 8, 1875, he remarked that "we do not notice any falling off in trade because of our shutting off our credit customers." Diary of Edmund Platt.

23. R. G. Dun & Co., GVK, pp. 62, 161-162, 351; vol. 74, pp. 472, 514.

24. R. G. Dun & Co., CB, pp. 70-71, 198; vol. 74, p. 479; GMVK, pp. 62, 143, 155, 304; LH & K, pp. 260, 396; *Poughkeepsie Illustrated* (1906), p. 15. Few firms advertising in the *Poughkeepsie Illustrated* in 1906 listed themselves as dry goods stores. Stores specializing in men's, women's, and children's clothing had taken their place.

25. R. G. Dun & Co., V & A, pp. 128, 330, 411; *A Tale of Fifty Years: Luckey, Platt & Co.,* p. 23.

26. "The C. N. Arnold Lumber Company," *Poughkeepsie Eagle,* Fiftieth Anniversary Edition, 1911; F. H. Champion, "The C. N. Arnold Lumber Company, 1821-1936," typescript prepared for the WPA; Platt, *Eagle's History,* 270-271. R. G. Dun & Co., JC, pp. B, 11, 176, 373; vol. 74, pp. 510, 575; WCA, pp. 69, 87; D & T, pp. 87, 236; vol. 74, p. 455.

27. "Collingwood & Seaman," *Poughkeepsie Eagle,* Fiftieth Anniversary Edition, 1911, p. 40. R. G. Dun & Co., ES, vol. 74, p. 598; LS & L, p. 311.

28. R. G. Dun & Co., P. & M, pp. 101, 105; BVV, vol. 74, pp. 484, 489; AD, vol. 74, pp. 484, 726. By the early twentieth century D. W. Wilbur had bought out the lumber business of the Collingwood firm and combined it with his own successful coal yards, which he had purchased in the nineties. Wilbur, the native son-in-law of a lumber dealer up the river, capitalized his firm at $100,000 in 1901. *Poughkeepsie Illustrated* (1906), p. 8; "D. W. Wilbur's Many Enterprises," *Poughkeepsie Eagle,* Fiftieth Anniversary Edition, 1911, p. 39.

29. R. G. Dun & Co., AD, p. 76.

30. R. G. Dun & Co., JB, pp. 148-149; vol. 74, p. 418; JC, p. 230; vol. 74, p. 532.

31. R. G. Dun & Co., JC, p. 230; vol. 74, p. 532; *Biographical Record,* p. 310; *Empire State,* p. 242.

32. R. G. Dun & Co., G. Bros., pp. 25, 325, 485; WWR, pp. 75, 95, 189, 379; vol. 74, pp. 421, 630. *Poughkeepsie Illustrated* (1906), p. 24 A; Helen Wilkinson Reynolds, *Annals of a Century Old Business: Wm. T. Reynolds & Co., 1819-1919.*

33. R. G. Dun & Co., GE, p. 246; WR, vol. 74, pp. 432, 553; JW, pp. 227, 365, 402; LC & Sons, pp. 39, 127, 322; vol. 74, p. 591; G. Bros., pp. 25, 325, 485.

34. R. G. Dun & Co., FW, pp. 256, 326; vol. 74, p. 573; RK, vol. 74, pp. 500, 599; CK, vol. 74, pp. 422, 465.

35. *Daily Press*, 2/25/1868; Record of Inmates, Poughkeepsie Alms House, *passim*.

36. R. G. Dun & Co., C Bros., p. 218.

37. While the available information on bookkeepers' salaries is limited, the 1866 income list provides some data. Men reporting themselves as bookkeepers accounted for 10 of the 30 clerical workers on the list, all but 2 of the 10 reporting between $750 and $1,200. Bank, dry goods, and government clerks as well as the clerking sons of proprietors made up the remainder.

38. *Biographical Record,* pp. 819, 200-201.

39. Quoted in Silverman, "Luckey, Platt & Co.," p. 5.

40. *Daily Press,* 8/14/1868; *Daily Eagle,* 7/27/1877.

41. Diary of Edmund Platt, *passim*.

42. R. G. Dun & Co., SKD, pp. 54, 177, 369, 293; CB, p. 216. *Daily Eagle,* 2/18/1879.

43. *Weekly Eagle,* 5/8/1875. R. G. Dun & Co., CWB, p. 350; vol. 74, p. 480.

44. R. G. Dun & Co., GB, pp. 197, 394.

45. R. G. Dun & Co., GHB, pp. 114, 179, 184; B & M, pp. 105, 130, 340, 429.

46. R. G. Dun & Co., GDH, pp. 214-215; vol. 74, p. 449; OT, pp. 10, 89, 108, 168.

7. Opportunity for Artisans during Industrialization

1. During the worst year of the depression, the *Eagle* commented, "Quite a number of Poughkeepsie mechanics will 'hay and harvest' in the country this summer." *Daily Eagle,* 2/15/1877. The general state of the trades often can be inferred from other notices. For example, the *Press* reported in 1868 that the livery business was not good; "The mechanics, the best patrons of the stablemen, are not so flush in stamps this winter as usual, and consequently cannot so well afford to ride." *Daily Press,* 2/13/1868.

2. *Commemorative Biographical Record of Dutchess County, New York* (Chicago, 1897), pp. 279, 556. Those reporting apprenticeships of five years included a native printer, an American born tinsmith of English parentage, an Irish moulder, and two Germans, a shoemaker and a tailor.

3. J. D. Burn, *Three Years among the Working Classes in the United States during the War* (London, 1865), p. 22. See also the report to Parliament by Francis Clare Ford in 1869, extracted in Edith Abbott, ed., *Historical Aspects of the Immigration Problem* (Chicago, 1926), pp. 382-383.

4. *Biographical Record,* p. 170. Susan E. Hirsch has found complaints in the Newark *Advertiser* in the late thirties about boys taken on as apprentices without legal indenture. She comments, "Boys looked for advancement and would switch jobs whenever something better seemed to be available. They not only went from employer to employer, but might switch crafts several times before coming of age." Hirsch, "The Household and the Family: The Effects of Industrialization on Skilled Workers in Newark, 1840-1860," a paper delivered at the 1974 meeting of the Organization of American Historians.

5. R. G. Dun & Co., HS, pp. 120, 257, 265; vol. 74, p. 705; GT, pp. C, 312.

6. *Biographical Record,* p. 124; R. G. Dun & Co., JJB, pp. 105. 130, 340.

7. *Ibid.,* PK, pp. 283, 319.

8. The editor retracted the article subsequently saying, "the pews probably will be made here." *Daily Eagle,* 3/27 and 3/31/1877.

9. See the analysis of the cabinet makers, esp. table 14 in Griffen, "Workers Divided," pp. 83-84.

10. *Biographical Record,* p. 576; R. G. Dun & Co., GH, pp. 176, 348; vol. 74, pp. 581, 615.

11. *Biographical Record,* p. 825.

12. R. G. Dun & Co., DSM, pp. 86, 178; vol. 74, p. 572.

13. *Ibid.,* JFC, pp. 37, 343; vol. 74, pp. 434, 665; *Daily Eagle,* 7/2/1879.

14. "Old Lasts Tell Story," Hudson Valley *Sunday Courier,* 2/12/1908; R. G. Dun & Co., AB, p. 313.

15. Hirsch, "Household and Family," pp. 7-8, 10, 13.

16. *Daily Press,* 10/28/1863.

17. R. G. Dun & Co., BK and JCK, pp. 98, 182; vol. 74, p. 612; BP, p. 100.

18. Report on Hermance in Record of Inmates, Poughkeepsie Alms House, January, 1876; R. G. Dun & Co., SW, p. 316; CW, pp. 316, 427; MS, p. 28.

19. *Ibid.,* AM, p. 193; vol. 74, pp. 446, 590; LH & Son, p. 259; vol. 74, p. 544; *Daily Press,* 5/7/1868.

20. R. G. Dun & Co., SBR, pp. 101, 199, PBC, p. 223; vol. 74, pp. 473, 556; HM, pp. 170, 399; vol. 74, p. 471; MT, p. 282; vol. 74, pp. 495, 603.

21. *Ibid.,* JFL, pp. 142-143.

22. *Ibid.,* DLH & Son, p. 395; vol. 74, pp. 518, 687; *Biographical Record,* pp. 104-105; Fiftieth Anniversary Edition of the Poughkeepsie *Eagle,* 1911, sketch of Gildersleeve.

23. R. G. Dun & Co., S & P, pp. 96, 103, 375; vol. 74, p. 582.

24. *Daily Press,* 1/7/1858; *Daily Eagle,* 4/24/1866.

25. *Ibid.*

26. *Daily Eagle,* 1/15/1867.

27. On the organization of the union and the strike, see *Daily Press,* 9/1, 10, and 10/7, 12, 15, 30/1863.

28. *Ibid.,* 11/4 and 11/13/1863; manuscript on the Standard Oil coopers by Herbert G. Gutman, p. 16, courtesy of the author.

29. Three immigrants appeared next at ordinary labor and one—a victim of intemperance—went to the poorhouse, but the other seven all found comparable and mostly better jobs. Two became brewers, three became grocers, and two appear next as saloon keeper and as merchant.

30. R. G. Dun & Co., L & Co., p. 14; vol. 74, pp. 420, 502.

31. *Ibid.,* OF, p. 187; vol. 74, p. 493.

32. *Daily Eagle,* 9/1/1879; 5/20/1876.

33. *Ibid.,* 9/22 and 10/20/1866; 12/27/1861; 11/7/1866; 4/24/1876.

34. *Ibid.,* 4/14/1870; 9/1/1879.

35. *Ibid.,* 4/24/1866; Franklin E. Coyne, *The Development of the Cooperage Industry in the United States* (Chicago, 1940), pp. 7-26.

36. R. G. Dun & Co., DVC, p. 30; *Daily Eagle,* 5/7/1877.

37. R. G. Dun & Co., JM, p. 148; S. & Co., p. 258; vol. 74, pp. 495, 594, 659.

38. *Daily Eagle,* 2/27/1877 for the partnership of three young mechanics: Dusenberry, Mastin, and Smith.

39. *Ibid.,* 5/10/1876; R. G. Dun & Co., ED, pp. 378, 457.

40. *Eagle* Anniversary Edition, 1911.

8. Immigrant Success in the Handicrafts

1. Edith Abbott, ed., *Historical Aspects of the Immigration Problem: Select Documents* (Chicago, 1926), p. 382. On the dominance of Irish tailors in Boston, see Oscar Handlin, *Boston's Immigrants: A Study in Acculturation* (New York, 1968), pp. 75-76.

2. R. G. Dun & Co., JD; pp. 73, 96, 97; LB, pp. 24, 68; vol. 74, p. 401.

3. *Telegraph*, 4/9/1851; R. G. Dunn & Co., JB and G Bros., pp. 50-51.

4. *Ibid.*, RT, pp. 34, 41; K Bros. & BL, p. 112.

5. This sole survivor happened also to be a local celebrity, John Bolding, a fugitive slave whose freedom had been purchased by Poughkeepsie abolitionists. Dutchess County Historical Society *Yearbook*, 20 (1935), pp. 51-55.

6. *Daily Eagle*, 5/26/1877.

7. R. G. Dun & Co., PBH & AFL, pp. 115, 182, 269, 370; GWD, p. 330.

8. *Ibid.*, JG, p. 208.

9. *Ibid.*, BFT & Co., pp. 81, 107, 111, 179, 347; H & L, p. 370; vol. 74, p. 477.

10. *Ibid.*, MS, pp. 135, 141, 331, 363; vol. 74, pp. 517, 579; *Daily News*, 7/11/1877.

11. *Poughkeepsie Illustrated* (Poughkeepsie, 1887), pp. 13-14.

12. *Daily Eagle*, 5/28/1866.

13. R. G. Dun & Co., JB, p. D; PL, pp. 247, 317, 472; *Biographical Record*, p. 266; John R. Commons, *History of Labour in the United States*, II (New York, 1918), 68-74.

14. R. G. Dun & Co., JS, pp. 118, 356; vol. 74, pp. 505, 649; *Daily Eagle*, 1/6/1868.

15. *Sixth Annual Report of the Bureau of Statistics of Labor, New York State* (1889), p. 606.

16. Platt, *Eagle's History*, pp. 295-296; F. H. Champion, "Ice Cream Industry, 1866-1936," WPA typescript (FEC Subject #633); R. G. Dun & Co., JS, p. 168; vol. 74, p. 431.

17. *Ibid.*, JB, pp. 35, 137, 73; WHB, pp. 36, 285; vol. 74, pp. 490, 645; *Poughkeepsie Illustrated* (1887), pp. 41-42; *Daily Press*, 11/11/1863; *Daily Eagle*, 9/1/1879.

18. New York *Times*, 1/13/1972, p. 43; *Poughkeepsie Illustrated* (1887), pp. 20-21; R. G. Dun & Co., JS and S Bros., pp. 12, 14.

19. *Daily Eagle*, 3/3/1868.

20. *Sixth Annual Report*, pp. 549-550.

21. *Biographical Record*, pp. 133, 263.

22. This analysis of German emigration and of the handicrafts in the German states is drawn primarily from Mack Walker, *Germany and the Emigration, 1816-1885* (Cambridge, Mass., 1964), pp. 49-57 and the same author's *German Home Towns: Community, State, and General Estate, 1648-1871* (Ithaca, N.Y., 1971), chapter 3 and pp. 315-318, 329-336, 364-365, 388-390; Wolfgang Kellmann and Peter Marschaich, "German Emigration to the United States," in *Perspectives in American History*, VII (1973), esp. pp. 516-532; Theodore S. Hamerow, *Restoration, Revolution, Reaction: Economics and Politics in Germany, 1815-1871* (Princeton, N.J., 1958); J. H. Clapham, *The Economic Development of France and Germany, 1815-1914* (Cambridge, Eng., 1936) and Herbert Heaton, *Economic History of Europe* (New York, 1948).

23. Abbott, ed., *Documents*, p. 833.

24. See the credit reports for Thielman on p. 84, Bahret on pp. 3, 415, Blankenhorn on pp. 338, 590, Kirchner on pp. 338, 426, 650, and Shwartz on pp. 135, 141, 331, 363, 517, 579 of volumes 73 and 74 of the R. G. Dun and Company ledgers. The detailed biographies for the 25 Germans are found in the *Biographical Record*.

25. Bruce Laurie, Theodore Hershberg, and George Alter have emphasized

differences in Philadelphia in 1880 between German immigrants and their native-born sons in relative concentration in the traditional handicrafts. They see the sons deserting these crafts at a very high rate and also achieving a greater representation in the building trades, printing, and the metal trades associated with producer goods industries. For the occupations they specify, the relative concentrations for Poughkeepsie and Philadelphia of both the immigrants and the second generation are quite similar, but for several reasons we do not find their analysis persuasive for Poughkeepsie and wonder whether they may even be overemphasizing for Philadelphia the shift from traditional crafts to trades—especially in the producer goods industries—which natives dominated. First, less than 9 percent of the native-born of German parentage in either city reported the occupations of moulder, iron moulder, boilermaker, machinist, printer, stonemason, bricklayer, carpenter, painter, and plasterer, not a very impressive proportion absolutely nor by comparison with whites of native parentage. These sons were narrowing the gap between their fathers' occupations and those of natives, but the gap remained substantial. Second, although the desertion in both cities from dying handicrafts like shoemaking and tailoring is dramatic, the proportion in more viable trades like baking and butchering either falls off much less or not at all. Third and more important, the authors do not include in their analysis several handicrafts with limited futures which in Poughkeepsie showed a dramatic shift in the other direction with the native-born sons of German parentage claiming a much greater concentration than the immigrant generation—notably cigarmaking and barbering. See table 13 and its interpretation in "Immigrants and Industry: The Philadelphia Experience, 1850-1880," *Journal of Social History,* 9 (Winter 1975), pp. 219-267.

26. Bricklaying itself does not conform to the generalization, but the usual way of learning the trade does. A bricklayer's laborer, sometimes called mason's attendant or hod carrier in the census, performed such heavy work as mixing the mortar and carrying the mortar and bricks to the journeyman. These tasks fell overwhelmingly to Irish brawn and it is not surprising that an increasing number of attendants became journeymen themselves.

27. See Robert A. Christie, *Empire in Wood* (Ithaca, N.Y., 1956), chapter 2, esp. on the separation between the speculative builder who supplied capital and the master carpenter-become-labor contractor.

28. Richard Weiss, *The American Myth of Success* (New York, 1969), pp. 100-101.

29. R. G. Dun & Co., WH, pp. 22, 34, 277.

30. *Ibid.,* JS, p. 110; JSP, pp. 87, 128; vol. 74, p. 531.

31. *Ibid.,* WT, pp. 167, 183, 334; CM, p. 345; SS, p. 215; vol. 74, p. 513.

32. *Ibid.,* C, D & VD, p. 154.

33. Griffen, "Occupational Mobility," p. 319; 60 percent of masons' sons who were employed in Poughkeepsie at two censuses reported the same occupation as their fathers in at least one census and the proportions for the sons of carpenters and of painters were 53 percent and 38 percent respectively. At last reported job 57 percent of these sons of masons still followed their fathers' trade, but the continuity among the sons of carpenters and of painters had dropped to only 39 and 31 percent respectively.

34. *Daily Eagle,* 9/22 and 7/11/1879; 9/16/1877.

35. *Biographical Record,* p. 914.

36. *Ibid.,* pp. 282, 588, and 198. Before the seventies Spross had hired an Irish Protestant trained by Harloe as his foreman for some years.

37. *Ibid.,* p. 790; R. G. Dun & Co., JBC, p. 223; vol. 74, pp. 473, 556.

38. *Sixth Annual Report,* pp. 200-201.

39. The success of Poughkeepsie's machine shops and foundries does not typify opportunities for self-employment in machine work in other cities. A few large establishments, notably the Buckeye Mower and Reaper Works, largely account for the rapid increase in the number of machinists employed in the city. These establishments did not spin off or encourage many auxiliary businesses. For whatever reasons of ability or situation, Poughkeepsie's machine makers collectively did not develop that ferment of inventiveness which so often spawns successful small businesses in young and rapidly developing industries.

40. R. G. Dun & Co., F, S & D, pp. 85, 86; CHR, p. 256; vol. 74, p. 578; M, vol. 74, p. 454; G & S, p. 305; O, C & D , p. 250.

41. *Sixth Annual Report,* pp. 218-219.

42. A similar evolution characterized Greensboro, North Carolina, between the 1870s and 1920s. Since the southern city was still a village in the earlier decade, the change in stratification was later in timing than in Poughkeepsie. See Samuel Millard Kipp III, "Urban Growth and Social Change in the South, 1870-1920; Greensboro, North Carolina as a Case Study" (Ph.D. dissertation, Princeton University, 1974), esp. chapter 6.

43. On the impact of rationalization, see David Montgomery, "Immigrant Workers and Scientific Management," esp. pp. 2-9 (paper delivered to the conference sponsored by the Eleutherian Mills Historical Library and the Balch Institute, November 1973).

44. Clarence Long, *Wages and Earnings in the United States, 1860-1890* (Princeton, N.J., 1960), pp. 98-104, 116-117.

9. Factories as Levelers

1. *Jubilee Year Book of the Church of the Nativity* (Poughkeepsie, New York, 1897), p. 9.

2. For example, when Irishman David Hughes died of heat exhaustion at the Hudson River Iron Co., the *Eagle* noted that he had not yet become accustomed to the strain of the work. The year before, the superintendent of the derricks at the Poughkeepsie Iron Works had been charged with negligence in the death of another laborer. The more highly skilled workers were not exempt from accidents either. In 1867 one of the Upper Furnace blasts "burst out suddenly, by which one of the leading employees of the concern was badly burned." *Daily Eagle,* 5/17/1877; 2/6/1867.

3. Eric Hobsbawm, *Industry and Empire: The Making of Modern English Society* (New York, 1968), p. 95; *Daily Eagle,* 6/14/1876.

4. "The Home of Dutchess Trousers," in the Poughkeepsie *Eagle's* Fiftieth Anniversary Edition (1911), p. 28.

5. Older men with long residence in Poughkeepsie comprised more of the work force at Buckeye than of any other large plant. Among the 66 skilled workers in 1879 whose ages can be determined, half were at least 40 years old and more than one fourth were over 50. Nearly two fifths had been employed in Poughkeepsie for twenty years or more and nearly three fourths for at least ten years. For a description of the factory, see *Daily Eagle,* 4/11/1866.

6. R. G. Dun & Co., EB, pp. 146, 346, 380; Smith, *History of Dutchess County,* p. 390.

7. The mould boy shut the sides of the mould for the blower and later removed the blown bottle; the snapping-up boy then placed the bottle in a "snap" for remelting the neck for finishing. After the "gaffer" or finisher had put the ring on the neck, the carrying-in boy took the bottle on a paddle and placed it in the

annealing furnace. For large ware, a gathering boy rather than the blower himself gathered the molten glass from the furnace at the beginning of the process. Hudson Valley *Sunday Courier,* 10/10/1937.

8. Wage differentials for ordinary operatives, skilled workers, and foremen have been inferred from wage data in a variety of sources, primarily newspapers and manufacturing censuses. The scale reported for a clothing factory in nearby Matteawan in 1876 suggests the range. The pay of skilled craftsmen averaged $15 per week, the remainder of the hands receiving from $6 to $9 per week; foremen there received a maximum of $2,000 per year, a higher figure than has been discovered in Poughkeepsie. *Weekly Eagle,* 2/5/1876.

9. *Ibid.,* 9/13/1879; John R. Commons, "American Shoemakers, 1648 to 1895," esp. pp. 255-256 in his *Labor and Administration* (New York, 1913).

10. *Daily Eagle,* 3/18/1870; R. G. Dun & Co., SF, p. 161.

10. From the Bottom Up

1. R. G. Dun & Co., JH, pp. 37, 161, 372; *Biographical Record,* pp. 278, 900; *Daily Eagle,* 5/16/1876.

2. *Daily Press,* 4/20/1868; *Daily News,* 10/2/1877.

3. Cook and Benton, eds., *Dutchess County Regiment,* p. 295.

4. *Biographical Record,* p. 925; *Daily Eagle,* 2/2/1877.

5. *Sunday Courier,* October 1903. In 1874, the first year of depression, the teamsters hired by the contractor for a new driving park received $4.00 per day for their labor and team, but struck for $5.00. The going rate for the most highly paid artisans, the stonecutters, did not exceed $4.00 that year but they did not have the teamsters' costs of maintaining their teams. *Daily Eagle,* 7/21/1874.

6. *Daily Press,* 5/10/1867; 10/6/1863. The premium on aggressiveness among hack drivers was, if anything, more intense. Of the city's eleven regularly organized livery stables in 1868, all but two employed drivers. The *Eagle* boasted that travelers could find a hack at the railroad depot night or day. But the drivers pursued customers so relentlessly and competitively that in 1877 a local assemblyman took it upon himself to hire a former night policeman "to protect passengers from the annoyance of hackmen." *Daily Eagle,* 7/19/1870; 1/20 and 1/23/1877.

7. *Daily News,* 7/17/1877.

8. *Daily Eagle,* 9/5/1868.

9. R. G. Dun & Co., UB, p. 109; JR, p. 328; whether Rhodes paid for his challenge through a subsequent loss in prosperity cannot be ascertained. In 1873, the year of his dramatic public gesture in taking his daughter to one of the city's previously all-white schools, a credit reporter described his dyeing shop as a "good business, making a little money" and Rhodes himself as a careful, close man who paid cash for what he bought and owned his house. By 1877 all his effects had been mortgaged to the Poughkeepsie Savings Bank and from then on he was described as worth nothing.

10. R. G. Dun & Co., W, S, and GD, p. 186; vol. 74, pp. 440-441, 462, 677.

11. *Ibid.,* HC, JHD and HVD, p. 154; vol. 74, pp. 434, 475; *Biographical Record,* p. 277.

12. Dutchess County Historical Society *Yearbook,* 36 (1951), p. 47.

13. *Daily News,* 7/30/1877.

14. On the accidents of brakemen see, for example, *Daily Eagle,* 1/5 and 9/28/1877; *Daily News,* 11/15/1877; and the annual reports of St. Barnabas Hospital for the late seventies, Adriance Memorial Library.

15. *Daily Eagle,* 8/20/1877.
16. *Ibid.,* 1/12/1867; 10/23/1866.
17. *Sunday Courier,* 3/3/1912.
18. *Daily Press,* 2/21/1868; *Daily Eagle,* 2/26/1867.
19. *Daily Press,* 10/21/1863.
20. Diary of Edmund Platt, 4/30/1861; *Daily Press,* 5/22/1866; *Daily Eagle,* 5/2/1877.
21. *Daily Press,* 5/12/1864.
22. *Daily Eagle,* 1/1/1877; *Daily Press,* 9/30/1868.
23. *Daily Eagle,* 2/3/1870 and 1/24/1870; *Weekly Eagle,* 2/14/1874; *Daily Eagle,* 2/10/1885.
24. *Ibid.,* 1/22, 1/24, and 1/25/1876.

11. The Employment of Women

1. Susan Kleinberg, *Historical Methods Newsletter,* 9 (December 1975), p. 16. Conceivably, the opening of Vassar College in 1865 could have made Poughkeepsie less typical. The college, however, was not located within the city limits so the employment figures for women do not include the professionals associated with the college. The surprising number of female doctors may have been related to the presence of Vassar, but we can find no other evidence that the college affected the employment of women.

2. Waitresses, designated in the census as restaurant clerks, have been classified as domestics. Although waitresses probably had more independence than other household workers, their work was too similar and their numbers too few to classify separately. The majority in 1880 worked in one restaurant and lived there as well.

Domestics sometimes were listed at both their places of work and their homes. In 1880, for example, 54 white women and 19 black women were counted twice. These women have been counted only once since there could be no mistake about their identity, but it was impossible to tell whether women with names such as Mary Burns were the same or different women. German and black women tended to have more unusual first and last names so it was easier to eliminate the domestic overcount for those groups. This overcounting of domestics may help explain why women between 15 and 25 or 30 so often outnumber men in nineteenth-century cities.

3. In 1860, the proportion in the youngest age group is based on those over 15 because the census only asked for the occupations of those over 15. The sharp increase in domestic servants in the female labor force is not explained by this discrepancy. If the composition of the female labor force is recalculated to include only those 16 and over, the percentages at the various skill levels in 1870 and 1880 never vary by more than one percentage point from the proportions given in the present tables.

4. Patricia Branca, "A New Perspective on Women's Work: A Comparative Typology," *Journal of Social History,* 9 (Winter 1975), pp. 129-153.

5. Edith Abbott, *Women in Industry* (New York, 1910), pp. 228-245, 359.

6. The number of those taking in boarders is slightly inflated. In 1880 the census taker sometimes neglected to record the relation of persons to the head of household and listed some people as boarders who can be identified as relatives from other sources. Unless such people were known to be relatives, they have been classified as boarders.

7. Diary of Edmund Platt, April 10, 1873.

8. *Biographical Record,* p. 131.

9. *Daily Eagle,* 1/7/ and 4/14/1862; *Biographical Record,* p. 287; "Nanci P. Monell" in Esther P. Lovejoy, *Women Doctors of the World* (New York, 1957), p. 221; *Tyro* (December 1883), Adriance Memorial Library; *Weekly Eagle,* 1/26/ 1878.

10. *Biographical Record,* p. 197; "Elizabeth Moshier" in *Notable American Women, 1607-1950,* II, 587-588; *Daily Eagle,* 9/22/1877.

11. *Daily Eagle,* 1/7/1862.

12. *News,* 7/10/1877; *Daily Eagle,* 10/8/1877.

13. *Daily Eagle,* 1/10/1867; *Annual Report of the Poughkeepsie Board of Education, 1886.*

14. *Eagle,* January 1902, *Eagle* scrapbook, Adriance Memorial Library.

15. *Annual Report of the Poughkeepsie Board of Education, 1898.*

16. R. G. Dun & Co., JW & WFM, 287; vol. 74, p. 451.

17. R. G. Dun & Co., Mrs. RCF, pp. 137, 337, 408; EBK, p. D; vol. 74, p. 459; Mrs. PRB, vol. 74, pp. 445, 442; Mrs. WOD, p. 216; vol. 74, p. 492.

18. R. G. Dun & Co., Mrs. MK, pp. 122, 325, 377, 446.

19. R. G. Dun & Co., Mrs. MB, vol. 74, p. 580.

20. R. G. Dun & Co., Mrs. DM, p. 49.

21. *Press,* 1/20/1858; *Telegraph,* 2/22/1859; R. G. Dun & Co., Mrs. RVC, pp. 177, 183, 333, 402.

22. R. G. Dun & Co., Mrs. EB, p. 42; Mrs. MF, pp. 205, 211; vol. 74, p. 525; Mrs. ML, p. 243.

23. R. G. Dun & Co., JSB and FEB, pp. 260, 407; EC & Co., p. 259; vol. 74, p. 525.

24. R. G. Dun & Co., Mrs. MP, pp. 55, 61; Mrs. RVC, pp. 177, 183, 333, 402; Mrs. EG, p. 337; Mrs. AD, p. 13.

25. Account books of J. J. Bahret & Co., Adriance Memorial Library.

26. R. G. Dun & Co., Mrs. RVC, pp. 177, 183; Mrs. JAD, p. 246.

27. Diary of Edmund Platt, May 10, 1871. Dressmaking at times was a part of the service expected of a domestic as seen in the following advertisement: "Wanted: a chambermaid and a seamstress, one who understands dressmaking." *Press,* 11/11/1867.

28. The overrepresentation of skilled workers is substantial if one considers only men over 40, the age group most likely to have working daughters. In this age group, only 29 percent of native men, 34 percent of German men, and 18 percent of Irish men were skilled workers.

29. Francis A. Walker, *A Compendium of the Ninth Census, June, 1870* (Washington, 1872), p. 603; Ralph Bartholomew, *Greenwich Village* (New York, 1920), p. 11.

30. *Press,* 11/19/1867.

31. *Eagle,* July 1902, *Eagle* scrapbook, Adriance Memorial Library.

32. Record of Inmates, Poughkeepsie Alms House, Margaret Dillon, Adriance Memorial Library.

33. City of Poughkeepsie Poor List, untitled, Adriance Memorial Library.

Index

Abramson, Harold, 270n
Abbott, Edith, 235, 277n, 278n, 283n
Age distribution: and persistence, 18; and occupational mobility, 61-63, 144-147, 215-216; and occupation, 176-177, 202, 209, 248-249; and household structure, 252-253
Agents, insurance and real estate, 136-137
Agriculture, 9-10
Agricultural workers, 218-219, 223
Albany, N.Y., 3, 7, 13
Alms house, 225-226
Alter, George, 264n, 279n
Arensberg, Conrad, 46, 267n
Artisans: and division of labor, 14, 141-142, 184-185, 191-192, 199-202; apprenticeship, 18, 21, 35, 142-143, 182, 201-202, 277n; migration of, 18, 153, 187; attrition in declining crafts, 19, 140-141, 149-150, 160-161, 163-164; attitudes toward success, 35; self-employment, 35-36, 63, 105, 147-148, 161, 165-166, 180, 192; occupational mobility, 143-149, 168-169, 186-187, 190-191; shops of, 151, 169-170; aristocracy of, 173, 191. *See also* Manufacturing
Assessment books, 85-87
Assimilation: attitudes toward, 28-29, 43-49; and Germans, 30, 44-46; and Irish, 30, 46-49
Associations, voluntary, *see* Fire companies; Temperance organizations; Trade unions; Jews; Protestants; Roman Catholics
Atlanta, Ga., 4, 5, 58

Bakers and confectioners, 175-179
Bankers, 89, 94
Barbers, 212-213
Beard, Mary, 275n
Binghamton, N.Y., 3
Blacks: education, 30, 77, 282n; compared with Irish, 31, 209, 214-215, 217; persistence, 31; migration, 77; occupational mobility, 77-78, 214-215; property ownership, 77-79; occupations, 123, 194, 208, 211-214
Blessing, Patrick, 267n
Blumin, Stuart, 263n, 267n
Boarders: as transients, 17; and household structure, 235-236
Boatmen, 223-224
Boorstin, Daniel, 50
Boosterism, 1, 10, 103
Boston, Mass., 4, 5, 33, 43, 58, 73, 77, 85, 87, 272n
Branca, Patricia, 233, 283n

HARVARD STUDIES IN URBAN HISTORY

The City in the Ancient World, by Mason Hammond, assisted by Lester J. Bartson, 1972

Town into City: Springfield, Massachusetts, and the Meaning of Community, 1840-1880, by Michael H. Frisch, 1972

The Other Bostonians: Poverty and Progress in the American Metropolis, 1880-1970, by Stephan Thernstrom, 1973

Urban Growth and the Circulation of Information: The United States System of Cities, 1790-1840, by Allan R. Pred, 1973

The Glassworkers of Carmaux: French Craftsmen and Political Action in a Nineteenth-Century City, by Joan W. Scott, 1974

The Lyon Uprising of 1834: Social and Political Conflict in the Early July Monarchy, by Robert J. Bezucha, 1974

Peasants and Strangers: Italians, Rumanians, and Slovaks in an American City, 1890-1950, by Josef Barton, 1975

The People of Hamilton, Canada West: Family and Class in a Mid-Nineteenth-Century City, by Michael B. Katz, 1975

Immigrant Milwaukee, 1836-1860: Accommodation and Community in a Frontier City, by Kathleen Neils Conzen, 1976

Class and Community: The Industrial Revolution of Lynn, by Alan Dawley, 1976

Cities and Frontiers in Brazil: Regional Dimensions of Economic Development, by Martin T. Katzman, 1977

People of Salé: Tradition and Change in a Moroccan City 1830-1930, by Kenneth L. Brown, 1976

Fortunes and Failures: White-Collar Mobility in Nineteenth-Century San Francisco, by Peter R. Decker, 1978

Natives and Newcomers: The Ordering of Opportunity in Mid-Nineteenth-Century Poughkeepsie, by Clyde and Sally Griffen, 1978